Educational Care:

*A System
for Understanding and Helping
Children with Learning Problems
at Home and in School*

Dr. Mel Levine

Educators Publishing Service, Inc.
Cambridge, Massachusetts

Educators Publishing Service, Inc.
31 Smith Place, Cambridge, Massachusetts 02138-1000

Cover art and bird illustrations by Lorrie Bonestelle
Text design by Joyce C. Weston

About the cover: The author's longstanding fascination and admiration for geese is reflected on the cover of *Educational Care*. The collaboration between parent geese and others in the gaggle to nurture and care for the hatchlings and fledglings is not unlike the mutual efforts of parents and teachers to foster the learning and development of young children and adolescents. The snow gosling on the back cover and at the head of each chapter strives valiantly to climb the bricks which represent the challenge of schoolwork.

ISBN 0-8388-1987-7

June 1994 Printing

This book is dedicated to innocent children whose stifled struggles to succeed have been misinterpreted.

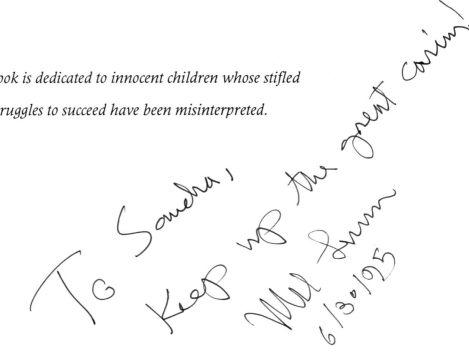

CONTENTS

ACKNOWLEDGMENTS

I would like to acknowledge the valuable assistance of a number of individuals who facilitated the writing of *Educational Care*.

Cheryl Hunter worked diligently and with great skill to create much of the complex graphic work for the book. Martha Reed carefully reviewed the manuscript and offered numerous superb suggestions. She also provided the writing samples from children that she and the author have evaluated together. Jim Montgomery read and made suggestions for improvement of the language portions of the book. Barbara Cassell handled much of the administrative detail with her usual care and efficiency. Special appreciation goes to Ralph Hines whose unique and brilliant insight into the minds of computers made it possible for this volume to emerge as a product of modern technology. Mary Troeger performed with expertise in her role as editor. Her very many perceptive comments and recommendations for modification influenced the prose style and content of all sections.

I am very grateful to the funding sources who have had enough confidence in my work to support research and demonstration activities that have enabled me to contribute to progress in learning about learning. I wish to acknowledge the following private foundations: The Carnegie Corporation, The Geraldine R. Dodge Foundation, The Ford Foundation, The Hancock Foundation, The Robert Wood Johnson Foundation, The Charles and Helen Schwab Foundation, and The Smart Family Foundation. In addition, I would like to thank the following United States government agencies for their support: the Department of Education, the Administration on Developmental Disabilities, and the Bureau of Maternal and Child Health.

Much credit is due my remarkably tolerant and inspiring wife, Bambi, whose encouragement catalyzed this writing. I am indebted as well to the geese, pheasants, swans, dogs, horses, cats, and mule (whose name is Rose), all of whom have provided endless evidence for the beauty of diversified patterns of ability and behavior.

CHAPTER ONE

Education as Care

NEEDLESS suffering occurs whenever children grow up disappointing themselves and the adults who care about them. Often they do so because they perform inadequately in school. Unfortunately, these children come to question their own worthiness, as they gaze about and compare themselves to others. Often they conceal profound concerns about their minds, believing that somehow they are defective or inferior. We are describing the sad plight of children who have difficulty performing certain highly age-specific roles that are needed to keep pace with the demands imposed in school. These young students often create confusion in their parents and their teachers. They bewilder themselves as well. This book sets out to diminish that shared confusion, to enable all concerned to construct a better understanding of the reasons for an individual child's exasperating and often futile struggles to keep pace and feel effective.

So much is at stake. Children who experience too much failure too early in life are exquisitely vulnerable to a wide range of complications. When these students are poorly understood, when their specific problems go unrecognized and untreated, they are especially prone to behavioral and emotional difficulties that frequently are more severe than the learning problems that generated them. It is not unusual for such students to lose motivation, to become painfully (and often secretly) anxious about themselves, to display noncompliance, to commit antisocial acts (including substance abuse and delinquent activity), and to lose ambition.

These struggling children comprise a very large and heterogeneous group. They differ from each other in their strengths as well as in the reasons for their learning difficulties. They come from diverse cultural

1

backgrounds. They emerge from conditions of affluence as well as poverty. However, they all share a deep desire to taste success and to feel good about themselves. Every one of them contains the seeds for mastery and gratification in life; none of them needs to fail.

A MODEL

This book presents what is called a phenomenological model. It is a model based on clinical, educational, and research experience, a model that favors informed observation and description over labeling and that takes into account the great heterogeneity of children with disappointing school performance. As its basis it makes use of analyses of phenomena that are known to hinder academic performance in children at different ages. This model places a strong emphasis on identifying and using the innate strengths of these children. This approach is also developmental in that it recognizes both that children's brains change over time and that school continuously changes in terms of the level and complexity of demands placed on children. Therefore, the phenomena that cause difficulty differ in their manifestations as children age.

In order to make use of this conceptual model, some basic ideas and terms need to be introduced. The first is the notion of an *observable phenomenon*, namely, a particular problem with learning or performing in school that is clearly visible as one watches a child over time and/or during some form of testing. For example, we might *observe* the phenomenon of a child having trouble remembering new material while studying for tests. Or, we might observe that a child exhibits great anxiety or that she or he has trouble organizing and allocating time. In *Educational Care*, we will be examining twenty-six common observable phenomena and their different forms. No doubt there are others, but these twenty-six are commonly written about and observed by educators, clinicians, and researchers and are thought to be especially prevalent and likely to interfere with a child's educational progress. While others may be inclined to trim or augment the list, they can still preserve a commitment to the direct observation of phenomena as a basis for understanding struggling school children.

Not surprisingly, there can be many different reasons why a child might exhibit a particular observable phenomenon. In some instances the phenomenon may be a manifestation of one or more *neurodevelopmental dysfunctions*, which are gaps, delays, or variations in the way a particular child's brain is developing. These can stem from many causes, including chemical/metabolic abnormalities, uneven brain growth, or a lack of appropriately dense nerve connections in specific regions of the brain. Then, too, they can be the result of unusual patterns of blood circulation in the brain. In most cases, we simply do not know (or need to know) the exact mechanisms responsible for a child's neurodevelopmental dysfunctions. We are certain, however, that the dysfunctions themselves have the potential to interfere with learning, with productive work output, and with behavior in school.

Not all observable phenomena result from neurodevelopmental dysfunctions. Some represent acquired behaviors, such as aggression in children who are trying to act "macho" to hide their inner fears about doing poorly in school. Other observable phenomena are delayed skills, such as poor reading, which may themselves result from one or more neurodevelopmental dysfunctions, a lack of experience, or inadequate prior teaching. Often a problem in school is likely to stem from more than one source. A child may have a genetic tendency toward a language weakness and also show evidence of excessive anxiety that is interfering with school performance.

In this book, we will place relatively little stress on the causes of a child's difficulties, because such causes are often very hard to establish and are not necessarily relevant to helping the child improve or overcome the difficulty. Instead, we will emphasize the accurate recognition and understanding of problems and different ways to manage them. Thus, our discussion of children who have difficulty processing language (page 85) will not stress whether the phenomenon is caused by genetic factors, cultural differences, environmental circumstances, or head trauma. Instead, we will explore the different forms of each observable phenomenon and then consider the implications that each of these will have for helping the affected student.

TASK ANALYSIS

Any learning task that a child is asked to complete in school demands the coordination of multiple behaviors, skills, and brain functions. Thus, if a young child is asked to write her name, she must make use of several neurodevelopmental functions that mobilize and regulate the muscles in her fingers. She must also draw upon several forms of memory to recall the letter formations and the correct spelling of her name. In addition, she needs to focus her attention on the task, use self-monitoring behaviors (i.e., watch carefully what she's doing to avoid careless mistakes), and apply spatial awareness in order to position her name in the right place on the page. If one or more of these essential functions or behaviors does not operate properly, the child may have trouble writing her name legibly and accurately.

So it is that every academic task represents a collaboration between multiple brain (i.e., neurodevelopmental) functions, acquired skills, and behaviors. This joint effort must be exquisitely integrated and synchronized for the task to be completed effectively and without excessive effort. Therefore, once we have a good understanding of the elements needed to perform a task, we can then begin to understand how to work with a child who has difficulty with that particular task. We can explore which of the called-for task elements is deficient. We can make the child and the adults in his or her life aware of that deficient element. We can seek ways to strengthen the identified weakness. Also, as we shall see, students with learning problems can find alternative ways to perform, often making use of their strengths to bypass the weak elements.

This process of analysis must be highly *developmental* because different skills and functions become critical for school success at different stages during a child's education. For example, the functions needed to acquire reading skills in the early grades include a keen awareness of language sounds and an ability to manipulate these sounds within words and to match the sounds with visual symbols. The functions required to be a proficient reader in tenth grade are quite different. They include the ability to recall prior knowledge quickly while reading, to interpret highly abstract and technical language while reading, and to hold in the mind the content of the beginning of a chapter while at the same time comprehending the material near the end of it. Reading in high school also is dependent upon acquiring good reading behaviors and having an orientation toward the printed word as well as a belief in its value. So it is that very different demands on the brain exist for a tenth grader from those that confront a first or second grade student. Children's functional abilities, academic skills, and adaptive behaviors are expected to evolve progressively and strengthen over time.

Because the expectations imposed upon students are changing during the course of the school years, becoming more demanding in depth of content and more taxing in the amount and complexity of material, it is possible at any point in their educational careers, for these expectations to exceed students' current mental capacities. It is not surprising, then, that children may be much more successful at one particular age than at another. While a learning problem may have its onset at any age, it is also true that students' strengths can become educationally relevant at a particular grade level, and they may experience success for the first time.

In interpreting children's school performances it is essential to understand not just their deficiencies but also the crucial role of inborn and acquired strengths. In fact, most children can compensate for neurodevelopmental dysfunctions, skill deficits, and poorly adapted behavior patterns by making good use of these strengths. There are many tasks or activities that can be accomplished in more than one way. For example, a child may have difficulty appreciating language sounds. Ordinarily this dysfunction could interfere with the ability to spell accurately. However, it might be the case that the student possesses a highly developed visual memory and is therefore able to picture the words so well that his or her weakness of language sound appreciation does not impair spelling. Often an understanding of children's neurodevelopmental strengths can be invaluable in trying to help them make use of their strengths as a way of overcoming the effects of dysfunctions.

A dysfunction, skill deficit, or poorly adapted behavior becomes a handicap when it interferes with a necessary component of performance in school. It is possible to harbor a form of neurodevelopmental dysfunction that is not a handicap. For example, a person may have trouble with the motor coordination of his cheek muscles. That motor dysfunction may make it very hard for him to whistle, but a whistling deficit is hardly a handicap in our culture! In fact, we all have neurodevelopmental dysfunctions or problematic behaviors or feelings, most of which do not cause great difficulty in our lives. It is unlikely that anyone could read this book without at some point recognizing himself or herself. After all, there are no perfect brains! It is only when our neurodevelopmental dysfunctions or inappropriate behaviors are sufficiently severe, when they occur in "clusters," when they deter critical areas of performance, and/or when they are hard to bypass with compensatory strengths that they become problematic.

VARIATION VERSUS DEVIATION

Sometimes it is difficult to decide whether a particular child's brain is "disabled" or whether it is "highly specialized." Unquestionably, some (perhaps most) minds seem to function very well in specific contexts or when confronted with certain demands but not so well under other circumstances. The adult world desperately needs a wide range of "kinds of minds." It is only during childhood that a young person is expected to be reasonably adept at everything. That expectation may discriminate against children who have uneven abilities. Furthermore, it may sometimes cause variation to be confused with deviation! So it is that some of the children who suffer from significant neurodevelopmental dysfunctions may ultimately perform very well in life but only when they are permitted to practice their "specialties," to pursue the areas where their abilities best serve them. In the adult world, such specialization is not only encouraged by the way jobs are organized, but is also highly desirable and likely to increase the chances for success. During childhood, specialization and/or the freedom to make use of a unique learning style may not be viable options.

THE CONCEPT OF EDUCATIONAL CARE

Too frequently education is viewed by both educators and students as a process in which skills and knowledge are conveyed or imparted by teachers to learners. In such a context, there may be little regard for the individual needs of the learner. Often it is assumed that what is good for one student is good for all students. In this book we will suggest a very different approach. We propose that just as health care is a system through which medical professionals tend to the specific needs of patients, so education needs to be a system that delivers care to individual students. Health care needs vary considerably from individual to individual. Not all medical conditions require the same medicine or the same level of health care. Education too should provide a form of individualized care and, in addition, it needs to do this with compassion. As we have described, children arrive at school each morning with a wide range of strengths and weaknesses and, therefore, with diverse educational care needs. While we cannot (and should not) individualize all learning for all students, in so far as this is feasible it is imperative to try to do this for those who are most in need. As with optimal health care, there should be good prevention (of complications), accuracy of diagnosis, strong advocacy, and responsible management.

The observable phenomena we shall describe in this book come together in a nearly infinite array of individual patterns. They are further altered by a child's strengths and by environmental circumstances. In view of this extreme diversity, no universal panacea will ever exist. Individualization must be the rule. But how this is accomplished is important. We certainly do not wish to isolate struggling children, to heighten any sense of feeling defective, or to remove them from the mainstream of education. And these steps are not necessary. It is possible to recognize and meet individual needs without segregation and stigmatization. The intention of this book is to portray some of the ways in which individual educational care can be provided with the least disruption to the lives of children.

COLLABORATION BETWEEN HOME AND SCHOOL

A major supposition in this book is that a child with a learning problem cannot receive the best educational care at school unless there is close collaboration with the adults at home. Throughout these chapters, therefore, we will stress *collaborative management*. After each observable phenomenon is described in its various forms, we will offer specific suggestions relating to the educational care children should receive at home and the types of care they ought to receive in school. In this model of mutual responsibility, there is a strong emphasis on consistency. Parents and schools need to share the same understanding of the child, work from the same conceptual models of strength and dysfunction, and communicate using the same terminology so as to minimize that student's own confusion. When a teacher bases his or her actions and communication with the student on one particular explanation of the child's difficulty, and the parents use a totally different frame of reference, this can only drain motivation and add to the student's anxiety.

THE PLAN OF THE BOOK

In the next six chapters of *Educational Care*, we will describe the twenty-six common, observable phenomena, grouping them according to particular educational themes (such as controlling attention, remembering, and understanding). (See table 1.1.) Under each theme, after a discussion of the different forms and manifestations of these observable phenomena, we will consider the effects of children's strengths. In each of these chapters, there are suggestions for parents and teachers to help in the collaborative management of these children. These suggestions are not intended to be "recipes" nor do they represent a whole cure for a child. Instead, they comprise a sampling of kinds of management techniques that are likely to be helpful. The suggestions cover the needs of a wide age range and therefore will need to be adjusted to fit each grade level. As they provide educational care to a child, parents and teachers should augment and customize the list while preserving a consistent collaborative approach.

Along with the management suggestions each chapter has a section on *demystification*, which is a process through which adults talk to children about the nature of their learning disorders and strengths. It is based on the belief that children cannot work on their problems if they do not really understand them. They desperately need a vocabulary to capture and describe what they are trying to work on. Suggested approaches to demystification relate to each of the areas covered in the book.

Chapter 8 provides an overview of the processes of assessment and management. There is a presentation of the forms of evaluation needed by children with learning disorders, followed by a general discussion of the systems and strategies that can be used for managing these difficulties. More general guidelines on demystification are included in chapter 8.

Table 1.1: Common Observable Phenomena

THEMES	OBSERVABLE PHENOMENA
Weak Attention Controls	Weak Mental Energy Control Weak Processing Control Weak Production Control
Reduced Remembering	Problems with Short-Term Memory Insufficient Active Working Memory Incomplete Consolidation in Long-Term Memory Reduced Access to Long-Term Memory
Chronic Misunderstanding	Weak Language Processing Incomplete Concept Formation Weak Visual Processing Slow Data Processing Small Chunk-Size Capacity Excessive Top-Down or Bottom-Up Processing
Deficient Output	Weak Language Production Disappointing Motor Performance Persistent Organizational Failure Problematic Problem Solving and Strategy Use
Delayed Skill Acquisition	Slow Reading Development Inaccurate Spelling Patterns Impeded Written Output Underdeveloped Mathematical Ability
Poor Adaptation	School-Related Sadness Bodily Preoccupations Noncompliant Behaviors Social Inability Lost Motivation

Chapter 9 offers an examination of the implications of educational care. There is some discussion of the policy issues for schools, for communities, and for our broad conceptualization of childhood and the needs of developing children. The Appendixes contain examples of interview formats that can be used with children, and other diagnostic materials. The book concludes with a list of suggested readings.

Ultimately, we hope that this book will influence the way in which adults think about children struggling with difficult personal profiles of strength and weakness that they did not select. These pages will have fulfilled their mission if and when conscientious parents, clinicians, teachers, school administrators, and policymakers can come to perceive education as primarily a form of care—and a way of caring.

CHAPTER TWO

Phenomena Related to Weak Attention Controls

ATTENTION can be thought of broadly as a complex system of brain controls that allows us to energize and regulate our thinking and our daily activities. In a sense, attention is like the conductor of an orchestra who does not actually create the sounds of music but who controls the players of instruments who in turn generate the actual melodies. Analogously, attention controls a vast number of "thinking players," individual brain processes that are essential for learning, for behaving, and for relating well to other people. It should not be surprising, therefore, that children who have problems with attention may possess strong abilities that they are unable somehow to control or use effectively. Their inability to direct any number of important brain functions may lead to problems in developing skills, adapting their behavior, and succeeding socially. Such problems, in turn, can disrupt the education and life adjustment of a developing child. For this reason, weaknesses of attention are of critical importance.

THE ATTENTION CONTROLS

In order to make clear what is taking place when attention is operating, we will define three key control systems that work together to make up attention and which are depicted in figure 2.1. These are mental energy control, processing control, and production control.

The aspect of brain function that energizes our alertness and enables us to exert mental effort we will call *mental energy control*. In a sense, this form of control is responsible for distributing the fuel needed for competency, productivity, and well-controlled behavior. Several different parts of the brain participate in turning on, allocating, and keeping up an

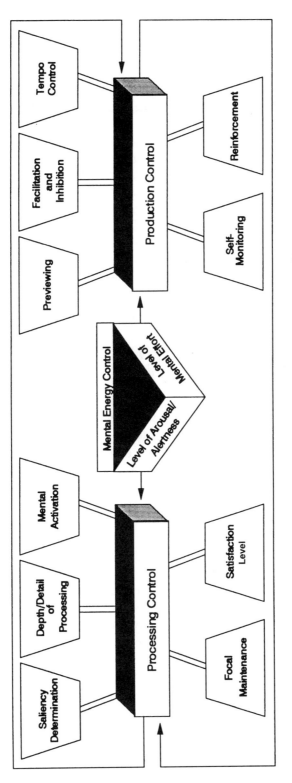

Fig. 2.1. The three attention controls are illustrated here, along with the three domains of function in which they have significant impacts.

11

appropriate flow of energy that is needed for an individual to concentrate and be productive. There are two principal forms of this control. The first of these promotes *alertness*, while the second is responsible for the exertion of *mental effort* to accomplish tasks and control behavior.

Several closely related controls are responsible for assisting with the processing of information. Together they provide control over the brain's *awareness* and *absorption* of relevant information from moment to moment. It appears that many different parts of the brain collaborate in the control of processing information that may come from external sources or from within the consciousness of the individual. We will identify five basic processing controls. The first of these is *saliency determination* which helps distinguish what is important from what is not, allowing an individual to filter out or ignore that which is unimportant. The second is *depth of processing* which sees to it that incoming relevant information is processed with enough depth or intensity so the material can stay in the mind. A third is *mental activation*, a control that turns on just the necessary functions of the brain and draws upon the appropriate background knowledge needed to interpret, relate, and/or use the selected information. A fourth control, *focal maintenance*, keeps concentration going as long as needed. Finally, *satisfaction control* determines continuously whether the current information or experience is satisfying to or fulfilling needs for the individual.

Another group of brain functions regulate the production of creations, activities, and behaviors. These controls are located mainly in the *prefrontal lobes* of the brain (just behind the forehead). They bear a large responsibility for material or actions that we produce. As with processing, we can describe five basic controls. One of these, *previewing*, enables an individual to foresee or estimate possible outcomes, that is, the likely result of what is about to be done or produced. Another is the control over *facilitation and inhibition*. This control facilitates actions or functions that are desirable or needed and simultaneously inhibits those that are not wanted or needed. A third, *tempo control*, governs how we pace our actions, allowing for the regulation of rate and synchrony. Another control, *self-monitoring*, helps determine during and after production how effective our efforts proved to be. Finally, control over *reinforceability* helps people gain from experience, for it provides the ability to use feedback, to learn from positively and negatively reviewed actions or good and poor products.

The controls over mental energy, processing, and production are highly interactive. Often good production is dependent upon good processing. For example, if children would like to contribute something in a class discussion, they must first "tune in" properly to process what others are saying. It is also the case that the different functions within each set of controls must constantly interact. Thus, it is easier for students to filter out distractions when they are maintaining a high level of alertness in class. Despite their interdependence, we will describe these controls individually as a way to better understand children who are having problems with attention.

Attentional Dysfunction

Many children exhibit signs of weak attention controls which can be referred to as attentional dysfunction. Problems with attention are the most common source of learning and behavioral difficulties in school-age children. Often these weaknesses are lumped as a syndrome called Attention Deficit Disorder (ADD) or Attention Deficit Hyperactivity Disorder (ADHD). Without denying the existence of these specific conditions, we will avoid the labels and explore in some depth the phenomena that reflect attentional dysfunction in this heterogeneous group of students.

Children with attentional dysfunction have weaknesses in some (and sometimes all) of the controls depicted in figure 2.1 and described above. They vary significantly in which controls are weak and in the degree to which the weak controls actually interfere with learning, behaving, and/or relating to other people. There are children whose problems with attention cause them to underachieve but not misbehave. Others have attention problems that lead to disciplinary actions, while still others find that poor attention control disrupts their ability to form friendships and maintain a good reputation with peers.

Children with attentional dysfunction clearly are highly diverse. To lump all of them together and say they have ADD or ADHD is to tell us very little about them. Not only do students vary in their precise traits and the severity of their manifestations, but they differ as well in their strengths and weaknesses in other relevant areas, such as motor skills, language ability, and memory capacity. These other functions (covered in later chapters of this book) have a potent effect on learning and behavior and can also have an impact on attention. If children are having trouble understanding, they are prone to become inattentive. Attention is fragile and depends on a range of factors (including success) to keep it running properly! So, in view of the conspicuous variety within this population of children, we feel there is justification for describing the individual characteristics of individual children rather than lumping them into one massive group or syndrome.

The process of describing individual children with attentional dysfunction will be achieved by returning to our model of attention controls and considering how weaknesses in each of the individual controls make up forms of observable phenomena (fig. 2.2). We will begin by discussing the two forms of weak mental energy control and their management at home and in school. Then we will continue with a description of the phenomena associated with weak control of processing and production.

WEAK MENTAL ENERGY CONTROL

Children with weak mental energy control may simply lack the stamina needed to maintain optimal behavior and/or learning. Their mental energy may be difficult to start up and, once started, quickly used up. They may also waste energy by assigning it to irrelevant actions or subjects. Inconsistent alertness and inconsistent mental effort are the two common forms of this lack of control of mental energy.

Inconsistent Alertness

Students with inconsistent alertness can find their classroom experience tedious and unrewarding. When they try to concentrate, they are apt to experience mental fatigue and/or incapacitating boredom.

These children often show the following tendencies:

- They may yawn, stretch, and appear tired in class more than do their classmates. They seem most exhausted when they are required to sit still. It has been said that nothing a child does requires more energy than sitting still!
- They may be fidgety, squirmy, and overactive in class as if they are moving around to try to stay alert. They may also assume various contorted body postures, seemingly attempting to get uncomfortable as a way of becoming more aroused.
- Their abilities to concentrate are markedly inconsistent as is their overall performance in school. This erratic functioning is evident in Susan's case. At times, these students seem "tuned in," while at other times, they are "tuned out." Their tuning-in phase may last for seconds or minutes, for hours or even days, before they inevitably enter a period of lost alertness. The inconsistency of their focus causes them to miss important information in school. They may be confused about directions, for example, because they are attentive to only part of them.
- On quizzes or examinations, these students may reveal bizarre error patterns due to their fluctuating attention. They may success-

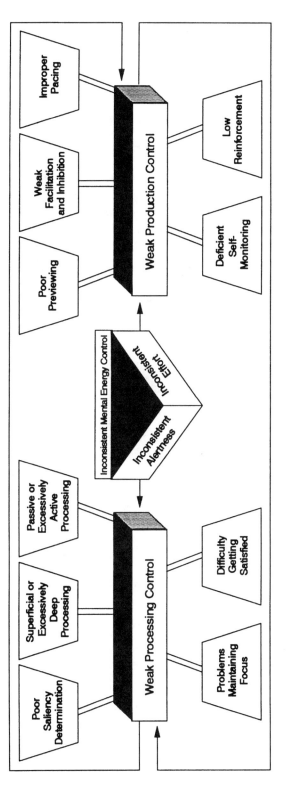

PHENOMENA RELATED TO WEAK ATTENTION CONTROL

THE THREE POSSIBLE DOMAINS OF IMPACT:

Cognitive/
Academic
Problems

Poor
Behavioral
Adaptation

Social/
Interpersonal
Difficulty

Fig. 2.2. The attention controls are shown here with descriptions of the forms they take when not working effectively. Children with attentional dysfunction show varying combinations of these weak controls.

15

SUSAN

Susan is a sixteen-year-old girl who is struggling to keep pace academically. She is a highly creative person who is capable of generating truly original ideas. However, in school she frequently appears to be bored and tired. Her teachers catch her "staring into space." They note that she yawns and stretches on many occasions. Susan is not a very hard worker. Her parents report that she is very resistant to doing homework. She insists that she did it all in school, but reports from her teachers contradict this. Susan's parents and teachers are baffled by her inconsistency. On some days she is highly productive. On many other occasions, her work output is inadequate and the effort required for an assignment seems too much for her. Her parents report that Susan has trouble falling asleep.

---

fully answer three successive items, then miss the next three. Likewise, they may provide an accurate response to a difficult question and then err on a subsequent simpler item.

- As a result of being tuned out, they may tend to miss the beginnings of statements or directions from a teacher or parent. They do not orient their minds toward a new important signal, such as an assignment about to be given.

A number of different observable phenomena are associated with inconsistent alertness. Some children have problems with alertness primarily when information is presented in a particular format. For example, a child may find it difficult to pay attention when information is spoken and may be described as having *weak auditory attention* or *weak listening skills.* That same child, however, might become highly alert when information is presented visually.

Children who have an imbalance in their sleep-arousal patterns may have problems with alertness. Often because it is hard for them to fall asleep, they remain awake until late at night and then they have trouble getting up and staying alert throughout the school day, a pattern evident in Susan. Some of these students may have a dysfunction relating to a part of the brain stem called the *reticular activating system.* This anatomical region working with other parts of the brain helps to control sleep and arousal, and when it is not working properly it can cause the kind of imbalance just described.

Finally, there are some children who have particular times of the day when they are more alert. They may ultimately emerge as the future morning or night people of the adult world!

Children with inconsistent alertness are easily misunderstood. They often are accused of not really trying when they are tuned out. Adults may incorrectly assume that if someone can be alert some of the time, she or he can be alert all of the time. It is important to understand that a student's inconsistent alertness is frequently beyond her or his control.

Inconsistent Effort

Many children with attentional dysfunction find that effort requires too much effort! When they try to do work, they experience mental fatigue similar to what was described in the section on inconsistent alertness. They often are prone to having trouble completing tasks, such as finishing homework assignments. They seem to "run out of gas" easily.

Often these students are very inconsistent in their supply of effort. They are able only to work in spurts, at times being extremely productive, and at other times accomplishing meagerly. This pattern represents another form of performance inconsistency that can make a student appear to be "lazy" or poorly motivated, yet often the child would like to succeed but is simply unable (as opposed to unwilling) to mobilize the needed mental fuel. When trying to work, the student is likely to experience disabling fatigue and boredom. Different students show somewhat differing patterns. Some have trouble getting started with work. Others can get started but can only work effectively for short intervals.

Children with inconsistent mental effort usually do not have trouble mobilizing and sustaining a steady flow of mental effort for pursuits they really enjoy. We might argue, in fact, that things that are fun actually consume very little effort. Many work-related activities, on the other hand, have content that is not very entertaining or highly motivating. So they demand large amounts of sustained mental effort. An appropriate question to ask about a child might be: how unexciting or personally uninteresting can content or subject matter be before she or he loses the capacity to mobilize and sustain effort? Effective students are able to work diligently at only moderate levels of interest. We all have trouble working when an activity is excruciatingly dull. Many children with attentional dysfunction can only exert effort when pursuing activities they consider fun.

Managing Weak Mental Energy Control at Home

Parents have a significant role to play in helping children with problems controlling mental energy. They need to be involved especially in the management of sleep patterns and in the facilitation of work output.

1. Children who show inconsistent alertness and reduced mental effort need frequently scheduled breaks when studying at home (e.g., every ten minutes). Such breaks can be set on a kitchen timer. Parents should encourage a child to stand up and walk around during these breaks, but to avoid activities that are too stimulating or too far away from the task at hand. For example, calling a friend may be excessively distracting.

2. For some students stimulant medication (page 264) may be helpful in improving mental alertness and fostering mental effort. The drug may allow a student to concentrate with greater intensity and duration. The dosage, the time of administration, and whether or not to use long-acting drugs all need to be considered by a physician who is helping to manage the child's difficulties.

3. Those children who have problems falling asleep at night require sensitive management. They may already feel very anxious about this. Parents can avoid adding to this anxiety by not dwelling on the importance of a good night's sleep. Instead, they should reassure these children that trouble sleeping will *not* affect their health or overall well-being. Children should understand that it is okay to fall asleep whenever they can, but that they should stay in their rooms in bed with a lamp on. They can read and/or listen to music while trying to fall asleep. Sometimes "white noise" (such as music or a fan) can help. In some instances, a physician may prescribe sleep medication as a temporary measure. Children who take a stimulant drug for attentional dysfunction may need to have the timing or amount of the medication adjusted if sleep problems worsen.

4. As we have mentioned earlier, these children are most alert when they are doing things that interest them. They should be encouraged to read about, write about, and talk about subjects they find compelling and areas of interest for which they show a clear affinity. Often these students learn better through direct active experience than

through reading and listening. Trips, tours, and other active projects are likely to induce the greatest levels of alertness and therefore the most learning. Whenever possible parents should reinforce the child's formal learning through direct experience of or exposure to the subject matter.

5. Sometimes using regularly scheduled breaks combined with a change of work site enables children to renew their mental effort. They may need to spend ten minutes working at a desk, ten minutes at the kitchen table, and ten minutes doing mathematics on the living room floor. Each time there is a change of locale, the student may experience a burst of productivity. Some children find it difficult to work where they sleep, so they should not be required to do homework in their bedrooms.

6. There are students who believe they can improve their alertness and mobilize more mental effort when they listen to music while they are working. It's worth a try!

Managing Weak Mental Energy Control in School

Children with weak mental energy control become exhausted during a day at school. Fortunately, there are measures that can be taken to enhance their alertness and bolster the amount of effort that are able to invest.

1. Teachers can help children with inconsistent alertness and mental effort by requiring them to put forth relatively small amounts of work or focused attention at one time. For example, there may need to be brief breaks interspersed between paragraphs they are writing or mathematics problems they are solving.

2. The teacher should have a private way of signaling a child when he or she is "tuning out" due to mental fatigue A gentle tap on the shoulder may be effective.

3. These children should be allowed to stand up and stretch, walk to the back of the room, or even visit the rest room a certain number of times per day or per period. They can keep a checklist documenting such breaks and should be praised for not needing to take all of them on some occasions. These "stretch breaks" may need to be explained to classmates. Children taking these breaks must understand that they cannot be disruptive or talkative.

4. Many of these students need to be doing something with their hands while seated at a desk. It may be that doodling, handling a piece of

clay, or performing some other manual activity helps keep them aroused and alert. Ultimately, note taking may serve this function optimally.

5. Teachers need to understand that the great *inconsistency* of children with limited alertness and/or erratic mental effort is not evidence of a poor attitude. It is very much a part of their attentional dysfunction and is most often beyond the easy control of a student. Statements, such as, "We know you can do it; we've seen you do well when you apply yourself," are not helpful to these students because they cause additional feelings of guilt. Instead, teachers should express an interest in the child's puzzling inconsistency and offer hope and encouragement for more frequent top performances in the future.

6. A teacher may need to signal a child with limited alertness when something especially important is about to be stated. Looking right at the child, she or he could say: "Now listen very carefully. I'm about to give you important instructions about tomorrow's field trip."

WEAK PROCESSING CONTROL

Optimal learning and behavior take place when the brain selects, prepares, and refines information that needs to be interpreted. That information can then be understood more clearly by relevant brain regions that deal with such functions as language comprehension, visual processing, and the interpretation of social cues. Children with weak control of processing are likely to be processing data that are inadequate in one way or another. The possible reasons for this inadequacy are reflected in the forms of weak control of processing described below.

Poor Saliency Determination

At any given moment in school, there is far too much detail to process and store in memory. While reading a book or listening to a class discussion, students are exposed to more information and stimuli than they can possibly make use of. Therefore, efficient learners must be selective and choose what is most salient. They have to decide instantly what information is most important or necessary to take in and process in depth and what information is not so important and therefore can be neglected or filtered out of consciousness.

Determining what is important is a serious problem for some children in school. They are constantly focusing on and sometimes remembering details of questionable relevancy (i.e., trivia) at the same time that they are likely to miss or disregard more important data. Such diffuse

---

JEFF

Jeff is six years old and in the first grade. His teacher has become exceedingly frustrated because she cannot seem to "reach him." He frequently stares out the window and shows a keen interest in irrelevant stimuli. He makes comments about sounds out in the hallway and seems to overhear better than he is able to hear. Jeff often disturbs other children in the classroom. He likes very much to stir things up. He appears to crave excitement and intense experience of any kind. His parents report that Jeff makes trouble at home, too. He is chronically restless and seems to require constant stimulation in order to feel content. In class, Jeff's mind is extremely active. He daydreams and fantasizes. His dreaming frequently prevents him from processing that which is occurring in the classroom. The very same dreaming, however, enables Jeff to draw fantastic images and to be remarkably inventive in his thinking.

---

attention is characteristic of Jeff's processing. Affected children overindulge in what has been called *incidental* as opposed to *central* learning. That is, a child may take note of some minor detail and miss the critical gist or message while reading a paragraph or listening to a verbal explanation. For example, while reading a science assignment, such a student may remember that a chart showing the process of photosynthesis was on page 226 but not remember anything that was in the chart. In addition, these children often are described as lacking in vigilance. That is, they cannot remain on the lookout for upcoming important information. If told to watch out for a particular road sign while in a car, the child may be able to do so only briefly; so when the sign appears six minutes later, the child misses it. Tests of vigilance are often used to evaluate children with possible attentional dysfunction.

Not surprisingly, children who have trouble with saliency determination may have a hard time knowing what to study for tests. They may also have difficulty finding the main idea in their reading or picking out relevant information for solving a word problem.

These children are all too easily distracted from meaningful concentration in school. A distraction is a departure from whatever current need or plan a child is attending to. While all students experience repeated distractions during class sessions and in the midst of home-work, some are more vulnerable to these than are others. In extreme cases, distractibility can seriously interfere with accomplishing or learn-ing anything.

Children with attentional dysfunction are prone to specific types of distractibility at home and in school. Various forms that distractibility may take and the ways they manifest themselves in children appear in table 2.1.

Distractibility is certainly not all bad. Distractible children are often very creative and insightful. They notice things others would miss or ignore. They are frequently described by their parents as incredibly observant. They perceive relationships between things that their more focused peers would never think of. Like Jeff, they tend to have vivid imaginations and uniquely interesting ideas and perspectives. In fact, one may wonder whether to be truly a creative individual, a person must be at least somewhat distractible!

Superficial or Excessively Deep Processing

When a child selects information he or she wants to process and perhaps remember, this needs to be entered in consciousness with the right amount of impact or intensity. It is common for children with attention-al dysfunction to have shallow concentration. In a classroom or while studying for a quiz, a student with this problem may seldom concentrate with enough intensity to retain what is said or written. Superficial pro-cessing often appears in children who show mental fatigue and limited alertness, but there are also children who even when alert are not think-ing very hard or intently. They are only barely concentrating on what they are supposed to be reading, hearing, or watching. These students often develop a partial or tenuous understanding and retention of the subject matter.

Children with superficial processing often have problems with short-term memory (page 57). They fail to register information deeply enough in memory for it to last. During class these children often appear detached or disengaged from what is occurring. When called upon, they may be able to answer a question, but only in shallow ways.

Often children with superficial processing abhor fine detail. They much prefer the big picture. Such students may have an excellent mastery of mathematics concepts, facts, and procedures but make numerous care-less errors because they fail to process detail (such as operational signs).

As children progress through their school years, they confront an ever growing mass of fine detail. Furthermore, the detail becomes in-

Table 2.1: Some Common Forms of Distractibility

FORM OF DISTRACTIBILITY	MANIFESTATIONS
Visual	Child stares, looks around aimlessly, focuses on irrelevant sights, notices things no one else notices.
Auditory	Child shows weak sustained listening, focuses on background noises, requires verbal repetition often.
Tactile	Child can't resist things that have the potential to be handled, fingers constantly exploring, touching.
Future-oriented	Child is constantly looking ahead to what is coming next or happening tonight or next weekend.
Social	Child has trouble "filtering out" peers, keeps watching, possibly provoking others.

creasingly *decontextualized*, that is, removed from familiar everyday experience. Ancient wars, scientific phenomena, and the study of foreign countries are examples of such material. This explosion of decontextualized detail places heavy demands on depth of processing. Some students whose progress was strong in the earlier grades may see this deteriorate in the face of such a challenge if they overindulge in superficial processing.

There are also children with attentional dysfunction who tend to process too deeply. They become so bogged down in details that they are unable to see the big picture. These overattending youngsters may have trouble moving from one idea or topic to the next. Some children show both problems with this form of control; sometimes they process too superficially, while at other times they are focusing too deeply.

Passive or Excessively Active Processing

Children may be able to focus attention, so that the information they want to understand or remember is registered in the brain. But once it is there, it needs to activate just the right prior knowledge and brain functions in order for the information to be used. A child hearing about a recent news event should quickly and actively relate it to similar events she or he has known about. Making use of the appropriate prior learning helps to develop a better understanding of or explanation for the recent event. Such association and activation of prior knowledge (and skill) involves control over *processing activity*. For some children this is very difficult. They are either excessively active in processing or very passive.

Children who show low processing activity find new knowledge inert; it fails to "ring bells." The subject matter they study in school remains fragmentary and unconnected in their minds. These children are sometimes called passive or inactive processors. They may display

- A distinct lack of interest in any of the subject matter in school
- An overuse of rote memory or imitation of procedures in school with only limited understanding
- A tendency to do many things the hard way with no thought-out strategies for completing challenging tasks (It may be that the relative inactivity of their minds prevents them from connecting with or activating the best ways of doing something.)
- A feeling of pervasive boredom in school

A child with passive processing may appear poorly motivated and uncaring. But often these are students who want to succeed but can't seem to "turn on the intellectual ignition." Commonly (but not always), other phenomena that suggest attentional dysfunction show up in these students.

Another group of children is just the opposite. They have excessively active processing. When they hear or see something, it triggers too many associations and ideas. Like Jeff, they are prone to the "free flight of ideas." A teacher mentions an airplane in class. The child starts thinking about the time he flew in a jet plane. That memory reminds him of a TV show about jet pilots which makes him think about astronauts and how much fun it would be to be launched in a satellite and explore outer space. He starts imagining what it would be like to live on Mars or the moon. While this free flight has been taking place, the teacher has begun pursuing another topic which the child has missed. Children with such active and irrelevant processing are often highly imaginative and inventive. During a class they are apt to draw pictures of their clever inventions or of dream-like figures. They frequently state unorthodox but interesting ideas in a class discussion, although their comments may not be relevant to what is being discussed. These students daydream regularly and are apt to lose track of the flow of ideas in a classroom, a textbook, or a dinner-table discussion at home.

Problems Maintaining a Focus

Ordinarily if a child is attending to useful information, she or he can do so until the entire message has been conveyed and processed. When the information is understood or used adequately, the child can then focus on the next piece of information. Often children with attentional problems have difficulty regulating the length of their concentration. Some of them are described as having a short attention span. In the middle of a story or an explanation, they simply stop focusing. There are also children, on the other hand, who concentrate for too long a period who often allocate too much time to unimportant stimuli or aspects of reading material that should be processed quite quickly. In some instances the same children have trouble concentrating long enough (on certain occasions) and also concentrate too long (at other times).

Problems maintaining a focus overlap substantially with the other forms of weak processing control. Children may tune out prematurely due to mental fatigue or because they are distracted or because they are feeling insatiable and what they are doing is failing to satisfy them. It can be helpful to observe children with problems maintaining a focus to see if any of these other control problems are contributing to their inability to persist.

Trouble Getting Satisfied

The control over feeling satisfied is a driving force in attention. The taking in and processing of information in school as well as in other domains of daily life should make a person feel at least momentarily that a need is being met and that a certain level of satisfaction is experienced. The critical question is: what does it take to satisfy the attention of an individual child?

Some children are exceedingly hard to satisfy. They are described in fact as *insatiable*. They require frequent high levels of stimulation to feel satisfied. This is a very conspicuous trait in Jeff, the boy we met at the beginning of this section. Focusing on and processing certain data in school does not quell their appetites for intense experience.

We find that two forms of insatiability seem to dominate in these children: *experiential insatiability* and *material insatiability*. Children with experiential insatiability crave excitement and require high levels of stimulation to satisfy their need for intense experiences. They may well become behavior problems (page 222). In their unending quest for excitement, they are likely to be provocative, to stir things up, to create intensity of experience even if it is negative. Some students can satisfy this longing for excitement in more adaptive ways, including bicycle riding, skateboarding, playing video games, or developing and pursuing a hobby or passionate interest.

Those with material insatiability crave things all the time. However, almost as soon as they acquire what they seek they desire something else. They may become hoarders and collectors. They want material satisfaction so badly that they cannot seem to delay gratification. They can wear out their parents with their incessant wants and overwhelmingly felt needs. They often have trouble taking turns, sharing with others, and waiting in line. Consequently, they incur the wrath and mostly justified resentment of classmates and of siblings.

It is important to recognize that insatiability during childhood can lead to high ambition and drive in adult life. However, it is also a potentially dangerous trait, one that could culminate in substance abuse, reckless driving, extreme risk taking, marital instability, and problems with feeling comfortable and satisfied in a career.

Managing Weak Processing Control at Home

Parents can help their children a great deal to work on their problems with the control of processing. Much can be done to assist students to become more selective and careful in sorting through and organizing the information and stimuli that constantly confront them.

1. When children with poor saliency determination have trouble deciding what is important while studying, parents can help by asking them to summarize the key points after reading a passage or chapter. They can discuss what's most important to study for a test and can help their children look at a word problem in mathematics with the purpose of determining what's relevant to the problem's solution and what's not. They can play games in which the child can guess what will be asked on a test or quiz and then be rewarded for good determinations.

2. Once parents understand the child's specific type(s) of distractibility, they can try to minimize the source either by reminding the child, "This is important, so don't listen to sounds from outside while you're doing this" or by creating an environment with minimal distraction (e.g., a very quiet place to work for a child with auditory distractibility or, alternatively, one with white background noise to help filter distractions). Parents should also build times into the schedule when children

can have an outlet for their distractibility. For example, a child with tactile distractibility may enjoy opportunities to work with clay or to engage in other forms of handicraft.

3. Parents can take advantage of the positive aspects of a child's distractibility. We have pointed out that distractible boys and girls may be highly creative. They are apt to notice things that others would miss. It is important to encourage and praise their creative talents and abilities and to provide them with opportunities to use and display them through art work, story telling, or inventing things. Such opportunities are also helpful for children with overly active processing or who are prone to the free flight of ideas. Their imaginary explorations can translate into highly creative and laudable insights and perceptions.

4. To help overcome the effects of superficial processing, parents may need to repeat instructions or directions to a child with attentional dysfunction. It may be necessary to stress the need to "really tune in to this." They can then ask the child to repeat what was just said. Parents should always try to achieve good eye contact when giving important directions. Such eye contact increases the child's depth of processing and makes it more likely that the information will be retained in short-term memory. It is not a good idea to blame children for needing to have directions repeated; most often it is not their fault that their processing was so superficial.

5. Children with superficial processing may read an entire chapter of a book and have no idea what they just read. They should be encouraged to underline, to keep summarizing, to whisper important ideas under their breath, and to have opportunities to stop and talk about what they are reading with a parent.

6. A child who shows passive processing can sometimes be helped by having parents show an interest in the subject matter that she or he is learning. Whenever possible, parents should share in some of the learning experiences of the child, even stating, "That's something I'd like to know more about; let's find out about it together." Children should be encouraged strongly to teach what they have learned.

7. It is important for children with passive patterns of processing to elaborate on their ideas as they discuss material learned at school. This may take place at the dinner table, during a car trip, and/or as a child is ready to go to sleep. This can be a time for parents to stress that what a child has just learned connects to what she or he already knows. It is also

helpful whenever possible to relate school learning to experiences and potential applications in everyday life.

8. Parents need to "model" active processing of intellectual content. A student with passive processing can benefit greatly from dinner table conversation that includes parental excitement over and elaboration of their own personal interests. At home there needs to be an atmosphere in which everyone is interested in the active pursuit of new knowledge.

9. If there is an intellectually active sibling, that brother or sister should not be allowed to dominate meaningful discussion at home and actively or subtly inhibit or deride the thoughts of the child with passive or superficial processing.

10. It is important to search for subject matter in school that has the potential to excite a child's passive mind. It is helpful to look over what a child is studying in school to uncover ideas or topics that might coincide with the child's interests or family activities. For example, if children are studying the ocean in school, parents can discuss how what they are learning can make the next trip to the aquarium more interesting. This also can be used as a means of encouraging elaboration and rich association.

11. Parents should set limits on passive processing experiences, such as watching television, listening to music, and playing electronic games. These activities in excess may prevent children with passive processing from becoming more active thinkers.

12. When passive processing is one aspect of a picture of overall attentional dysfunction, stimulant medication may be helpful in activating learning. However, such treatment is unlikely to provide the whole cure. These children need explicit reminding and modeling to become more active learners.

13. If students have become passive largely because of peer pressure, it is exceedingly hard to alter their approach to learning. They need as much encouragement and as little belittling from their parents as possible. They must realize that improvement in school performance even to a modest degree will please their parents.

14. Children with excessively active processing need periodic reminders to return to reality. They need to be reminded when they are

straying off the subject during a conversation or when they make an irrelevant comment at the dinner table. Such reminders should be offered in a low-key manner that does not connote disapproval or criticism. A parent might say: "There goes your active mind again. It took off and you lost track of what we were saying; so now let's get back to the subject. I know you have a lot of good ideas about it."

15. Children with problems maintaining a focus can benefit from being told in advance how long they will have to concentrate. They can actually practice maintaining their concentration (perhaps while reading) by using a clock or timer. They need to understand that they are doing so in order to get better at focusing longer. Such measures should never be perceived by the child as punishment or criticism.

16. It is important that children with problems maintaining a focus do not become chronic "dabblers." Their long-standing pattern of jumping from one subject to another may cause this to happen. They need to be helped to develop a small number of interests that they are able to explore in depth and over long periods of time instead of pursuing many interests superficially and incompletely. These are individuals who can benefit greatly from becoming "experts" in a focused area of knowledge or skill.

17. Students who become overly focused need periodic reminders that it is time to move along and change the subject. They need to be keenly aware of their overattending and the problems it is causing them (such as reading too slowly).

18. Children who are highly insatiable need to understand fully what this means. They may require careful, ongoing counseling to help them recognize the risks as well as the potential advantages of their insatiability. Then they should practice conscious delay and substitution processes. That is, they need experience at postponing gratification and practice substituting something else when they can't attain a goal. One method of delay is to allow them to do or receive what they want only after they have been able to remain focused on some other necessary activity. Another method is to set aside certain periods of the day (insatiability office hours) during which children can talk about things they want to have or do and possibly get their needs satisfied. At other times of the day they should write down or record these needs. These children should be asked to think about other possibilities that will be nearly as satisfying when they want something very badly.

19. Many children who show insatiability and have good language production skills become extremely argumentative at home. By the age of thirteen or fourteen they can usually out debate their parents as they present their arguments for getting or doing whatever they want. These children come to believe that if they can state a demand eloquently, it must be right. It is very important for parents to let these children know as early in life as possible that the home is neither a place for debates nor a democracy and that the parents are fully in charge of decision making. Allowing a child to excessively develop his debating skills at home is inevitably destructive.

20. It is important not to overindulge insatiable children with material possessions and excessively stimulating daily experience. Parents should avoid a constant succession of planned play activities, shopping trips, and intensely exciting electronic games. The constant feeding of an insatiable appetite tends to increase the level of a child's insatiability.

Managing Weak Processing Control in School

Children with poor control of processing need to have teachers who can keep them focused and properly oriented to the subject at hand during class sessions.

1. Children who have problems with saliency determination benefit from a strong stress on prioritization and relative importance. They need to be corrected in a nonthreatening manner when they express or recall irrelevant information during a discussion and/or in their writing. When working with them, it is important to emphasize the process of determining what's really important.

2. It is inappropriate to call on children when it is obvious they have not been listening. Such an approach just adds anxiety to inattention.

3. Activities that stress relative importance can help children with weak saliency determination. They might be asked to read a text and circle the most important ideas. They need opportunities to develop skills at summarizing, finding main ideas in paragraphs, paraphrasing what a teacher has said, and giving the most important characteristics of a person, a place, or an event. In providing these experiences, a teacher should keep explicitly emphasizing that the human mind can't take in everything; a person just has to keep deciding what's most important.

4. A child's specific form(s) of distractibility requires good management in school. A visually distractible child needs periodic verbal

reminders to look at the teacher or the book. A child with auditory distractibility may need to have instructions repeated when there is considerable background noise. Some distractible children respond well to reminder cards on their desks or attached to the cover of their notebooks. The cards can ask: "Am I tuning out? Am I listening to noises instead of the teacher?"

5. Children can be asked to rate their distractibility during certain periods. On a particular day, students can keep score of the number of times they catch themselves looking out the window, listening to voices outside the classroom, etc. They can give themselves points every time they can refocus their attention.

6. When giving verbal instructions to children with superficial processing, teachers should try to make them short and direct and to deliver them with good eye contact. These children also benefit from advanced warning when something very important is about to be communicated by the teacher. Additionally, they may process more deeply when information is delivered in more than one way (e.g., verbally and with a diagram on the chalkboard).

7. Children with superficial processing may fail to understand directions in class. The teacher should check to make sure that a child really processed the instructions for a homework assignment.

8. As students with superficial processing come to understand their problem, they can be encouraged to engage in strategies to improve the depth of processing. They can try whispering under their breath to repeat something they've just heard, forming relevant pictures in their minds while a teacher is speaking, and learning to ask themselves whether they really heard something. Since these children often experience difficulties with short-term memory, the suggestions for management of short-term memory problems (chapter 3) may be helpful.

9. It is important for students who show passive processing to be asked questions that encourage the *interrelating* of what they have learned. There should be significant emphasis on the comparing and contrasting of ideas, events, facts, and procedures, for example, "Tell me how percentages and decimals are alike and how they are different." Teaching and testing should follow this practice.

10. Teaching styles may need to change to accommodate students who are accustomed to the passive absorption of ideas. More interactive, hands-on participatory modes of learning may be needed.

11. Subject matter to which a child is romantically attracted can be used intermittently to get that student into an active learning mode. Reading or writing in a specialty area may rekindle enthusiasm and active attention. If children love horses, they should be given opportunities to focus on this affinity, read about it, talk about it, and write about it. Teachers may need to be highly creative in integrating children's interests outside of school with the content of the classroom to bolster their enthusiasm.

12. Children with passive processing need practice in elaborating during class. However, their teachers should give them advanced warning before calling on them for such a response. They should also be given some leeway with respect to topic selection.

13. It is sometimes helpful for students with passive processing to have a reminder card on their desk or attached to their notebooks. On it should be inscribed: "Am I being passive or am I being active in my learning today?"

14. The teaching and testing of children with passive processing should discourage rote memorization and the passive regurgitation of knowledge or imitation of skill. There should instead be a stress on applying and extending what was learned.

15. The use of some kind of agreed-upon signal can be helpful for students whose minds become overly active in class. Children need to be informed when they are "getting carried away" or dreaming excessively. It can also be good for these children to have a way of informing the teacher when they realize they have been off on the free flight of ideas and have missed an instruction or explanation.

16. For children with excessively active processing, the kinds of creative outlets that are encouraged at home should coincide with those that will be nurtured in school. These students need opportunities to demonstrate their original and imaginary thinking through artistic activities and oral presentations.

17. In collaborative activities children with excessively active processing can often serve as brainstormers, coming up with unique ideas and approaches.

18. Children who have trouble maintaining their focus need to be reminded gently in school as at home to get back on track. They may benefit from being told in advance how long they will need to concentrate on something.

19. Students with insatiability should be encouraged to take turns, share, and delay gratification, just as at home. Once children understand their problem with insatiability, the teacher can let them know when their need for instant gratification is out of control.

WEAK PRODUCTION CONTROL

We have looked at the kinds of weak attention control that interfere with the flow of mental energy and with processing. In so doing we have limited our discussion to the taking in and preparing of information or stimuli by a child's brain. We will now scrutinize the effects of weak control of production or output while acknowledging that much of what we produce in the form of writing, speaking, or behaving is affected by how we took in or processed information initially. As a result, it is not always easy to separate processing and production entirely. Although many children have problems with the control of both, there are still those who reveal difficulties with production control primarily or only.

Forms of Weak Production Control

There are many types of production that students undertake and control throughout a school day. First, there are the various academic produc-

---

S A M

Twelve-year-old Sam is always on the go. He shows a great deal of overactivity. In fact, he readily admits that he is "hyper." Everyone agrees that Sam means well, but he frequently gets into trouble in school and at home. Most of the time it is because he does or says things too quickly without predicting their consequences. Sam's academic work could be excellent, but he constantly rushes through things and fails to notice any mistakes he makes. Sam is not well liked by his peers. This is because he often offends them with his odd comments and actions. When he says something that irritates other children, Sam just doesn't notice their reactions. His unpopularity saddens Sam deeply. He is a sensitive and kind person who would like very much to succeed with friends and with academic pursuits.

tions, such as written assignments and tests or activities in a physical education class. Second, there are behavioral productions, such as actions that demonstrate a child is complying with rules of the classroom or daily schedule. Third, there are social productions, efforts at forming and maintaining relationships with others. An inability to control any or all of these three types of production may have serious negative effects on a child's life at school and at home.

In the sections that follow, we will describe several common forms of weak production control. As we shall see, these manifestations are closely related, and some or all often coexist in an individual child.

Poor Previewing

One aspect of producing good results, whether it is with behavior or work, is to estimate beforehand or preview the likely effects if the intention is carried through. Such previewing serves as an important blueprint or plan for action. Many children with attentional dysfunction are prone to accelerate or neglect this previewing stage for much of what they do. Consequently, they may do, say, or produce things in a random, haphazard manner without regard to the probable consequences. They may find themselves in behavioral trouble because of having committed an act too quickly and without sufficient forethought. This is seen in the case of Sam (above) who often gets in trouble because of his failure to look ahead before acting. Similarly, such a child may offend a peer because of a behavior or statement that was produced without predicting its possible social effects.

Children with poor previewing tend to operate like a photographer who is using a camera without a viewfinder—they act but have no idea what the results will be. They fail to ask themselves various "if . . .?" or "what if . . .?" questions: "If I pick this topic, will I be able to write a good report?" "What if I act this way? Will I get in big trouble?" "What if I say this to her? Will she still like me?" Instead of looking ahead and predicting likely outcomes, they are apt to engage in the first possibility that comes to mind. If negative consequences follow, these children will not believe they caused them. Often they feel no responsibility for what they have produced!

Children with poor previewing may have difficulty estimating answers to mathematical problems. It may be hard for them to plan a project for school because they have trouble imagining what it will look like upon completion. Some of these children become discipline problems because they fail to foresee how an action will be in violation of the rules. They are also vulnerable to rejection by their classmates, as they behave poorly or make unpleasant comments without predicting what effects these will have on their reputations.

Many children with poor previewing deal inadequately with transitions in their daily lives. Because they fail to preview what is coming next, they are forever unprepared for it. They become highly disorganized as a result. They get on the bus without their homework because they never actually stopped and pictured themselves in school and wondered what they would need at that future point. They are most disorganized and sometimes very anxious at key transition times because they feel so unready and have had so many negative past experiences at these times. Forms of organizational problems are discussed further in chapter 5.

Weak Control of Facilitation and Inhibition

Another aspect of production control involves facilitating actions that will help a person carry out a plan and inhibiting actions that might get in the way. This control usually is an important part of the planning stage of production. For example, let us suppose you are driving your car and you have a plan to arrive at a particular restaurant to meet some friends. Because you have a plan, you can preview in your mind or foresee what it will be like getting to the restaurant on time and finding your friends there. But to meet this planned expectation, you must look at all the possible ways of getting there. You can then facilitate the best route and inhibit any temptation or need or inclination to take a less desirable pathway to your planned destination.

There are many students who seem unable to control facilitation and inhibition dependably. They keep inhibiting what they should have facilitated and facilitating what they ought to have inhibited! Such poor judgment interferes with completing tasks or achieving planned goals.

Once a goal has been selected because it is likely to represent a positive outcome, the brain has the job of facilitating just the right functions or pathways to get that job accomplished well and efficiently. This represents an important part of facilitation and inhibition. If students need to write a report about what they did last summer, then they activate their long-term episodic memories (i.e., they recall events in their lives). If they are going to do some creative writing, then they facilitate various divergent brainstorming pathways of thinking in their minds. When they are solving equations in algebra class, they use certain memory and problem-solving functions while simultaneously inhibiting the aforementioned creative pathways and episodic memories because thinking about the horses they rode last summer will not help them balance the equation. Some children have great difficulty with this kind of selective facilitation and inhibition, so they are prone to go astray while executing a cognitive/academic task.

A child's motor coordination and skill may also reflect selective facilitation and inhibition problems. If one observes such a child running, kicking a ball, or riding a bicycle, it is possible to detect that too many different muscle groups seem to be working during the particular activity. For example, while running the arms may be moving excessively. When such a child writes, his or her tongue and lips may be moving. Such extraneous muscular activity occurs because the child's brain is not properly inhibiting certain specific muscle groups that are unneeded for the task at hand. As might be expected, this lack of selectivity can cause overall motor coordination problems. During a neurological examination, a physician may actually try to elicit these superfluous movements (often called *synkinesias* or *associated movements*) as a sign of neurological dysfunction in a child. Such movements are normal in very young children but gradually disappear as they grow older. However, they may persist in older children with weak production control.

The inability to facilitate desired actions and to inhibit undesired ones can affect children's behavior and their socializing with others. A child may consciously decide to behave well in class today so she can earn points toward an award. But then she talks continuously to a friend and finds herself losing points instead of gaining them. A child may decide he wants to be a friend of a particular student, but then he says something that is insulting to that potential friend. His temptation to insult should have been inhibited, while a positive comment should have been facilitated.

Some children with attentional dysfunction are described as showing *low frustration tolerance*. For example, during a soccer game, the other team scores a goal and a child walks off the field and quits playing. Often, such a child has problems with facilitation and inhibition. She or he has little ability to think about possible ways of dealing with the setback and then facilitating the best response (e.g., "I'll play harder and I'll help cheer our team on").

Previewing skill and selective facilitation and inhibition are often thought of together as *planful* behaviors. They enable an individual to undertake actions that are truly intentional and thought out. Children who have difficulty with these production controls commonly are said to be *impulsive*. Many of their actions are not consciously intended and adequately thought out. Children with impulsivity, in addition, are susceptible to problems accomplishing things at an appropriate rate which we shall discuss as the next phenomenon.

Improper Pacing

There is an optimal rate for accomplishing most goals. A competent student is often a well-paced student, finishing work neither too rapidly nor excessively slowly. But among children with weak production control improper pacing is very common. They may do their work too fast (like Sam), committing careless errors which affect the overall quality of the result, or they may work too slowly some of the time and too hastily at other times, but seldom at the right tempo for the task at hand. Some of these students are not able to judge how much time to allow for different parts of an assignment or they may have difficulty predicting how long a particular task will take.

Many such children also think too fast. They are said to have a rapid *cognitive tempo*. They have trouble slowing down and thinking through a conflict or a problem or a task. As a result, they are apt to jump to conclusions or to do things in a way that is not well thought through because they did not give their minds the time to reason before acting or coming up with an answer.

The control of pacing is also related in many cases to the level of motor activity. Children with pacing problems in their school work may also show poor control over their motor tempo. They are said to be *hyperactive* or *hyperkinetic* because they appear driven. They are perpetually on the go. They have trouble sitting still in a classroom or remaining in a seat long enough to finish lunch. They can't seem to slow down. In some cases hyperactivity may be a manifestation of a child's mental fatigue, that is, the youngster may be using physical activity as a way of waking himself up, becoming more aroused and alert. In other instances the high activity level may represent a form of motor disinhibition or part of the overall picture of improper pacing.

It is important to emphasize that not all children with attentional dysfunction are hyperactive. In fact, some are quite normal in their activity levels, while others are actually lethargic or hypoactive. In general, girls with weak attentional controls are less likely than boys to be hyperactive and older adolescents of both genders are less prone to be hyperactive than are younger students.

Deficient Self-Monitoring

In accomplishing a task or attempting to behave in a certain manner, it is critically important to know how we are doing. Are we remaining "on task," or are we going astray in one way or another, deviating unknowingly from our chosen goal and pathway? It is of equal importance to monitor a task or action after its completion, asking ourselves: "How did I do?" Such essential controls are known as self-monitoring functions.

It is common for children with attentional dysfunction to use little or no self-monitoring. The absence of this skill has been a significant handicap for Sam in his academic work, behavior, and relationships. This shortcoming reveals itself in many ways. Students may have

- A great reluctance to check over or proofread work in school
- Trouble "reading" social feedback cues (e.g., knowing when they have just said something that offended or annoyed another person)
- Difficulty adhering to a topic during conversation and/or writing (i.e., not noticing that they are wandering off the subject)
- A tendency to behave in a manner that is becoming progressively worse without noticing that people around them are displeased
- Difficulty detecting their own mistakes while taking a test
- An inability to evaluate how they did after completing something (e.g., sensing how they performed on a quiz)
- A problem interpreting feedback from others (e.g., parents or teachers or friends)

It is common for children with inadequate self-monitoring to lack sufficient sensitivity to feedback that would enable them to be aware of how they're doing or how they've just done. They have trouble comparing actual outcomes to intended outcomes. This lack of discrimination can compromise performance in many areas.

Low Reinforceability

Some children have trouble learning from experience. They may be relatively insensitive to the effects of positive reinforcement (i.e., rewards) and negative reinforcement (i.e., punishment). Affected children may get into trouble for a particular inappropriate act. They may truly regret and feel remorseful for having done it. However, the very next day they repeat the crime! Somehow the unpleasant consequences of their action were not reinforcing. They failed to teach them not to do it again.

Low reinforceability is also encountered in relation to cognitive/academic tasks. Children may be taught a new technique for reducing fractions. The strategy works remarkably well for the students, but then the next time they are faced with the need to reduce a fraction, they don't use this method. It does not become part of their cognitive repertoire despite the fact that it worked so well before. Success fails to reinforce the strategy. Likewise, children can bask in praise for having submitted their homework assignments on time but then neglect to repeat the performance the next day.

Their low reinforceability may make these children relatively unresponsive to traditional methods of punishment and reward which can be very frustrating to parents, teachers, and school administrators. Adults need to keep seeking ways to help these children reinforce what they learn from experience.

Managing Weak Production Control at Home

There is much that parents can do to help their children to plan and carry out responsibilities and to become more aware and in control of their behavior. The following are some suggestions.

1. To help develop previewing skills for school work, parents can encourage children to come up with a plan before writing a report, starting a project, or drawing a picture. Children need to preview consciously, to visualize and describe what the outcome or result is likely or desired to be. Parents should inquire specifically about children's preview of a task. Sometimes students can make a sketch, a brief summary, or an outline to use as a blueprint. Children should understand that they are doing these things to build up their previewing skills. It is often especially helpful to stress previewing in a child's area of talent. For example, a child who is good at carpentry or knitting might be asked to draw a rough sketch of what the final product will look like prior to starting the actual work. Parents should spend time discussing this sketch and helping the child think through possible revisions in advance. It is also helpful to engage in previewing activities related to everyday life. For example, a parent can ask a young child such questions as, "How do you think Susan will feel when we tell her we won't be home this weekend for her visit?" The child should be told occasionally that it is good to think up questions like this because they help a person look ahead and decide how to act.

2. Many impulsive children with behavior problems can benefit from discussions that stress previewing. Parents can think up hypothetical situations and also discuss real predicaments the child has been

through or is going through. With the child they can play the "what if . . .?" game. "What if you said this, what would happen? What if you did this to him, what would your teacher think? What would your friends think about this?" Such previewing of responses can increase the child's awareness of the need to look ahead and foresee outcomes before acting. When an impulsive child gets into trouble, some previewing of alternative actions can be instructive. "What if you had done this instead?" A strong emphasis on previewing and the exploration of alternatives also helps those children who have behavioral difficulty with facilitation and inhibition. These kinds of activities are not usually effective during the "heat of battle," but they can be excellent ways of reviewing what went on at a later and calmer time.

3. To work on the academic aspects of facilitation and inhibition, parents can ask questions like: "What are the different ways we might do this? What do you think is probably the best way? What would be the worst way to go about this?" This sort of reviewing of alternative strategies can occur before preparing a report, studying for a test, or trying to a solve a new kind of mathematical problem. Such techniques can also help with overall problem-solving skills (chapter 5).

4. The same kind of help can be related to behavioral and social planning (e.g., "What's the best thing to do about that boy who called you a bad name in school today? What are some other things you could consider doing? What would work best? Which of these possibilities is a bad idea?"). These kinds of discussions when feasible can be conducted at home with an individual child or, when it seems appropriate and relaxed, with the whole family.

5. To help children with improper pacing, parents should discourage frenetic work patterns by avoiding statements such as: "You can watch television when you finish your work." Offers of this kind may inadvertently encourage children to work as quickly and carelessly as possible.

6. It can help a child's pacing to set aside a certain amount of time each evening (or each weekday evening) for cognitive work. The whole family should be engaged in such activities. There is then no incentive to finish quickly, since it will only mean having to find some other brain work to do.

7. Some of these children work too quickly, in part, because they are convinced that quality is unattainable. They may require a great deal

of encouragement at home and in school to shed this belief. They need to see progress in their grades and the real possibility for improvement in the future. A tutor may help them improve their work, so they can feel some optimism about their school performance. Tutors can offer positive reinforcement, showing these children that they can turn out high-quality products by working slowly and systematically.

8. Sometimes it is helpful to urge a child to work more rapidly or more slowly. A parent can set a certain time allotment for a task. Children who work too slowly can practice speeding up, while those who proceed too rapidly can strive to pace themselves more deliberately. It is important to discuss with them the relationship between pace and result. Children who are perfectionists need to see the advantages of a quicker pace and also be reassured that perfection is not really necessary. Those for whom speed is the highest priority need to learn of the benefits of high quality rather than the advantages of always finishing first.

9. Improper pacing sometimes leads to behavioral and social problems. A child may act too quickly and get into trouble with adults or peers. When a child is showing frenzied behavior, a parent should take him or her aside and encourage slowing down and thinking things out. This should be undertaken in a way that does not embarrass the child and does not seem critical or punitive. A parent might say, "Things are moving a little too fast, and that can cause trouble for you. Let's slow down and think some more about what's happening."

10. Students who need specific help with self-monitoring and proofreading can benefit from looking for discrepancies or errors in their work or in the work of others. They should be required to proofread their own work but only after an interval of hours or days has passed since the work was completed. It is very tedious for anyone to correct something immediately after completing it.

11. Parents can help children engage in behavioral and social self-monitoring. Through discussions at home children can have an opportunity to review the quality of their relationships with various friends and teachers. They can talk about how their behavior in school is going, whether it seems to be in the right or wrong direction.

12. When students with weak production control are having serious behavior problems at home, parents should find a professional with whom they can meet regularly to discuss ways to handle the issues. The child, of course, must be included in these conversations. Often, the

whole family needs to be involved. The therapy should take the form of advice and coaching. Even the most competent parent needs objective advice when dealing day in and day out with a child whose poor control over production is causing behavioral chaos at home! Several different formal approaches to counseling have been advocated for these children. Some children with weak control of production can benefit from a form of counseling called *cognitive-behavioral therapy*. This kind of treatment is often carried out by a psychologist. Like the suggestions in this list, the approach places a stress on educating the child about his or her problem and offering appropriate activities and exercises for working on it. Such therapy, at the very least, may help affected students understand themselves much better.

13. Low reinforceability can present the greatest challenge to management. Children who somehow fail to respond to punishment and reward can frustrate themselves as well as the adults in their lives. However, they may benefit from very consistently administered behavioral modification programs. Such systems of rewards usually need to be organized and supervised by a trained professional. In the absence of such professional support, parents should strive to be as consistent as possible in establishing and maintaining rules, keeping close score of behavior, and charting it from day to day. Additionally, some of these children benefit from signing behavioral contracts with their parents (page 238).

14. It is important that parents communicate to impulsive children that they know how really hard it is for them to control their behavior. It is also useful to point out that no one expects perfection, only some improvement from week to week.

15. When there are other family problems at home, these are likely to complicate the child's own innate difficulties. It is not at all unusual for a parent to have some of the same production control problems that are present in the child and there may, of course, be a strong genetic basis for this similarity. In fact, it can be very beneficial to explain this to the child. In such cases, broad family problems may need to be addressed professionally.

16. Children with weak production control may benefit from stimulant medication. In particular, the medication may markedly reduce a child's impulsivity, through improving previewing, pacing, and facilitation and inhibition. This form of treatment is never the whole answer, but it should be considered as part of a broad management plan.

Managing Weak Production Control in School

There is much that teachers can do to deal with students whose working pace, overall productivity, and/or behavior is notably out of step with that of their peers.

1. Teachers, like parents, can help children by stressing previewing. Whenever possible teachers should design and model activities that accentuate the blueprints for production. For example, students should periodically submit their work plans and be graded on them before starting an assignment. Teachers can also model good previewing through the use of advance organizers or of questions to consider while reading a story or chapter (page 173).

2. An art or woodworking class can provide an excellent opportunity to discuss and practice previewing. Children should be expected to picture in their minds and then actually depict what a project will look like when completed.

3. Children with poor previewing may need help with their estimation skills which are often very deficient. In mathematics there should be a stress on estimating answers. In discussions of current events, history, science, and geography, these children can gain from experience in estimating. For example, a teacher might ask, "About how many people do you think live in London?" "About how far away is the moon?"

4. Whenever possible teachers should offer these children practice in behavioral previewing. The kinds of "what if?" questions described under home management should also be asked in school.

5. Children's awareness of facilitation and inhibition can be enhanced through a constant emphasis on reviewing alternative strategies before undertaking a task or other activity. Such exercises also contribute to the development of good problem-solving skills (chapter 5). In as many contexts as possible, children should be taught to develop problem-solving plans that reflect consideration of alternative approaches. An example of this can be found in Appendix 1. To model this practice, a teacher might distribute a sheet that includes different techniques that might be used to study for a spelling test. Students could look over this list and write comments about which method or methods would work best for them and why.

6. As part of a work or study plan, students with improper pacing should document in advance how long they think the different stages of

a task ought to take. They should review these estimates with an adult to help determine if they are realistic. While working on the activity, children should keep track of the time actually taken.

7. Children who keep on facilitating behaviors they should have inhibited can become serious discipline problems in school. For them there needs to be a continuing stress on how they could have acted differently. After they have impulsively violated rules, children might be asked to go back and describe the situations that led to their actions as accurately as possible (in writing, on a tape, or directly to an adult). They should then record how they reacted and what some other reactions might have been. They can rate these possibilities to decide what would have been best.

8. When children get in trouble for impulsive acts (i.e., without previewing and proper facilitation and inhibition), they should never be called bad. A teacher or school administrator should say, "It looks as if you were out of control today. Your attention problem [or your impulse problem] is acting up. How are we going to get it back in control?" Parents also need to keep impulsivity out of the realm of good and evil.

9. When a student works too quickly and carelessly, the teacher should make it clear that such rapid pacing is not what he or she is looking for and that being the "first one done" is not the goal of the assignment. The child should be praised when discovered to be working "slowly enough."

10. Sometimes it can be effective to tell a child in advance how long a homework assignment ought to take. The child should then record on the paper how long it did take. Similarly, it can be helpful for these children to be told how long they should study for a test; they can then report back on how long they actually did study. Teachers may also improve students' pacing by requiring them to work in stages and to submit work in progress at these designated stages.

11. As children become better at organizing their time and their space (see chapter 5), they may improve in achieving an appropriate work tempo.

12. When children with improper pacing move about too quickly and get into trouble, they should be taken aside and encouraged to slow down and think about what they are doing. When there are signs of hyperactivity, teachers need to allow these children to have chances to move around. Responsibilities such as erasing the board, taking a mes-

sage to the office, and collecting papers can offer appropriate outlets for activity. Teachers should never criticize or embarrass children for being fidgety or showing bizarre postures at their desks. Many children with hyperactive tendencies actually need to keep moving. It is good to try to find acceptable nondisruptive ways for them to be active. They should never be made to feel that they are bad or "weird" just because they need to stay in motion.

13. Children with inadequate self-monitoring should be rewarded for finding their own errors. They can learn also by finding mistakes in the work of other (hypothetical) people. When they take a test, it can be helpful for these students to look over what they have done and record at the top the grade or score they think they will get. They might be given bonus points if their self-monitoring is accurate. In addition, children should look over their mistakes on tests or other assignments and try to explain why they made specific errors (e.g., "I did it too fast" or "I didn't understand the question" or "I couldn't remember how to do that"). Again, there should be strong incentives for engaging in this kind of analysis.

14. When inadequate self-monitoring is associated with behavior problems, children can be encouraged to engage in daily self-assessments. A teacher can design a custom-made score sheet for children to rate each day the state of the controls they are trying to improve. This activity can also take place at home, using the same system of rating. Appropriate rewards can be offered for improvement. Again, it is important that such ratings focus on being in control rather than being good or bad.

15. When low reinforceability hurts academic performance, there should be a constant emphasis on doing things the way that has worked best in the past, that is, learning from experience. As part of a work plan, children might review things that they have done well and consider how to incorporate them into the next assignment.

16. When low reinforceability makes the management of behavior problems very difficult, often professional advice is needed. A school psychologist should consult with classroom teachers to develop a consistent behavioral management plan.

17. In communicating with children who have poor control over production, it is especially important that the same terminology, the same methods, and the same interpretations of behaviors be used at

home and in school. It is confusing and discouraging for children to be told by their teachers that they are bad and told at home that they have a problem with attention control that they were born with and need to work on. These mixed signals will seriously interfere with any attempts to help them. Therefore, with this condition (as well as with others described throughout *Educational Care*), close coordination and communication between home and school are essential.

The Variabiliity of the Traits

We have stressed the fact that children with weak attention controls vary markedly in the particular traits that they display. Some may have much more trouble with processing than production, while others show predominantly problems with the control of mental energy. In considering the management needs of an individual child, it is important first to document the status of specific controls. The Inventory of Traits (fig. 2.3) provides a way of doing this.

Sources of Weak Control of Attention

In this chapter we have examined attentional dysfunction as it involves various forms of difficulty with the mental energy flow and weak control of processing and production. It is likely that fundamental inborn (possibly genetic) weaknesses of attentional function are the most common causes of these phenomena. However, it is important to stress that breakdowns in these controls may resemble primary attention deficits, but they actually may result from other causes. The following are some examples:

- A child with weak language processing (chapter 4) may have trouble understanding her teacher. She may experience extreme mental fatigue in striving endlessly to do so. Ultimately, she becomes distractible and fidgety. Her problems with attention are the result of her weak language processing. Other kinds of processing weaknesses may likewise erode attention.
- A student who has problems with active working memory (chapter 3) keeps rushing through his work because when he works slowly, he forgets what he's doing. He often looks frenetic and impulsive in class. His weak production control may be a result of his memory gaps rather than primarily a dysfunction of attention.
- A child is very preoccupied and depressed because her parents are having serious marital and major financial problems. She feels partly responsible for their plight. She is very worried about the

ATTENTIONAL DYSFUNCTION:
AN INVENTORY OF TRAITS

Child's Name _____ Date _____

Grade _____ Age _____ Teacher/Administrator _____

Others Involved in Assessment _____

Part A—Mental Energy Control

[– = A definite finding; +/– = A possible finding; + = Not a finding]

Parameter	Trait	–	+/–	+
Arousal/Alertness	Has trouble falling or staying asleep			
	Shows evidence of fatigue (e.g., yawning, stretching) during the day			
	Is fidgety when needing to concentrate			
	Reveals highly inconsistent/erratic patterns of attention			
Mental Effort	Has trouble getting started with work			
	Has difficulty finishing work			
	Can only work on things that are particularly interesting to him/her			
	Effort is unpredictable; can work well at some times but not others			

IMPACT(S): Cognitive/Academic_____   Behavioral_____   Social_____

Fig. 2.3. This inventory is intended to help parents, teachers, or clinicians document the presence of specific weak or strong attention controls in a particular child. The results can help establish priorities for the child's management at home and in school. It can also enable different adults to compare their observations of a child's attention controls.

Part B—Processing Control

[– = A definite finding; +/– = A possible finding; + = Not a finding]

Parameter	Trait	–	+/–	+
Saliency Determination	Can't tell what's important when *listening* or *studying* (cross one out if necessary)			
	Seems to remember unimportant information better than important facts or ideas			
	Is easily distracted by irrelevant sounds/background noises			
	Concentrates on visual stimuli that others would ignore			
Processing Depth and Detail	Requires repetition of instructions			
	Has trouble with fine detail in school work			
	Does best with "the big picture": conceptualizing, generalizing			
	Has trouble entering new material in memory			
Mental Activation	Seems passive in learning; doesn't relate new information with what is already known			
	Is unusually creative/inventive/imaginative			
	Has trouble getting involved/engaged in school subject matter			
	Has a mind that is too active, free associates, daydreams too easily			
Focal Maintenance	Often doesn't concentrate long enough			
	Concentrates too long at times			
	Is not a good listener			
	Misses key parts of directions/explanations			
Satisfaction Control	Is hard to satisfy; seems to want things all the time			
	Can only concentrate well on exciting stimuli			
	Has trouble delaying gratification			
	Is notably restless; craves excitement			

IMPACT(S): Cognitive/Academic____   Behavioral____   Social____

Part C—Production Control

[– = A definite finding; +/– = A possible finding; + = Not a finding]

Parameter	Trait	–	+/–	+
Previewing	Fails to look ahead and consider possible consequences before doing or saying things			
	Does school work without planning or thinking enough before starting out			
	Has trouble accomplishing transitions from one activity or task to next			
	Has trouble estimating or foreseeing solutions or work outcomes in school			
Facilitation and Inhibition	Does inappropriate things without realizing it			
	Does a lot of things the hard way			
	Has a way of doing the wrong things at the wrong times			
	Says inappropriate things without realizing it			
Tempo Control	Seems to have trouble allocating, organizing, and/or estimating time needs			
	Often dawdles, is late, misses deadlines			
	Does many things too slowly			
	Is "hyperactive"			
Self-Monitoring and Self-Correcting	Loses track of what she/he is doing during a task or activity			
	Doesn't notice when others seem displeased			
	Doesn't realize when he/she has said or done something wrong			
	Makes frequent careless work errors without noticing			
Reinforceability	Doesn't seem to learn from her/his mistakes			
	Is not greatly affected by punishment			
	Doesn't use methods that have worked well previously			
	Doesn't really respond properly to rewards			

IMPACT(S): Cognitive/Academic_____   Behavioral_____   Social_____ future. As a result, she has trouble concentrating in school. Her attentional problems are caused by anxiety and preoccupation.

- A child has a learning disorder that has never been properly identified and managed. He thinks he is "retarded." He tunes out and does very little work because he has given up on school and on himself. His lost motivation masquerades as a primary attention deficit.
- A child keeps tuning in and tuning out in class. He is found to have seizure disorder that is causing this pattern. There are, in fact, a number of medical conditions that can seriously diminish the flow of mental energy and interfere with processing and production control. There are also health problems that may contribute to the development of attentional problems. These include lead poisoning, recurrent ear infections, extreme prematurity, some disorders of chromosomes, and serious head trauma. Children with weak attention control need to be evaluated to consider the role of these conditions (chapter 8).

Sometimes attentional dysfunction in a young child may be the beginning of some other condition. For example, often cases of adolescent and adult depression or manic depression (chapter 7) seem to start out as attentional dysfunction in childhood. Children with Tourette Syndrome who eventually show tics and possibly other unusual behaviors frequently manifest weak attention controls years before their other symptoms appear. Adults with narcolepsy (a condition where they suddenly fall asleep during the day) often have a history of attentional dysfunction during childhood.

The above examples should serve to illustrate the fact that the phenomena described in this and other chapters of *Educational Care* are relatively nonspecific. That is, they can go together in infinite patterns and represent the effects of many different possible causes. In fact, most children who are having trouble in school have more than one reason for their difficulties.

The Demystification of Attentional Dysfunction

Children who have trouble with attention are often confused by their own day-to-day performance at the same time that they are disappointed by it. They are likely to sense the disparity between their true abilities and their actual accomplishments. They may condemn themselves for their inconsistency of alertness and effort, as they are so often told that they can do better "when they really try." These students are therefore prone to believe that they are lazy or that there is something damaged in their brains. Demystification needs to aim at allowing them to understand that they have a problem that is not their fault and one that can be worked on.

In educating a child with weak controls of attention, it is important to be specific about the phenomena that are showing up in that individual. The person who is demystifying should show an understanding of what it feels like to have trouble with attention. It is reassuring for a student to hear: "Many kids with attention problems say they feel tired and bored a lot in school, especially when they have to sit and listen; some of them feel like moving around, but they have to just sit there."

The following are examples of points that can be stressed.

1. Lots of smart and "cool" kids are having trouble with their attention controls; having this problem doesn't mean they're dumb or crazy or weird.

2. When students have this kind of problem, it is something they're probably born with; it's not their fault.

3. A mind with attention problems keeps "tuning in" and "tuning out," so it misses important things in school and is very inconsistent. Sometimes it works really well and other times it doesn't.

4. People who have trouble with attention get distracted very easily. They may look out the window, listen to noises in the hallway, watch the clock, think about the weekend, dream about all the things they want, or just daydream too much.

5. A lot of kids with attention problems do things too quickly without thinking enough; they are impulsive which sometimes gets them into trouble or makes them do schoolwork too fast and carelessly.

6. It is not all bad to have trouble with attention. Kids with weak attentional controls are often very imaginative and interesting people. They notice things and think up ideas that are different and frequently exciting.

7. Many people with attention control problems become very successful when they grow up. They can be great at thinking up original ideas and inventing new things or ways of doing things.

It can be helpful to use diagrams to explain to a child how attention is supposed to work and what happens when someone has problems with the attentional controls. One such example is the Concentration Cockpit (fig. 2.4) that likens attention to the controls in the cockpit of a

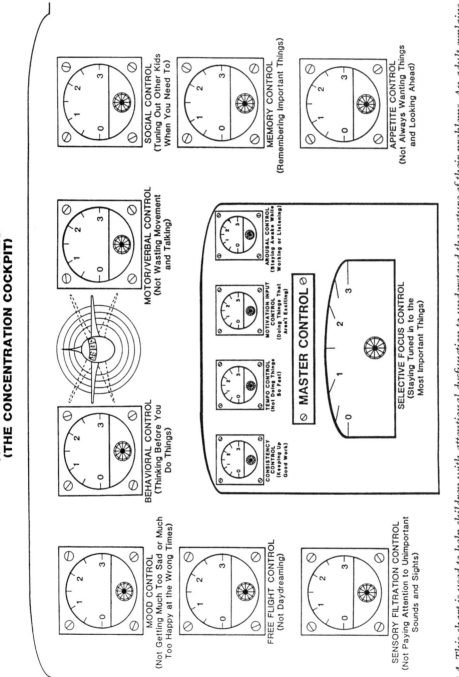

Fig. 2.4. This chart is used to help children with attentional dysfunction to understand the nature of their problems. An adult explains each of the controls on the cockpit, and the child draws her or his needle on each dial (0 = I have a big problem with this, 1 = I have a little problem with this, 2 = I have no problem with this, and 3 = I am excellent at this).

jet airliner. An adult explains each of the controls and then the child rates himself or herself on each of them.

Recognizing Attentional Strengths

There are many children whose attention represents a definite asset. They are able to concentrate with great depth and selectivity and their output is effectively planned and executed. They can use their well-regulated attentional functions to compensate for deficiencies in other aspects of their education.

Most students show what might be called *specialized attention*. That is, they are able to control mental energy, processing, and production remarkably well when engaged in certain kinds of activities or topics. It is important to identify areas of strong attention control for any child and let the child consciously practice his or her strong attention control in those areas. Someday it may be possible to generalize that control to other subjects or pursuits. Also, the area in which children display strong attention controls may be highly revealing, as it may represent the context in which their kind of mind operates most effectively. That may have significant implications for their ultimate choice of career!

We have seen how attention controls occupy a central position in all learning and much of behavior. They do so by regulating and collaborating with a multitude of other brain functions. One of attention's closest allies is memory. Attention and memory are invariably intertwined during learning. It is therefore appropriate that our next exploration of observable phenomena should take place within the territory of memory.

CHAPTER THREE

Phenomena Related to Reduced Remembering

A T NO time during life are we required to store and retrieve as much diverse information and skill as we are during our school years. As a student progresses through school, the demands imposed upon memory become increasingly stringent and strenuous. Some children simply are unable to keep pace with these heightened demands. They suffer from one or more of the different forms of *memory dysfunction*. In this chapter we will consider some of the memory functions most relevant to formal learning and productivity in school. We will explore the ways in which specific forms of memory dysfunction may interfere with learning in certain students, and then we will present some ways to manage children with these problems.

MEMORY FUNCTIONS

Memory is an extremely complex and only partially understood system of brain processes. When looking at aspects of memory that are most important for the kinds of learning that go on in school, we need to tease out those components that promote the retention of relevant facts and skills. For our purposes, we will concentrate on four broad aspects of memory function and dysfunction. These are: (1) entering new information or procedures in short-term memory, (2) temporarily maintaining material in active working memory, (3) consolidating new knowledge and skill in long-term memory, and (4) drawing upon the knowledge and skill stored in long-term memory with accuracy and timeliness. These aspects of memory function are illustrated in figure 3.1.

Memory Pathways

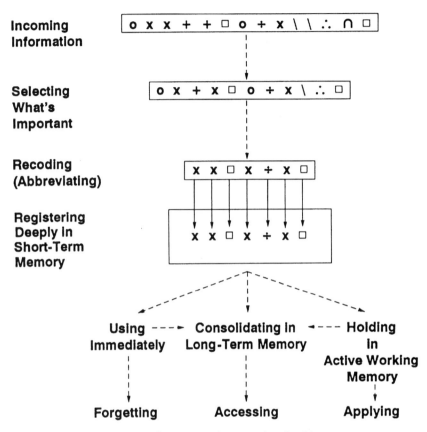

Incoming Information

Selecting What's Important

Recoding (Abbreviating)

Registering Deeply in Short-Term Memory

Using → Consolidating in ← Holding
Immediately Long-Term Memory in Active Working Memory

Forgetting   Accessing   Applying

Fig. 3.1. The flow diagram indicates some key steps involved in memory. One can see a wide range of data is available to memory. A person must select what's important, condense it further (recoding), and then register it in short-term memory. The information can then take several different pathways, including temporary maintenance in active working memory, consolidation in long-term memory, or immediate use (with the possibility of forgetting or consolidating it). Children with memory dysfunctions may exhibit weaknesses at specific points along these pathways.

PROBLEMS WITH SHORT-TERM MEMORY

Short-term memory enables us to hold information for a brief period, a matter of seconds. Such information can be used immediately, held in temporary suspension (i.e., transferred to active working memory) while it is being further developed, or it can decay and be forgotten almost

CARLETTA

Her teachers feel that thirteen-year-old Carletta doesn't really try very hard in school. However, Carletta's parents are aware of how frustrated she becomes when she needs to learn new material. They have worked with her for hours, trying to help her to master vocabulary words or a spelling list. Despite frequent repetitions she is unable to do so. In class, she has trouble remembering directions. She is often confused when she gets home because she never really is able to retain homework assignments or other detailed instructions. Her parents have observed that Carletta has no real sense of how to go about learning something new in school. She appears unable to think about how best to enter new facts or skills in her memory. Instead, she just stares at a page and repeats things over and over to herself, yet little information really "sinks in."

instantly. Alternatively or in addition, the information can be consolidated in long-term or permanent memory. Entering new material in short-term memory is a process called *registration*. To be effective, registration must take place with sufficient intensity; the degree of intensity is called the *depth of processing*, a concept that was introduced in chapter 2.

Short-term memory is strikingly limited in its capacity. For example, we know it can hold only about seven numbers. Consequently, we are forced to be highly selective in deciding what to register there. Also, because short-term memory accommodates so few data, much of what we want to remember must be abbreviated (encoded or recoded) in order to fit into its "space." Finally, it is important to recognize that information we consciously try to remember must pass through short-term memory before it can be stored in long-term memory.

It is not at all unusual to see children who experience difficulty registering new material in short-term memory. This is certainly a major barrier for Carletta. Children like her may go over something repeatedly, but somehow it fails to stick. When they are quizzed shortly after studying, often only a small proportion of what they worked on has registered effectively. The following list identifies some common signs of a problem with short-term memory.

- Inconsistency when following verbal instructions
- A history of trouble studying math facts, spelling words, historical dates, and/or vocabulary
- A tendency to know things quite well once they are learned but to have difficulty with their initial mastery
- A failure to use strategies of any kind while studying
- Confusion with multistep inputs (such as a sequence of directions) and/or large chunks of verbal and/or nonverbal material
- Poor ability to paraphrase or summarize recently presented information

Forms of Problems with Short-Term Memory

It is possible to divide problems with short-term memory into four forms that are commonly observed among children.

Attentional dysfunction affecting short-term memory. Many children with weak mental energy and processing controls also have difficulty with short-term memory. There appear to be several reasons for this. First, they are apt to have inconsistent alertness and mental effort while studying. Second, they often engage in superficial processing (page 22). In a sense, nothing gets very deeply into memory! Third, because of their rapid pacing while studying, such students may fail to employ various strategies that other children use to improve the depth of processing. These include such tactics as visualizing what they are trying to register or whispering under their breath (subvocalizing) that which they are trying to remember. Such strategies are common practices of competent memorizers. Fourth, because of their poor saliency determination these students have trouble deciding what to register in short-term memory. They are apt to study or memorize inappropriate or trivial information.

Weak processing affecting short-term memory. Material that is not clearly processed by the brain is exceedingly difficult to register. When ideas or facts are not understood, they are unlikely to be registered effectively in short-term memory. Therefore, when a child is having short-term memory problems, it is important to consider the possibility that he or she is having trouble processing information in one or more ways. Often this kind of difficulty results from an inability to accurately interpret information that comes to the brain in a particular format or modality. There are three common formats that merit consideration. These are described in the following table.

Table 3.1: Formats for the Presentation of Information

FORMAT	DESCRIPTION	EXAMPLES
Visual-Spatial/ Configurational	Material that enters mainly through the eyes as a configuration or pattern	Letter shapes, map locations, geometric forms, facial features
Linguistic	Information that is conveyed through spoken or written language	Spoken instructions or explanations; reading materials
Sequential, Linear, and/or Procedural	Data coming into the brain in a particular temporal or linear order, where that order is critical and must be preserved	Steps in a math process, digits in a telephone number, list of events leading up to a war, sequence of letters in a spelling word

As children move from grade to grade, they are expected to take in and process information that is presented in these three formats and to do so with increasing speed and in larger and larger amounts. Some children are unable to register information fast enough. Others have trouble with short-term memory if the amount of information is great in a particular format. For example, some students are weak at registering verbal material with sufficient speed or when long sentences and extended discourse prevail. Others may have trouble with the rapid registration of lengthy sequences whether in mathematics or in history (see also page 139). It is important to recognize short-term memory problems that are related to format, speed, and/or amount of material, as these phenomena can cause significant academic frustration, failure, and misunderstanding.

Weak paraphrasing skills. As we have noted, because short-term memory has such small capacity, much of what we want registered needs to be abbreviated or recoded. Obviously, no student can repeat verbatim a teacher's detailed instructions or explanations; such material needs to be condensed to be registered in short-term memory. Children who have deficient paraphrasing or summarization skills may register only fragments of what they have read or heard. They may arrive at home and realize that they don't really remember what the assignment is. Consequently, they are apt to feel overwhelmed. Recoding does not always need to involve verbal summarization or paraphrasing. It is possible and necessary sometimes to recode visually and register the salient details of a design, a map, a geometric figure, or a chart. Such visual abbreviating may be a problem for some students.

Failure to use memory strategies. Effective students are aware of the need to use good strategies to strengthen registration in short-term memory. It has been mentioned that some children with attention deficits work too quickly to deploy strategies. There are also students who pace themselves well but fail to make use of these strategies. They seldom subvocalize, form visual images of what they are trying to remember, change information to a different format (e.g., make a diagram of a paragraph), or test themselves. This lack of strategies is a conspicuous feature of Carletta's problems. These techniques which could enhance registration are seriously neglected by her and many students with short-term memory gaps. Often these are children who also lack other strategies needed for success in school.

Managing Problems with Short-Term Memory at Home

Parents are in a good position to observe children's short-term memory functions as they assist them in various learning activities. There are several ways parents can help these children.

1. Studying for tests can be an exercise in short-term memory building. Students should deploy a stepwise approach to such studying. Older students can actually formulate a memory plan using a guide such as the one shown in figure 3.2, which can be adapted for use with elementary school children. They should consider ways to enhance the depth of processing and engage in appropriate self-testing or collaborative testing with a peer, parent, or sibling. Such approaches can be especially helpful to students with excessively rapid pacing and to those who lack registration strategies.

2. Parents can help children to improve their depth of processing by teaching them to use various *rehearsal strategies*. These include the previously mentioned whispering under their breath and visualizing, along with making up rhymes, acronyms, or anagrams to represent

A MEMORY PLAN

Name _____ Date _____
Class _____

Material to Be Remembered

Ideas _____ Facts _____ How to Do Things _____

Topic or Subject Matter

_____
_____
_____

Information Sources

Textbook _____ Notes _____ Other Books _____
Other Sources _____

Ways of Condensing Material

Diagrams _____ Underline/Highlight _____
Written Summary _____ Taped Summary _____
Key Words/Concepts Lists _____ Questions _____
On Computer _____ Other _____

Registration in Memory

Estimated time needed _____hrs/mins
Best hours for registration _____
Breaks _____
Methods: Whispering _____ Imaging _____
Tricks (specify) _____
_____

Consolidating and Connecting

Elaboration alone _____ On tape _____
Discussion(s) with _____

Self-Testing

Times _____
Alone _____ With Family Member _____
With Friend _____

Fig. 3.2. This form is intended to help students learn to study for tests. They may complete it and submit it before preparing for a test. The form encourages them to think through the methods of using memory strategically. Students can be graded on the quality of their memory plans.

what they are attempting to register. It can also be helpful for them to form associations while trying to remember. For example, when learning the name of an important historical figure, students can think about what the name sounds like or makes them think of. Parents can practice this kind of activity with children while they are studying.

3. In some cases short-term memory can be enhanced through the use of stimulant medication (see page 264). This is likely to be the case when a child's short-term memory dysfunction is accompanied by weak control of mental energy and processing. The administration of the medication may need to be timed so as to have an effect when the child is registering material in short-term memory. For example, a short-acting methylphenidate (Ritalin) tablet might be given one to two hours before studying for an examination.

4. Parents can help their children improve their paraphrasing skills by giving them practice. They can allow them to watch an extra television show or go to a movie if they will summarize it (orally or in writing) afterward. They can encourage them to retell chapters or sections of a book after reading them. Not all summarization needs to be verbal; a child can make a diagram or chart that summarizes information. Such graphic representation may be especially helpful to a student who has difficulty paraphrasing language.

5. Students may need help recognizing which of the three formats is the easiest for them to use. Then they should be encouraged to use it. They can convert data into the format they use most successfully. A strong visual processor may need to make a diagram; a linguistically oriented student may verbally paraphrase written material (perhaps into a tape recorder). Sometimes it may be necessary to change the sequential nature of some inputs. For example, if students can't learn the order of steps needed to complete long-division problems, parents might help them put the steps into language by describing them verbally into a tape recorder. The tape can then be played back several times. Alternatively, each step can be depicted visually on a separate card.

6. Parents need to realize that children with limited short-term memory may not retain instructions. They need to keep such inputs short and offer repetition without being critical.

7. As they grow older, children who have problems in this area need to keep lists and take good notes in order to relieve the burden on short-term memory.

Managing Problems with Short-Term Memory in School

As they come to recognize problems with short-term memory, teachers can use various techniques to make it easier for students to retain recently presented information.

1. Sometimes it helps students who have problems with short-term memory if they sit close to the teacher, especially if they also have attentional dysfunction.

2. The teacher can assist these children by regularly repeating instructions and explanations.

3. Placing a strong emphasis on paraphrasing and explaining how it is important in remembering things will benefit these students. A teacher can model for them how to paraphrase material and then provide them with opportunities to practice this skill. Children can take turns paraphrasing important inputs during class or serving as the paraphraser for the day.

4. Teachers should also encourage students to paraphrase while they read something important. For example, students need to learn to pause at a key sentence or group of sentences and repeat the information in a shorter form. They can write their paraphrases in a book margin, take brief notes, or record them on tape.

5. Related to paraphrasing is the skill of note taking. This ability can enhance registration. A teacher may want to take some time illustrating how to take effective and concise notes and then to include note taking as part of various assignments. For example, children can interview each other and submit notes from these interviews.

6. When children demonstrate that they have a strong format for processing, as much information as possible should be presented in that format. If they are strong at visual processing, they are likely to retain material written on the board better than information presented orally.

7. Some students require that information be delivered in smaller units or portions. This may mean that a teacher uses shorter sentences, allows more time to copy from the board, and simply speaks more slowly.

8. All students can benefit from learning about how short-term memory works and about the kinds of strategies that can be used to make it work better. Once children have learned this, they can be asked to submit memory plans (see fig. 3.2, page 60) before studying for a test. The plan should include: how they will decide what's important, how

they will paraphrase the material they need to remember, what strategies they will use to register it deeply, and when and how they will test themselves or have someone else quiz them.

INSUFFICIENT ACTIVE WORKING MEMORY

Active working memory can be conceptualized as a critical intermediate stage of memory function. Its capacity is not as large as long-term memory, nor is it as limited as short-term memory. Information can be held in active working memory longer than in short-term memory but not nearly as long as in long-term memory.

This essential component of memory serves as a temporary way station, a place where ideas are stored while they are being developed further, manipulated, or used as part of an activity. Table 3.2 describes and provides examples of these roles of active working memory.

Forms of Insufficient Active Working Memory

Problems with active working memory can take a heavy toll on learning and academic productivity. Todd's case illustrates this vividly. Some or

---

TODD

Todd is an eleven-year-old boy who has shown very uneven academic performance. He is motivated and enthusiastic about acquiring new knowledge. In the past, he has had no trouble learning mathematical facts and acquiring other kinds of knowledge in school. However, recently, Todd has experienced difficulties in mathematics, in reading, and in his written output. His parents have observed that Todd forgets what he is doing in the middle of a mathematical problem. His teachers have found that when Todd tries to write, he often loses track of what it was that he intended to get down on paper. Sometimes while trying to remember the correct spelling for a word, he forgets why he needed that word in the first place. When Todd reads he seems to understand what he is reading while he is reading it, but then he has trouble summarizing or remembering the overall content of a chapter or passage. Todd is a boy with excellent language skills. He is quite eloquent, fluent, and sophisticated when he expresses ideas during class and at home.

all of the functions summarized in table 3.2 may be impaired when active working memory capacity is significantly limited. Students with insufficient active working memory have

- A tendency to lose track of what they're doing while working on mathematical problems (a serious impediment for Todd)
- Trouble sustaining the logical development of ideas while writing or speaking
- A pattern of forgetting one part of a task while working on some other part of that task, that is, not recalling what they were going to do
- Trouble remembering reading material (sometimes called "leaky reading") with a possible disparity between reading comprehension (adequate) and reading memory or recall (relatively poor as noted with Todd)

Children with insufficient active working memory can become exceedingly frustrated in school. They simply have inadequate mental space in which to hold ideas, facts, or parts of procedures while working with them.

Managing Insufficient Active Working Memory at Home

Difficulties with active working memory often show up while a child is attempting to study or complete homework assignments. Confusion, disorganization, and performance anxiety can follow. Therefore, the following suggestions can be useful.

1. As children with this limitation grow older it is important for them to know which of their homework activities require active working memory. They will need to be aware of the importance of having special tactics for such pursuits.

2. These children need to be especially active readers. They need to underline as they read. At the end of each page they need to reread what they have underlined. They might even do their rereading into a tape recorder and later listen to what they have transcribed. In addition to underlining, they should asterisk very important points, write key words or brief comments in the margins, and in general use many different ways of indicating different degrees of importance (e.g., double underlining, circling, etc.). The use of highlighters should be discouraged because they provide only one way to mark what is salient. When children are reading books which are not their own, they can use "Post-it" stickers, placing two or three on each page and writing key words or

Table 3.2: Active Working Memory—Roles and Examples

MAJOR ROLES	SOME EXAMPLES
Holding an idea in mind while developing, elaborating, clarifying, or using it	Thinking further about a new concept the teacher has just introduced; comparing and contrasting two countries or two people
Recalling from long-term memory while holding some information in short-term memory	Trying to recall the answer while remembering the question
Holding together in memory the components of a task while completing that task	Carrying a number in multiplication while remembering what you were going to do next
Keeping together a series of new pieces of information so that they remain meaningful	Remembering material at the beginning of a page while reading to the end of that page; being able to retell or summarize the contents of that page or passage; or retaining the first sound or phoneme in a new word while decoding the last one, in order, ultimately, to blend them
Holding a long-range plan while thinking about a short-range need	Remembering what you want in the picture you're painting while selecting the color for one part of it

phrases on them. At the end of a chapter, they can remove the stickers and place them on a board where they can then read across to resynthesize the chapter in their minds. In this case and in using a tape recorder (mentioned above), students are, in effect, transferring their active working memory to some external space.

3. While doing math problems, these children should rely as little as possible on mental computations. For example, as they carry numbers they should write them down. While solving word problems, they should

use scratch paper to write out all the steps, so that they don't lose their place or forget what they are doing in the midst of their problem solving.

4. Whenever possible students with insufficient active working memory should develop a stepwise plan *before* engaging in a task and then they should check off various stages upon completion. They can benefit from reviewing carefully what they have read or done.

5. Some students with active working memory problems seem to benefit from verbalizing what they are doing while they are working. Whispering under their breath or intermittently summarizing what they have done and what they still need to do may bolster active working memory capacity.

Managing Insufficient Active Working Memory in School

School can be made considerably less traumatic for students with insufficient active working memory if specific accommodations can be made for them within the classroom. The same recommendations suggested for home management should be carried out in school along with these additional strategies.

1. Children whose decoding of multisyllabic words is impeded by insufficient active working memory (i.e., they somehow lose the initial sounds while working out subsequent ones) will need to spend a great deal of time and effort becoming automatic with the individual phonemes and the letter combinations that represent them. It will be very hard for them to decode lengthy words until these individual sound-symbol associations are known completely. Then a teacher can proceed very gradually to two-, three-, and four-syllable words.

2. Because students with insufficient active working memory have trouble working rapidly on tests, they may need to be given more time or told they can write less or solve fewer problems.

3. Before writing a paragraph or a report, these students should jot down the topic, key ideas, and any other pertinent material they need to preserve while writing. In other words, they should make liberal use of scratch paper during writing activities.

4. Ultimately, these students need to become very good note takers during class. Before they acquire note-taking skills they may be apt to get disoriented in the presence of prolonged explanations or directions. Some repetition may be required for them.

5. Calculators and word processors are especially helpful for children with insufficient active working memory. Their use should be encouraged.

INCOMPLETE CONSOLIDATION IN
LONG-TERM MEMORY

Long-term memory is sometimes called *permanent memory*. It is where a person stores the facts, ideas, and skills he or she needs to remember for a long time, ideally forever. Thus, multiplication tables, letter formations, and critical personal data (such as one's address and telephone number) are all held within long-term memory. The process of placing or filing material in long-term memory is called *consolidation*. It is a process that takes from hours to days to accomplish and it is a process that is easily subverted in certain students.

Consolidation involves organizing information or skill in memory in such a way that it will be easy to recall when one needs it later. Consolidation is thus the mind's way of storing material for future use. The more systematic a person is during consolidation, the easier it will be later to find or recall what one needs from memory. Consolidation seems to occur especially well during sleep and also when a person continues to think about or elaborate upon what he or she is learning.

ANTONIO

Antonio is generally a good student, but at age thirteen certain kinds of academic work are a problem for him. In particular, he has had a hard time learning vocabulary words in Spanish and in English. He works hard at it, going over lists of words and their definitions multiple times. His mother tests him on these words before Antonio goes to bed, and he seems to know most of them. Then the next day on the quiz, he can recall hardly any of the words. As Antonio puts it, "They get lost inside my brain while I am asleep." Antonio has good language skills and is an excellent reader and writer. He has had some problems remembering facts in mathematics; he was especially slow to master the multiplication tables.

Consolidation is interrupted when one switches subjects rapidly or makes a series of telephone calls immediately after studying.

Table 3.3 identifies four common ways in which information or skill becomes consolidated in long-term memory.

Forms of Incomplete Consolidation in Long-Term Memory

There are some children who often are unable to succeed at consolidation in long-term memory. In most instances, these students display very discrete forms of difficulty with specific aspects of the consolidation process. We shall describe these forms below.

Paired association deficits. Virtually all of us find it difficult to pair certain kinds of data in long-term memory. Some people are excellent at associating names with faces, while others find this utterly exasperating. There are individuals who are extraordinary in their abilities to link names with telephone numbers while others are forced to make liberal use of directories. Other examples of such variation include differences in the ability to associate songs with their titles, vocabulary words with their proper definitions, automobile logos with car brands, dates with specific historical events, and, most importantly, phonemes (language sounds) with graphemes (letters on a page).

A student may exhibit recurring problems with a specific form of paired association but usually does not have difficulty forming all paired associations. In Antonio's case, we encounter a boy who has specific problems associating words with their definitions despite having good memory for other things. Because the problem is often limited to certain very specific kinds of pairs, it is important for teachers to be keenly aware of the *types of paired associations* that they are demanding of students in their classes. This will help them to detect those students who are having trouble. Typically, these children, like Antonio, seem able to register one or more paired associations in short-term memory and hold them in active working memory, but somehow they then fail to consolidate the linkage firmly in long-term memory, so that it is unavailable on a test the next day. The child may lament, "But I knew it all when I studied last night!"

Poor categorization. Some students are not very good at taking in new knowledge and putting it in pre-existing categories. Successful students do this very well and, in addition, they frequently file new information in multiple, pre-existing categories. For example, a biology teacher might mention in class some new ideas about rain forests. Students who are very good at consolidating information in categories will take in the

Table 3.3: Modes of Consolidation in Long-Term Memory

MODE	EXPLANATION	EXAMPLES
Paired Associations	Two pieces of information stored together in memory	A word and its spelling; an historical event and a date
Categories	Classification of knowledge into pre-existing or new groups that go together	Plants, animals, minerals
Rules and Recurring Patterns	"If . . then" regularities that govern facts/procedures—may be either rules we are taught or patterns of occurrence we discern through experience	If this is a proper noun, it will be capitalized; when we see such dark clouds, it usually rains; if this is a tiger, it will have stripes
Chains	Information or steps in a very specific serial order	Steps in long division; motor movements for cursive writing or playing a minuet on the piano

new information and think about how they learned the locations of rain forests when they studied Asian and Central and South American countries last year. They are also reminded of a television program they saw recently about the destruction of rain forests in Brazil and Ecuador; then they remember reading about environmental groups trying to slow down the loss of plants and wildlife in these areas. This new information about rain forests has been richly represented and elaborated in their long-term memories. It is filed under geography studied last year, television programs, and recent readings about the environment. Unfortunately, many students do not make these connections to categories in memory, so that they are left with impoverished recollections and ultimately a lack of good access to the material. Often these categorization problems appear in students in the following ways. They may

- Rely excessively on rote memory, needing to repeat the material unaltered to themselves over and over again in order to learn it

- Know things in fragments instead of as an integrated meaningful whole
- Lack interest in the subject matter (it's hard to enjoy ideas you can't relate to what you already know)
- Refrain from participating in class discussions
- Recall learned materials very slowly or inaccurately, showing poor performance on tests
- Exhibit an overall pattern of passive learning (page 23, it takes good mental activation to classify new knowledge)
- Fail or show reluctance to elaborate on what they are learning
- Be unable or have difficulty mastering new concepts (page 96)

Earlier in this chapter it was stated that most information needs to be *condensed* or paraphrased in order to "fit into" short-term memory. Yet it then must be *expanded* (i.e., richly represented in multiple categories of knowledge) to become well consolidated in long-term memory. Certain kinds of material may need to be learned by rote (such as math facts), but the most effective use of long-term memory demands a more active and elaborative process which is extremely difficult for some students.

Problems with rules and patterns. There are students who experience their greatest frustration in subjects that require the mastery and ready application of factual and/or procedural rules. The learning of mathematics, grammar (in English and in a foreign language), and certain sciences may be affected by these problems. These students do not master new rules easily nor do they retain how and when to apply them. For example, their writing may be marred by poor use of punctuation and capitalization. They may have trouble because they cannot apply spelling rules—not only the formal rules of spelling but also the self-generated rules that come about through experience. Thus, a child might not internalize the insight that certain letter combinations just do not occur in English, *xns*, for example, or that all English words have at least one vowel. In addition, they may fail to accumulate acquired rules which most children discover and consolidate on their own.

Unstable serial chaining. There are other students who have great difficulty preserving serial order in long-term memory. They are apt to struggle with many of the procedures that are stored as *serial chains*, the sequential plans for accomplishing tasks. These plans include the procedures for forming letters when one writes, tying shoelaces, reducing fractions, and remembering a play in basketball. These students may also have trouble with *factual sequences*, such as the order of the months of the year, the events in a story, the successive occurrences in an historical period, or the steps that occur in a scientific phenomenon (such as internal combustion or the digestion of carbohydrates). Children who have this kind of difficulty are likely to make very unstable chains, omitting important components or confusing their order. They are likely to have some of their severest academic difficulty in those areas that stress knowledge and/or skill that must be stored in a set serial order.

Before we present suggestions for managing incomplete consolidation, we will examine another topic, reduced long-term memory access. This is because both difficulties involve long-term memory and require similar educational care.

REDUCED ACCESS TO LONG-TERM MEMORY

We will use the term access to refer to the processes through which students find information or skill in long-term memory. Access enables them to respond to questions in class or on a test, recall spelling words while writing, and remember arithmetic facts as needed. Information or skill is generally found or remembered in one or more of three ways: association, pattern recognition, or total recall.

When students encounter one half of a paired association, they are able to bring forth the other half. For example, during a concert they hear a melody and immediately associate it with the title of a song.

If students encounter a pattern or set of stimuli that they have met with previously, they may be able to recognize how that pattern was used successfully in the past. They see some wording in a mathematical problem and recognize it as a pattern that suggests the need for multiplication.

Often students are expected to recall from long-term memory some information or skill with little or no cueing. They may be asked in class to name the capital cities of all the countries on the African continent or younger students might have to recall the letters of the alphabet in the correct order.

Over time students must access information and procedures with increasing speed and precision. In addition, the nature of their school work requires that what they have learned be accessible instantly and with little or no expenditure of mental effort. This frees up their minds for sophisticated thinking or problem solving to take place at the same time that the retrieval is occurring. For example, letter formation needs to be automatic so that a student can be developing ideas while he or she is writing them.

ROSA

At age fourteen Rosa understands virtually all of the content of her subjects, but has trouble remembering specific facts. When called upon in class, she is very hesitant and quite often unable to respond with accuracy. While performing mathematical problems she is slow to recall facts. In all of her subject areas, nothing is automatic. The recall of knowledge and skills is a laborious process for her. When she tries to write, she cannot remember prior knowledge, letter formations, spelling, punctuation, grammar, and vocabulary all at the same time. As a result, her written output is slow, and, in fact, she is reluctant to write very much at all. When Rosa generates her own ideas, she is often quite brilliant. She displays sophisticated knowledge about a wide variety of subjects. However, when she has to come up with a very specific detail from memory on demand, her response is most often inadequate.

Forms of Reduced Access to Long-Term Memory

Unfortunately, for some students access to long-term memory is slow, imprecise, and unrewarding. Such reduced access presents great difficulty for Rosa in the case at the beginning of this section. Several forms of such reduced access can be described.

Reduced memory for associations. Some students have an inability to remember specific kinds of paired associations. Usually, these will be of the same type they had trouble consolidating (page 68).

Reduced pattern recognition. Other children have trouble recognizing patterns they have encountered in the past. The elusive patterns can be visual (as in a geometry class), linguistic (as in a word problem or a story), or even social (as in a recurring conflict with friends). By failing to recognize patterns, these students are unable to make use of what worked in the past or to avoid what was unsuccessful.

Reduced retrieval memory (recall). Finally, there are students who simply are unable to keep pace with the ever-growing academic demand for rapid and accurate recall of facts and procedures, a weakness clearly detectable in Rosa who finds such recall laborious. This inability to retrieve information or skill can come in several forms, which are summarized and illustrated in table 3.4.

It is important to note that many children with reduced access to long-term memory are able to recall certain kinds of information or experience remarkably well. A child who has trouble remembering mathematical facts and spelling words may be incredible with episodic memory (the ability to recall details associated with events from the distant past) or that youngster may be remarkable at recalling the lyrics of songs. Such areas of enhanced access are commonly found in students who are having problems handling the memory demands in school.

Children who have reduced access to long-term memory may also show some of the other forms of memory dysfunction described in this chapter. It is not unusual for a student to manifest three or four observable phenomena related to reduced remembering.

To effectively manage a long-term memory dysfunction, it is important to identify it as precisely as possible. By specifying the problem, parents and teachers can tailor their management to the relevant gap(s) and minimize the confusion that so often prevails in children with reduced remembering and in the adults who care for them.

Managing Incomplete Consolidation and Reduced Access to Long-Term Memory at Home

Many children with long-term memory difficulties are reluctant to undertake any studying outside of school because they feel they are not really learning well. Often this relates to the fact that they have had so much trouble in the past remembering material they were supposed to master. Parents can help a child to consolidate what he or she is studying and in this way improve subsequent recall.

1. Material will not consolidate in long-term memory if it was not initially registered in short-term memory with sufficient depth. Therefore, the kinds of techniques recommended for enhancing short-term memory (page 59) pertain to the improvement of long-term memory as well. In addition, the more successfully a child consolidates, classifies, and elaborates on information in long-term memory, the more likely he or she will be able to recall it when necessary.

2. Parents can help their children by getting them to elaborate on what they are studying. Elaboration enables a child to store new knowledge in multiple pre-existing memory categories. A parent can ask critical questions like: "What things that you already know does this remind you of?"

Table 3.4: Forms of Retrieval Memory Weakness

FORM OF WEAKNESS	DESCRIPTION
Convergent Retrieval	Trouble locating very precise data in memory on demand, while often much better with less exact, "free" recall (divergent retrieval) as when there are multiple, possible correct responses
Simultaneous Retrieval	Trouble recalling multiple items or procedures at the same time, usually impairing writing (page 187)
Rapid Retrieval	Trouble recalling fast enough (e.g., not able to answer within the usual three seconds when called on or unable to recall rapidly enough to complete a quiz on time)
Cumulative Retrieval	Trouble remembering in the spring what was learned in the fall—a big problem in courses where current understanding depends on what went before (e.g., foreign language, math, chemistry)
Content-Specific Retrieval	Trouble recalling facts or procedures only within a specific content area (e.g., history, geography, or biology)
Format-Specific Retrieval (verbal, visual-spatial, sequential/linear)	Trouble recalling material in a particular format (e.g., remembering a poem or lines in a play, recalling the appearance of a parallelogram)
Automatization	Trouble recalling previously learned material with great ease (i.e., rapidly and with little or no expenditure of mental effort), such as letter formation during writing, word decoding for reading

3. Paired association (page 68) is best consolidated through rote drill in many cases. Making up games and entertaining scoring systems can make it easier for a child with consolidation weaknesses to learn spelling words, definitions, and mathematical facts.

4. Serial chains (page 70) or procedures can be well consolidated by making diagrams with arrows pointing from step to step. Children should be helped to "talk through" serial steps in a procedure (such as reducing a fraction or forming letters) or a chain of events (such as United States involvement in World War II).

5. Whenever rule-based learning is needed (as in studying grammar or punctuation), a combination of practice and discussion can improve consolidation. It can be especially helpful to play games in which the child is given examples, some of which obey a rule while others violate it. The child must identify both and articulate the rule. Correcting mistakes is often an excellent way to consolidate knowledge.

6. In general, all consolidation is improved when multiple sensory pathways are recruited for the effort. Thus, if children are learning visual material, it is helpful to verbally elaborate what they are seeing. If they are trying to consolidate verbal material (as in a history text), the process is strengthened by making diagrams on cards that can be studied visually. Moreover, if children have a particular format or mode of expression that works best (e.g., if they are good at art), this asset should be used as often as possible to enhance consolidation.

7. Studies show that knowledge is best consolidated right before going to sleep. Children should get into the habit of reading, practicing, or reviewing material just before dozing off. They should not watch television, listen to music, or conduct telephone conversations right after studying.

8. Long-term memory self-testing skills need to be developed in all children. To ensure consolidation, this should be done the morning after studying, even for a brief period of five or ten minutes before school if this is feasible in a busy household.

9. The kind of memory plan illustrated earlier in this chapter (fig. 3.2, page 60) is likely to contribute to improved long-term memory access as well as deeper registration in short-term memory. Parents and teachers can collaborate to help children apply such a conscious and systematic approach to better memory performance.

10. Parents need to be aware that when long-term memory doesn't work efficiently, homework can take a very long time (since not much prior knowledge or skill is being accessed fast enough). Affected students may need some breaks. They should not be made to feel guilty or anxious about their slow work pace. Their speed may improve if they have the use of some devices that aid memory, such as a word processor, calculator, or thesaurus.

Managing Incomplete Consolidation and Reduced Access to Long-Term Memory in School

Problems with long-term memory can be among the most humiliating conditions for students to bear. To understand something and then not remember it is exceedingly frustrating. Teachers need to be sensitive to the plight of such children. The students themselves need to feel that their teachers sympathize with them and also respect them for their good understanding. The following suggestions can offer a humane approach to children who have difficulty using long-term memory in school.

1. Affected students need more time to remember when taking tests, when called upon in class, or when solving a problem. Appropriate "private" accommodations need to be made. These tactics might include more time on tests and advanced warnings about questions to be asked.

2. For many of these children, recognition memory is easier than retrieval. A question to them might be: "Isn't it right that . . .?" or "It has been said . . . . . what do *you* think of that?" Such questions enable a child with memory problems to participate in class discussions without having to rely heavily on the rapid, precise recall of large portions of material from long-term memory.

3. Open-ended questions that have more than one possible correct answer are often preferable for these students.

4. Whenever it is practical, they need opportunities to demonstrate their understanding of concepts and procedures without heavy reliance on memory. Writing a report or completing a project instead of taking a test are ways of accomplishing this.

5. Collaborative learning experiences can be reassuring for students with long-term memory weaknesses. These children should be teamed with one or more students who are good at recall. They should

study together, even take team tests, and collaborate on projects in which children with memory weaknesses can show their strengths in understanding, problem solving, or thinking up original ideas.

6. In every subject area teachers should take some time to identify the kinds of memory children will need in order to learn that subject well. Then they should discuss different techniques that can be used to make those forms of memory work. Children should share their own ideas and experiences connected with long-term memory use for school. Such discussions can enhance *metamemory* or an awareness of how memory is supposed to work in each content domain.

7. Every effort should be made to sustain a child's motivation, academic progress, and enjoyment of a subject area in the presence of long-term memory weaknesses. Take-home tests, devices (such as a calculator in math), and open-book quizzes may allow a child to continue to learn without experiencing a discouraging memory overload.

8. Teachers should be selective in what they expect students to remember. While this applies to all students, it is especially true for those with long-term memory weaknesses who easily may lose motivation if there is too much to remember. Excessive amounts of material to be memorized is particularly needless in an age when the technology of information access is so rapidly advancing that we can now afford to stress deep understanding over memory.

The Demystification of Phenomena Related to Reduced Remembering

Children with memory difficulties need to be able to separate the trouble they have remembering from their overall intelligence. They should be taught the difference between understanding and remembering. The following points can be included in this demystification process.

1. Many intelligent people have trouble remembering. No one has a memory that is completely bad, but everyone has certain parts of their memory that need improvement. It's a problem when the weak part of your memory interferes with learning in school.

2. There's much more memory work to do when you're a kid learning in school than when you're a grown-up in a career or working at a job. So students with memory problems can find it easier to be successful when they grow up!

3. A child needs to hear an explanation of the specific form(s) of memory weakness that is a problem for her or him. This should be explained in simple, direct language making use of any of the myriad concrete analogies for memory. Some examples are contained in table 3.5. These kinds of explanations must be customized to fit the child's age, grade level, and specific domains of difficulty.

4. Children with memory weaknesses always have aspects of their memory that work well. These too should be pointed out to the child.

5. Students should be encouraged to give examples of incidents in school when their memory weakness has been a problem for them.

6. It is good to mention that memory can be like a muscle; the more it gets used the stronger it becomes. If a person gets discouraged and stops studying, then his or her memory never gets a chance to improve.

7. Students should be told that it is possible to give their memories some extra help so they will work better. The kinds of extra help are called memory strategies and all kids need to use them. Examples (such as the rhyme: *i* before *e* except after *c,* and ROY and GBIV for the colors of the spectrum) can be given, and children asked if they have any they already use.

8. The vocabulary of the dysfunction is of critical importance. Children need to be able to name and understand their particular memory weaknesses as well as to be able to talk about them.

9. All children (and adults) can benefit from learning more about memory. Diagrams, such as the one shown in figure 3.1 (page 55), can be used to explain some of the memory processes covered in this chapter.

Recognizing Memory Strengths

Memory assets are of tremendous value during school. Some students are conspicuously efficient at registering, consolidating, manipulating, and recalling information and skill. When learning is working well, memory is enhancing understanding while understanding is facilitating memory. It is likely, however, that with so many different forms of memory operating, no one has universally excellent memory just as no one's memory is entirely inoperable. Therefore, we must seek strengths in particular aspects of memory function. As we have discussed, a child may easily remember information when it is presented visually but fail to recall when it is given verbally. There can also be content or domain-specific memory abilities. A student may be excellent at consolidating

Table 3.5: Examples of Demystification Statements

DEFICIENCY	SAMPLE STATEMENT
Short-Term, Sequential Memory	"It's really hard for you to put things in your memory in the right order. That's why when the teacher tells you to do several things in a row, you get all mixed up."
Short-Term, Verbal Memory	"Your mind doesn't hold on to language too well in class. That makes it hard for you to take notes because you keep forgetting what the teacher just said."
Active Working Memory	"A lot of times you forget what you're doing while you're in the middle of doing it. It would be like a television screen where parts of the picture disappear in the middle of a program."
Access to Long-Term Memory	"Your memory is like a closet with a sticking door. It's hard for you to remember things in school because the door keeps getting stuck. We have to figure out how to make the door for that closet open more easily!"
Simultaneous Retrieval Memory	"It's really tough for you when you have to remember a lot of things at the same time—like spelling, punctuation, vocabulary, and facts while you write. That's why you can spell okay on a quiz and then misspell the same words in a paragraph you write."

mathematical facts but not nearly as adept at filing new vocabulary words in a Spanish class. Some children remember best through direct hands-on experience. This is especially true of students with excellent episodic memory who may surpass all classmates in recalling the details from a field trip to the local shoe factory despite their problems remembering the countries of South America. Identifying highly specific memory strengths is very important for helping a child with learning problems maintain self-esteem. The recognition of such strengths can be tremendously valuable in devising strategies for improving learning by allowing individuals to make optimal use of the more effective parts of their memory function.

Good memory greatly facilitates school success. However, remembering by itself is an incomplete learning process. After all, it is not very fulfilling to remember without truly comprehending. In the next chapter, therefore, we will investigate phenomena related to understanding, memory's active partner in learning.

CHAPTER FOUR

Phenomena Related to Chronic Misunderstanding

T HROUGHOUT their school years children confront an unremitting tide of ideas, facts, and procedures that they need to interpret reliably. The process of understanding is highly cumulative because students must continually use their existing prior knowledge and interpretations to create or clarify new insights. New information must modify or reconstruct what they already know to form the basis for future learning. As they encounter different subjects they have to process information in multiple ways to understand it. Often they must comprehend with great speed, so as not to miss whatever information is presented next. Over the course of their school years, they are required to interpret increasingly large chunks of complex data, which become more densely packed within language, within diagrams, and within the direct experience of accomplishing academic tasks.

The processes of understanding do not operate in isolation. They are highly dependent upon attention controls, discussed in chapter 2, and upon the accuracy and speed of the various forms of memory, presented in the last chapter. In addition, other factors, including the motivation, interest, and previous learning experiences of students as well as the methods used by teachers all affect understanding,

In school, children regularly face a multitude of issues relating to the quality or extent of their understanding. Usually they are not even consciously aware of these issues. Yet, they need somehow to know when they understand something and when they do not. They must develop a sense of how much understanding of something is enough. None of us ever totally understands; understanding of anything grows over time.

When their comprehension is challenged, children must decide whether they are capable of understanding the idea or concept, how much effort will be required, to what extent prior knowledge and/or outside resources will be necessary for clarification, and how the understanding arrived at can be validated or verified. Comments such as: "I don't get this" or "That's too hard" or "This stuff is a cinch" or "We've already had this" reflect such self-evaluations of comprehension. Children need to understand their own understanding. (Such personal knowledge of learning is part of what is termed *metacognition*.) They should have insight into the steps involved in comprehending. They must learn how to clarify and what to do when they don't sufficiently understand. They also need to learn a kind of intellectual tenacity that will enable them to keep seeking understanding rather than giving in or resigning themselves to confusion, disorientation, or meaningless rote learning.

Being able to understand in depth substantially facilitates the enjoyment of learning. The feeling of having mastered a new and difficult challenge to one's comprehension is intellectually energizing, motivating children to inquire further, to work to disentangle and resynthesize the densely packed network of ideas in a subject area.

In this chapter we will look at ways that phenomena related to chronic misunderstanding manifest themselves in students. The word *chronic* is significant. Everyone on some occasions in some contexts has the experience of not understanding. But those students for whom misunderstanding seriously impedes learning are at serious risk. Six observable phenomena that are common deterrents to understanding in school are: (1) weak language processing, (2) incomplete concept formation, (3) deficient visualization, (4) slow data processing, (5) constricted chunk-size capacities, and (6) excessive top-down or bottom-up processing.

WEAK LANGUAGE PROCESSING

School in our culture depends almost entirely upon language for transmitting knowledge, putting children with reduced language abilities at a clear academic disadvantage during their elementary and secondary school careers. Language consists of a highly interconnected series of functions that operate at different levels for effective communication. Some of these levels and their components are illustrated in figure 4.1. It is customary when discussing language to make the distinction between receptive language (the *comprehension* of language) and expressive language (the communication or *production* of language). In this chapter we

BILL

At age seven, Bill is having serious problems in school. It has been very hard for him to acquire reading skills. His teachers find that it is difficult for him to rhyme words, analyze and reblend multisyllabic words, and sound out new words. They say he has a diminished vocabulary compared to his classmates. Bill also has trouble understanding his teachers' explanations and verbal instructions and is often confused in class. He frequently looks disoriented. His teachers observe that Bill is very much a "visual learner." His parents note that he is quite good at figuring out how things work and at remembering small visual details from the past. On the other hand, they are aware that often they have to repeat instructions and that Bill loses interest quickly when they try to read stories to him and his younger sister.

will consider only receptive language, as we deal with issues of language processing. In chapter 5 we will examine phenomena associated with expressive language (i.e., language production).

Language processing occurs at multiple levels. For our purposes, we will concentrate mainly on four of them: (1) language sounds (often called phonology), (2) word meanings (semantics), (3) sentence word order (syntax), and (4) paragraph and passage organization (discourse).

At the phonological level of language processing, students perceive individual language sounds with precision and speed. Good phonological awareness allows a child to discriminate between similar sounds (e.g., "bill" and "bell"). This facility is crucial for reading, writing, spelling, and general comprehension in school.

At the semantic level, children build a strong vocabulary and develop a rich understanding of the relationships between different words (antonyms, synonyms, derivatives, etc.) and figures of speech. Good word knowledge facilitates reading and all aspects of oral comprehension. Children who engage in rich comparisons and associations between words are said to be building a *semantic network*, a rich set of interrelationships that will facilitate and enrich language experience and learning.

Levels of Language

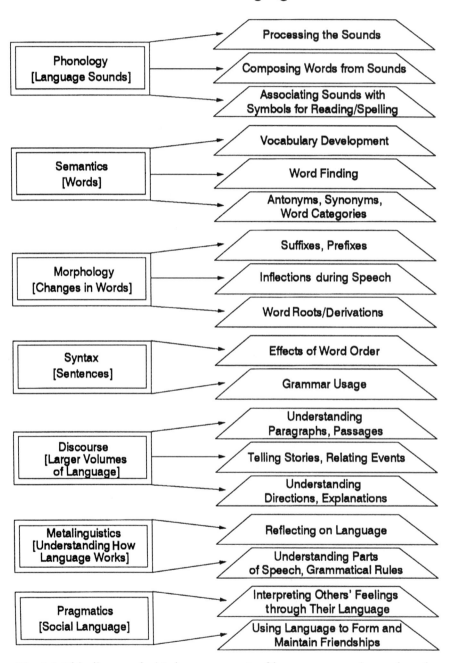

Fig. 4.1. This diagram depicts key components of language processing and production. These aspects of language ability are critical for optimal learning in school.

Comprehension at the sentence level is dependent upon a child's appreciation of the effects of word order, punctuation, and grammatical construction. In particular, a listener or reader needs to be aware of how syntax and intonation influence the meaning of a sentence.

Discourse processing involves grasping the cohesion between sentences. It requires considerable active working memory (page 63), the use of prior knowledge, and, as we have stated, good function at the other three levels of language processing. Effective processing of discourse enables students to follow narrative story lines and to interpret ideas described in their textbooks.

Students may show uneven degrees of competency at each of these four levels. However, success with the lengthier units (syntax and discourse) depends heavily upon the quality of performance with the more concise units (phonology and semantics). It would be hard for students to understand a paragraph if they had trouble with the meanings of the words, but even if they could understand the definitions of all of the words, it would still be possible for them to have an incomplete understanding of the paragraph because problems with syntax and discourse could interfere with their comprehension.

Forms of Weak Language Processing

We will now look at several observable phenomena associated with difficulty at each of these different language levels along with some problems that may interfere with comprehension at any of the four levels.

Problems with language sounds (phonological deficits). Some children have an incomplete appreciation of the distinctiveness of individual sounds in their native language, a phenomenon called poor phonological awareness. This condition affects Bill in the case cited at the beginning of this section. Somehow the reception of language sounds is insufficiently clear for him and others with phonological problems. In some cases this may be because students are unable to process certain sounds quickly enough. This is especially the case when the sounds are very brief in their duration. For example, the stopped consonants, "p," "t," and "g," are pronounced rapidly (in just a few milliseconds) and therefore may elude these students. Other sounds (such as "ing" and "sh") can be appreciated at a significantly slower rate. Some children also encounter problems holding language sounds in short-term memory and manipulating them in active working memory. It is hard for them to break words down into their component sounds and reblend them or to try to substitute a new sound for an existing one in a word. They may also have problems with rhyming.

Whatever the cause, children with phonological problems find it hard to process language in the classroom and often misinterpret words and sentences. These students depend heavily upon visual configurations and context clues; by making use of what words they do process well, they form educated guesses regarding overall meaning. This technique of *probabilistic processing* may be reasonably effective in the early grades when a lot of learning is about familiar content and everyday practical life. However, in secondary schools students are more apt to encounter decontextualized material, information that is remote from everyday life (e.g., Greek myths, Chinese dynasties, or electromagnetic forces). As a result, probabilistic language processing becomes increasingly ineffective.

A number of critical academic skills are undermined by a poor sense of phonology. Typically, decoding skills in reading (page 165) are delayed because these students have trouble forming associations in memory between language sounds (phonemes) and written letter combinations (graphemes). They expend enormous amounts of time and effort to master and automatize the decoding process. They often have serious problems with spelling, producing visually close but phonetically improbable spellings (e.g., "fught" for "fight"). Fortunately, with considerable help many children eventually can overcome or bypass these phonological weaknesses and learn to read. But, their underlying weaknesses may emerge again when they try to master the sound system of a second language and they may also be left with persistent spelling difficulties.

Problems with word meanings (semantic deficits). There are many ways in which difficulties with words and their meanings show up. In some instances, students may have very limited vocabularies, while in others they may possess sufficient vocabularies but have trouble with precise word meanings or be slow to associate meanings with the words they already know. Some students interpret word meanings too literally, completely missing the versatility and multiple possible meanings and uses individual words have or they may simply recite definitions without truly understanding them. Some of these children also experience difficulty with *morphology*, that is, not grasping the meaning-laden modifications that can be made in root words by means of prefixes, suffixes, and tenses.

Children with these semantic deficits do not elaborate on the meanings of words, nor do they think about their shades of meaning, the contexts in which these new words might be used, or the ways in which new vocabulary is similar to and different from words they already know. Instead, they are likely to hate learning new vocabulary and to overuse rote memory when they do. These children often don't recognize words when they are reading. Ordinarily when children see a written word, they instantly associate it with a meaning in the brain's "dictionary" or "lexicon." But children with a weak sense of semantics may be slow, vague, or inaccurate when associating written words with their stored meanings. In the absence of such precise instant associations, rapid word recognition is likely to be significantly impaired. Without rapid word recognition their reading comprehension suffers as well.

As their education proceeds, children have to learn and apply a growing number of words that can be described as technical vocabulary. These are the highly specialized words that are used almost exclusively in school. They include vocabulary like hypotenuse, subtrahend, and subjunctive. For students with semantic deficits such vocabulary may be especially hard to learn.

Problems at the sentence level (syntactic deficits). Some students have specific difficulty interpreting sentences. For example, they are often confused by the following aspects of sentence construction:

- Deciding which noun a pronoun refers to
- Knowing which noun or noun phrase a subordinate clause refers to (e.g., deciding who fled in the sentence: "The boy saw the girl who ran away quickly")
- Interpreting passive tenses (e.g., "The girl was seen by the boy")
- Understanding the effects on meaning of specific prepositions and conjunctions (e.g., distinguishing between *until* and *unless*)
- Responding accurately to "wh . . ." questions (e.g., Question: "When did you go on that trip?" Answer: "To Florida")
- Dealing with clauses embedded in the middle of sentences (e.g., "The girl whom the boy saw ran away down the street")

Children who experience these difficulties at the sentence level may have trouble understanding questions and explanations in class as well as word problems in mathematics. In many cases, reading comprehension is reduced. Their deficits in processing sentences may also impede the study of grammar and punctuation. The rules governing these functions may not make any sense to children with very limited appreciation of how sentences work. They may overuse rote learning of rules without understanding. They frequently show distaste for any exercises covering grammar, identifying parts of speech, parsing sentences, or conjugating verbs. Problems with sentences also make it difficult for these students to learn another language.

Since sentences are so governed by rules, in some cases poor processing of sentences stems from difficulty with the understanding of rules in general. These children may be having difficulty in other areas of school in which the mastery of rules is important (e.g., mathematics and certain sciences).

Problems with paragraphs and passages (discourse). Discourse processing involves interpretation of meaning that goes beyond the boundaries of sentences. To be effective at understanding discourse a student must discern *cohesion* in the material or be able to impose it. The understanding of discourse demands the use of active working memory (page 63). Listeners and readers must temporarily store the gist of one sentence while processing the subsequent sentences and drawing appropriate inferences. They also must be sensitive to pronouns, conjunctions, and other linguistic details that infuse cohesion into discourse. This is an elusive challenge for some students.

Two major forms of discourse children are expected to deal with in school are *narrative* and *exposition*. In narrative, the intent is to convey the movement of events. This is usually expressed as a temporal sequence. Most fiction coheres as narrative. In exposition, the intent is to inform the reader. This can be done in a number of ways (e.g., a list, a comparison, or an argument). Students who can process discourse well recognize the structure of what they are listening to or reading whether it is a narrative, an exposition, or some other form of discourse. Such recognition helps them find cohesion in the discourse. For children with poor skills of processing discourse, the material they read or hear may remain disconnected or fragmented. Because they are not able to recognize or make use of valuable structural clues to meaning, there is no flow of ideas.

Some additional language processing weaknesses. Now we will consider some forms of language processing weakness that are potentially detrimental at all four of the above levels.

First, a reduced *rate of processing* can cause particularly serious problems. There is probably nothing in school that must occur at a more rapid rate than the processing of oral language at all levels. Children who cannot take in and understand language quickly enough experience a kind of mental exhaustion which may reveal itself in the form of inattention in class. These children may be much more comfortable dealing with a slower-paced, visual-spatial challenge (such as drawing, making, or repairing something) than with a linguistic one. In the former, the material they're working with stays around. Spoken sentences vanish nearly instantly!

Second, there are children who can only handle a small amount of verbal material at one time. They may understand language reliably, but not when the quantity becomes too great. Long sentences, extensive discourse, multistep language may confuse these learners. Students with attention deficits, more generalized chunk-size problems (page 110) and/or short-term or active working memory limitations are likely to have trouble with the quantity of verbal material they can handle.

Third, comprehending abstract terms, figurative language, metaphors, analogies, and symbolic words (higher order language processing) can be a hard challenge for many students. Any language that is not concrete (e.g., words like honesty, sorrow, irony) or that has no obvious visual reference (e.g., words like corruption, altruism, patriotism) gives them trouble. Two other aspects of higher-order language processing reveal themselves in the ability to draw inferences (to supply missing information in language) and in the appreciation of ambiguity (to recognize that a sentence or paragraph or word may have more than one possible interpretation). Both necessitate careful consideration of the intended meaning of the speaker or writer. Over time in school, more and more implicit and ambiguous communication occurs. Students who have difficulty with drawing inferences and/or appreciating and resolving ambiguity often suffer.

Fourth, a person's ability to learn is influenced by the extent to which he or she reflects on language, thinks about how language works, and develops strong and helpful insights regarding his or her own understanding of language. Such consciousness is called *metalinguistic awareness*. Children with proficient language skills begin to show evidence of these insights during their preschool years. Some children with language processing weaknesses never acquire them.

Finally, there is a vital process called *comprehension monitoring*. While students are listening in a classroom, not only must they understand the teacher, but they also must understand *whether* they understand the teacher. Some students with weak language processing not only don't understand the teacher, but their woes are compounded by the fact that they don't understand that they don't understand the teacher. In other, words, they are not *monitoring* the quality and depth of their understanding, a process that is nearly automatic in students with effective language processing.

Language processing in school is always influenced by cultural factors. For example, children from families that speak in a dialect different from that of the school may be at a disadvantage. Some bilingual youngsters have problems meeting the demands of literate English in school. It should be pointed out, however, that many bilingual children who have persistent difficulty learning to process their second language are found to have weak language processing in their native language as well. Finally, there are some home environments that are simply more verbal and English literate than others, so that children are likely to vary in the extent to which language at home reinforces language at school.

Children's language processing problems may cause difficulty beyond the academic sphere. Some children have trouble interpreting language that has social meaning. It may be hard for them to determine when a speaker is angry, is sympathetic, or is trying to be friendly. They have difficulty using cues of word choice and intonation to help them understand the intent of what people are saying to them. This is often referred to as a problem with *verbal pragmatics* and is discussed further in chapter 7.

Various components of weak language processing are summarized in figure 4.2.

Managing Weak Language Processing at Home

A sympathetic approach to the child with weak language processing can go a long way toward preventing misunderstanding and even conflict at home. Parents can do a great deal to minimize the effects of this difficulty while, at the same time, striving to strengthen language comprehension.

1. Parents need to be aware that children with language processing problems sometimes fail to understand directions. Therefore, it may be necessary to repeat instructions, speaking slowly and trying to make good eye contact with the child whenever the communication is especially important. They should avoid becoming angry, tense, or accusatory when instructions have to be repeated

2. Parents can help their children follow instructions from school. A child with a language processing weakness often may not fully comprehend what is expected on a homework assignment because she or he never interpreted adequately the teacher's instructions. The child may also have trouble interpreting written instructions, worksheets, and texts. By establishing excellent communication with the teacher, a parent can often help the child understand what is required.

Possible Components of
Weak Language Processing

PHONOLOGY
- Deficient Processing of
  the Sounds of Language

SEMANTICS
- Limited Understanding and Relating of
  Words to Each Other

MORPHOLOGY
- Poor Appreciation of Word Roots,
  Tenses, Inflections

SYNTAX
- Weak Understanding of Grammar and
  How Word Order Affects Meaning

DISCOURSE
- Trouble Interpreting Language beyond
  the Boundaries of Sentences

METALINGUISTICS
- Being Unable to Think About
  How Language Works

PRAGMATICS
- Poor Understanding of Language in
  Social Contexts

Fig. 4.2. This diagram shows common areas of weakness in language processing.

3. It is important to collaborate with the school in helping children with weaknesses of phonological awareness. There are many games that can be played to strengthen the processing of language sounds. These include rhyming activities, pig-Latin games, and tasks requiring a child to break words down into their individual sounds and to reblend them. Sound substitution activities also help, as children substitute a sound for

an existing one in a word and try to create a new real word (e.g., "What word would you get if you changed the 'p' sound in pet to a 'g' sound?"). Many such phonological activities can be found in remedial reading texts. It is good if the same kinds of activities are taking place in school and can be reviewed at home.

4. Parents may need to help these children acquire new vocabulary. They can make use of various word games. They should also try to work with their children on any new vocabulary in daily lessons. Going beyond literal definitions of new words, talking about the ways in which new words are like (or unlike) words the child already knows, and thinking of different ways in which the new words can be used, all will strengthen the comprehension of children with weak language processing. Both at home and in school these children should learn new vocabulary words in categories of related meaning. For example, they might learn a group of words that describe different people (i.e., altruistic, egocentric, compassionate, hostile). They should have opportunities to compare and contrast these words as they learn them. This method of vocabulary building encourages the development of a rich semantic network.

5. Reading may be one of the best ways for children with weak language processing skills to strengthen them. These children need to be encouraged, perhaps even required, to read at a specified time and for a specified amount of time each day. Children with serious reading problems can try to read each day and also listen to books on tape (see page 170). Regrettably, many children with language difficulties hate and therefore avoid reading. Their inexperience in reading eventually weakens further their language skills. This snowballing process must be prevented. Parents can seek well-illustrated reading materials covering subjects of high interest to their children. Subscriptions to magazines on these subjects can be helpful, especially if a parent reads the same articles and discusses them with the child on a regular basis.

6. Parents can read to younger children and have their older children read to them as a way to bolster language processing.

7. While studying, older children with weak language processing need to be helped and encouraged to transform the material in their textbooks into some form of visual representation (e.g., a list, a chart, or a diagram).

8. Parents (and teachers) can help children listen to discourse and try to identify main ideas. They can also listen to stories or narratives that contain some contradictions or absurd statements and try to detect

these discrepancies. These activities can improve attention as well as language processing.

9. When cases are severe and when treatment is available and affordable, parents should try to arrange regular sessions for their children with a language therapist. Such a professional can make use of specific exercises to enhance a child's appreciation of language sounds, words, sentences, and/or discourse. The language therapist can guide both the parents and the teacher to remedial activities which they can continue at home and in school.

10. In some cases a child's difficulties with language may be the result of a hearing loss. When a child has weak language processing, the parents should make sure that she or he has a careful and complete hearing evaluation.

Managing Weak Language Processing in School

Teachers need to be keenly aware of their students with weak language processing. These youngsters can learn despite their deficits. However, specific accommodations must be made for them in the classroom.

1. Teachers should avoid embarrassing students who may not be understanding the language communication that is going on in class. They should not criticize them when they misunderstand. Student incomprehension often masquerades as noncompliance, indifference, or even, seeming defiance. These behavioral symptoms are most likely to occur when a child feels embarrassed about his or her poor comprehension.

2. When calling on a child with language processing weaknesses, teachers need to be aware that the student may not understand the *question*. They may need to repeat it, reword it, or simplify it.

3. Similarly oral directions or explanations should be communicated in short sentences, at a slow pace, and with strong intonation to emphasize critical points.

4. These children often benefit from as much visual reinforcement as possible. Writing or diagramming on the board while explaining something or right afterwards often helps them to bypass their language problems.

5. Children with weak language processing can consciously try to visualize during oral directions. They should picture in their minds what it is they are being asked to do.

6. The kinds of phonological awareness activities suggested for use at home should also be incorporated into a child's program in school. Additionally, various musical/rhythmic activities with lyrics may reinforce language sound appreciation.

7. A teacher can encourage children with semantic weaknesses to keep a personal illustrated dictionary, especially for technical vocabulary and words they find particularly hard.

8. Word mapping activities often help children develop a more extensive semantic network, as they seek and come to perceive the many relationships between words and their meanings. An example of such a word map is shown in figure 4.3. In this case the word *geese* is represented in a highly elaborated manner. These maps can also suggest structural similarities between words derived from the same roots. The act of creating such a map can enhance a child's recognition of the rich implications of individual words.

9. Teachers should encourage students with any aspect of weak language processing to keep a small notebook beside them in which they can record ideas, facts, or words they don't understand. Later they can review and discuss these with a classmate, a teacher, a parent, or a sibling. Such a log can also serve as a constant reminder of the need for ongoing comprehension monitoring (i.e., "Do I 'get' this stuff?").

10. When children have trouble understanding oral discourse, teachers should introduce the unfamiliar words and concepts of the subject prior to presenting it as a whole to the class.

11. Students can benefit from specific help processing complex sentences. Sometimes cloze procedures can be used. In such activities, students are given sentences with certain words missing, such as conjunctions or prepositions, and they must fill them in. Students can try out different words and then discuss how each one affects the meaning of the sentence. Other activities concentrated at the sentence level might include sentence repetition tasks and games such as twenty questions in which a teacher, using sophisticated syntax, asks questions of the child. These activities can also be pursued at home.

12. Children with weak language processing may need considerable help understanding abstract language—metaphors, figures of speech, and proverbs.

13. As with some of the problems described in earlier chapters, children with weak language processing can benefit from sitting close to

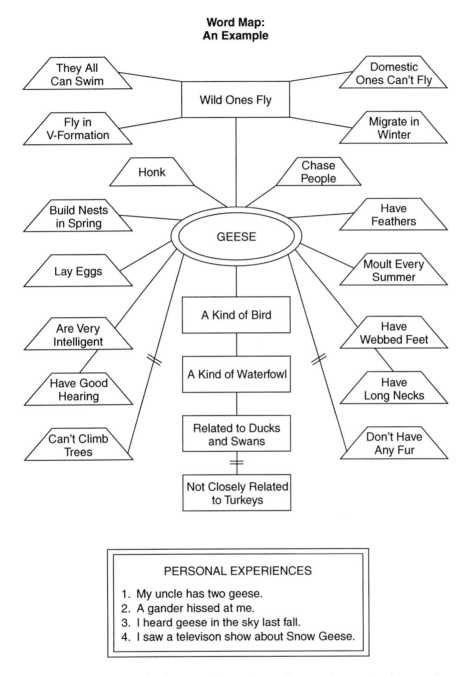

Fig. 4.3. Children can develop an understanding of semantic networks by mapping word meanings. The technique is illustrated in this example by using the word geese.

the teacher. They should have some inconspicuous way to signal that they are not understanding.

INCOMPLETE CONCEPT FORMATION

Success in school depends upon the firm mastery of a great number of concepts. To understand optimally is to acquire a very solid grasp of the varied concepts that comprise every subject area.

In order to deal with the phenomenon of incomplete concept formation, it is important to consider what is meant by a concept. A concept is a grouping of specific critical features that often go together to create a category or generic idea. For example, there is the concept of juice whose critical features include its liquid consistency, its origins (usually from a fruit or a vegetable), its creation (through squeezing or extraction), and its frequent suitability and desirability for human consumption. To really understand the concept juice, you need to grasp at least most of its critical features. If you don't you might blur the distinction between juices and the broader concept of beverages or the narrower concept of citrus drinks.

Children are expected to master many kinds of concepts which include

- Concrete concepts—those that refer to things we can see or hear or touch or smell or taste (like juice)
- Abstract concepts—those that relate to intangible ideas (like democracy or generosity)

TESS

Tess at age seventeen shows very little interest in the content of school. She has well-developed social skills and spends much of her time thinking about her many friends. Her teachers report that Tess has only a minimal grasp of the important ideas from their classes. She wants very much to succeed academically and tends to overrely on memory without really comprehending very well. Her history teacher recently commented that Tess has little understanding of the true differences between governments or the issues at stake in a war. She prefers simply to memorize facts. All of her teachers have agreed that Tess has the most trouble mastering abstract concepts as they occur across subject areas.

- Process concepts—those that explain a process or how something happens (like photosynthesis, atomic energy, or internal combustion) in which case the critical features are actually the steps that occur to make it happen
  - Verbal concepts—those that are readily explained and elaborated with language (like due process, sportsmanship, or simile)
  - Nonverbal concepts—those that are easier to understand without relying completely on words, because they can be visualized readily (like proportion, hypotenuse, symmetry, or trapezoid)

As children are able to master these types of concepts they acquire a vital kind of mental shorthand. Concepts allow a person to organize issues or ideas in a broad way, that is, to generalize, which takes a great deal of the strain away from memory. Thus, a child can think about the conservation of natural resources without having to consider separately water, forests, and fossil fuels.

Forms of Incomplete Concept Formation

Some children endure chronic misunderstanding in school because it is difficult for them to make the jump mentally from many particular examples to a general idea. They are not able to grasp concepts. Such incomplete concept formation creates serious obstacles for Tess, described at the beginning of this section. By looking at what students like her are able to do, we can identify several different levels or depths of understanding with respect to concepts (see table 4.1).

A history of weak conceptualization can make a child feel academically overwhelmed and hopeless. As the school years progress, the concepts which are taught become increasingly abstract. Such progressive abstraction has made things especially difficult in Tess's case. These abstract concepts can create serious problems for some children who have only barely mastered concrete concepts. Furthermore, in secondary school many abstract concepts have other abstract concepts within them as one or more of their critical features. For example, the critical features of the concept of democracy include the concepts of due process, equal rights, and representation. In this way, the conceptual demands intensify as students move to the higher grades.

Children with incomplete concept formation may reveal some or all of the following tendencies:

- A lack of awareness of the critical features of concepts.
- Heavy reliance on rote memory in school (as with Tess).

Table 4.1: Depths of Conceptual Understanding

DEPTH	DESCRIPTION
None	Student is unable to identify any critical features of the concept or to cite examples
Tenuous	Student can name one or two critical features but is vague about how the concept differs from others
Rote	Student can mimic the teacher's explanation but can't use concept or think of examples
Imitative	Student can apply the concept but doesn't really understand what he or she is doing and can't generalize its use
Explanatory	Student can explain the concept in own words, cite examples, as well as compare and contrast with other concepts
Innovative	Student can apply the concept in ways never directly taught

- A pattern of doing things without understanding why they are doing them or exactly what they are doing. A student may be able to add and subtract fractions but not understand what fractions are. In mathematics this is called the extreme *algorithmic approach.*
- Difficulty mastering abstract as opposed to concrete concepts.
- Confusion with concepts presented in a specific mode. Some children desperately need language to clarify all concepts for them, while others are just the opposite and require visualization in order to understand.
- Inability to understand concepts related to specific kinds of content. Students may grasp concepts in current events very well but struggle excessively when dealing with arithmetic.
- Difficulty perceiving relationships between parts of a curriculum or subject area. This may manifest itself as an inability to compare and contrast or to relate new ideas to prior knowledge. An affected student may see no relationship between fractions, decimals, or percentages. This phenomenon, sometimes referred to as a *lack of horizontal threading,* occurs when the individual concepts are too

vaguely formed and therefore not especially distinctive. The result is that learning may be fragmented and even incoherent. When learning is so poorly integrated, it is also unlikely to be of much interest to the learner.

- Inability to link concepts to examples (or prototypes) or vice versa. When asked to name countries, a child with an incomplete concept of a country may list: Italy, New York, South America, and Korea. Or when asked, "What is a whale an example of?", he or she might respond, "A fish."

Managing Incomplete Concept Formation at Home

Parents can work with a child to make sure that the concepts introduced in school are being grasped. Sometimes they are the first to discover that a child is not fully understanding.

1. Parents can help their children by discussing with them whatever key concepts they are currently learning in school. Children should be encouraged to talk about concepts in their own words as if they were explaining them to a younger child. Parents can also play concept games with their children. A parent can list some critical features and the child tries to name the concept.

2. When children are studying, parents can make sure that they are not just memorizing but, instead, attempting to understand the conceptual content of the subject matter.

3. Parents need to show that they too are still learning. They can ask their children to teach them about important new concepts. Such learning can take place at the dinner table, in the car, or in other settings. It is also important for parents to discuss with a child concepts that they are dealing with at work. The process can create an intellectual ambiance at home that makes school seem much more relevant to rather than widely disparate from home life.

4. Parents can help a child review. If a student feels overwhelmed and helpless when faced with the basic concepts in a certain subject, it is often beneficial to return to the earliest stages of learning in that particular area and reestablish or strengthen the fundamental concepts.

5. Parents should try to include discussions based on concepts in everyday life at home. The subject matter need not relate directly to

what a child is studying at school. Ideas from reading or issues in local or national news can provide conceptual material (e.g., "Do you think a dress code in school is a good idea?").

Managing Incomplete Concept Formation in School

All students need to develop a greater understanding of how concepts work. This need is greatest in those whose concept formation is incomplete. They require help in order to avoid falling so far behind that they give up on learning.

1. Teachers need to make certain that children know what concepts are and that they understand the critical features defining them and distinguishing them from each other. They can help students recognize different kinds of concepts and become aware of different levels of understanding.

2. In any subject area children should be forewarned when a key concept is being introduced.

3. Teachers can ask students with weak conceptual understanding to describe a concept in their own words (orally or in writing) before, during, and after applying it. For example, a student may be able to solve problems using equations but still not understand what he or she is doing. Having the student talk or write about equations may help this understanding to develop.

4. These students can benefit as well from conceptual mapping exercises. Teachers should show them how to make diagrams of important concepts. The diagrams can delineate the critical features, provide examples, and reveal relationships to other concepts. A format for mapping and a prototype are illustrated in figures 4.4 and 4.5. A student can create a book or "conceptual mapping atlas" to contain various diagrams of concepts. This can be reviewed periodically in school (and at home).

5. Teachers can work with students who only have difficulty with a specific kind of concept formation to make use of their strong modality for conceptualization. For example, a student who is highly verbal may need to use spoken or written language to understand geometric shapes.

6. Because students haven't formed concepts firmly, they aren't stored reliably in long-term memory. Therefore, teachers may recommend that students work with a tutor to review key concepts frequently.

7. Students with weak conceptual understanding need help and practice in highlighting key concepts. They should develop the habit of reviewing and/or mapping all the key concepts after completing a passage or chapter.

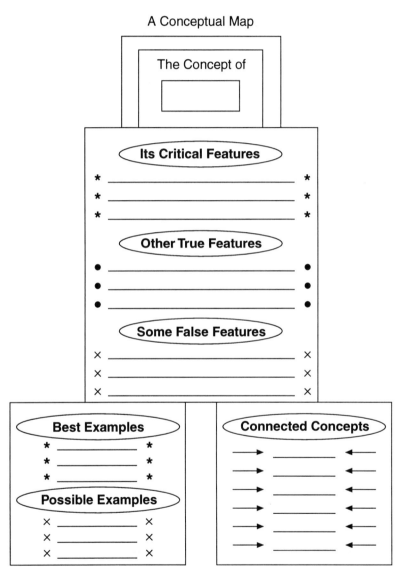

A Conceptual Map

The Concept of

Its Critical Features

Other True Features

Some False Features

Best Examples

Possible Examples

Connected Concepts

Fig. 4.4. By creating conceptual maps, children can strengthen their grasps on key concepts. This blank form can be used to help children map concepts.

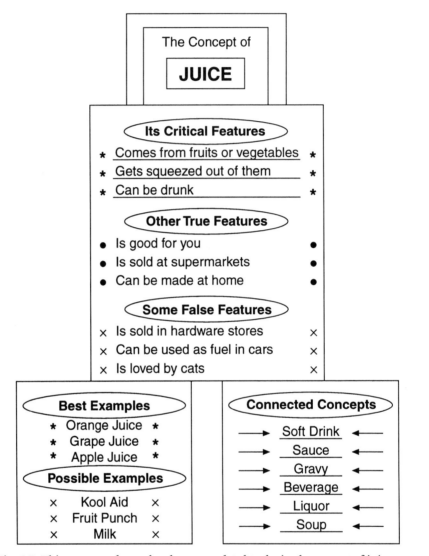

Fig. 4.5. This conceptual map has been completed to depict the concept of juice.

WEAK VISUAL PROCESSING

Although we have emphasized how critical language is as a medium for learning, it is also true that the ability to process visually is important for school success. Being able to form a visual image is sometimes essential for optimal understanding. Visual processing is especially helpful in mathematics, in the sciences, and in a variety of artistic, motoric, and mechanical activities.

The interpretation of spatial relationships depends on accurate visual processing. Knowing how different objects relate to each other in space (e.g., in terms of relative position, size, whole-to-part interactions, foreground-to-background determinations, perspective, or scale) is critical for maximally understanding graphic art and the inner workings of machinery. Such insights can play an important role in developing certain problem-solving skills (chapter 5) which might be applied in building scenery for a school play, repairing a broken toy, or solving a geometric proof.

Visual processing assumes great importance as young children begin to recognize letter symbols. Their ability to differentiate between similar appearing letters and numbers is dependent upon accurate processing in the visual mode. For older students the visual processing of letters and words is likely to be less relevant to reading ability. The language and memory aspects of the reading process assume much greater importance.

Visual processing helps us to preview (chapter 2). Collaborating with the attention previewing control, it allows us to form an idea beforehand of what something will look like or is supposed to look like

---

MARIO

Mario is an extremely verbal child. At age eight he loves reading and is a very good speller. His teacher reports that Mario is very quick to understand spoken instructions and explanations. However, he is having some difficulties drawing in art class. He is also very slow to copy from the chalk board. His teacher feels that somehow Mario does not have a good understanding of arithmetic. He overrelies on memory and seems unable to picture what is going on during operations such as addition and subtraction. The school thinks that Mario may eventually have difficulty picturing geometric shapes in mathematics. Mario's parents report that he is very disorganized with his possessions. He seems to lose things easily and can never remember where he last saw anything!

when it's completed. Being able to picture in our minds the steps in-volved in making something happen (such as water going over a dam to create kinetic energy which later is converted into electrical energy) strengthens our understanding of that process.

Visual processing also plays a role in grasping concepts. The under-standing of some concepts is enhanced when children form strong visual images in their minds. For example, the image of a sliced pie helps many children conceptualize fractions.

Some of the important functions of visual processing are depicted in figure 4.6.

Forms of Weak Visual Processing

Children with weaknesses in visual processing (like Mario in the case just cited) may reveal this gap in one or more of the following ways:

- Poor performance in subjects or with activities requiring substan-tial conceptualization and problem solving (page 147) that is non-verbal.

- Difficulty with spelling and writing because of inability to visualize the letter forms or whole words quickly and accurately. Often these children produce phonetically correct but visually inaccurate spell-ings.

- Possible delays in acquiring reading skills. It should be pointed out that many children with weak visual processing have little or no difficulty learning to read. They may compensate through strong language skills.

- Slow and possibly inaccurate copying from a chalkboard or over-head projection.

- Dependence on a strong verbal approach to mathematics and sci-ences.

- Difficulty with making and interpreting graphs, diagrams, charts, and maps.

- Trouble in art and design classes, trouble understanding how to use tools for woodworking and/or problems succeeding in physical education classes when the activities depend on visual-motor inte-gration, such as catching or hitting a ball.

- Manifestations of weak visual recognition (e.g., a tendency to for-get faces).

Visual Processing Roles

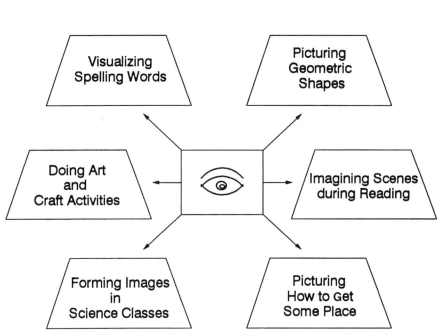

Fig. 4.6. This diagram illustrates some common roles of visual processing.

- Possible trouble forming and/or recalling associations between visual configurations and language (e.g., difficulty with recalling the names of geometric forms).
- Problems following directions from an instructor in a physical education class. Although children may have good language processing skills, they may have trouble picturing or previewing the action while the teacher is speaking.

Weak visual processing does not always become a significant handicap in school. A student with strong language skills, good memory functions, and other strengths may be able to compensate for weak visual processing and be quite successful academically. A student whose weak visual processing occurs in the presence of attentional, mnemonic, or other processing gaps is likely to experience much greater difficulty.

Managing Weak Visual Processing at Home

Parents may need to provide additional assistance when weak visual processing is causing learning difficulty. The interpretation of graphic representations (maps and diagrams) or the visualization of certain word meanings (e.g., in geometry) are often important areas in which parents can provide valuable help.

1. Parents can assist these children in interpreting graphs, diagrams, maps, and other such materials by discussing their meanings and providing practical experience in using them.

2. Parents can encourage a child to explain certain visual relationships that are hard to describe verbally but that may be even harder for that child to picture. If the child is effective linguistically, she or he should begin by striving to verbalize the material and later adding pictures to it. For example, a student who finds it hard to visualize ratios or proportion can try to talk about these entities as a parent listens. Parents should suggest metaphors, examples, and analogies from the child's daily life (e.g., "Think about when we go get pizza and your brother takes the largest portion of the pie. What's left for the rest of us?").

3. Through careful questioning parents can guide their children through visual material step by step. While looking at a map or a diagram, the parent can ask a series of simple questions that reduce the possible sensory overload the child may feel: "Let's see, which way is north on this map? How many miles are there to an inch? Which are the main highways?". This method can also be used to help children perceive the component parts and most salient features of a scene, a diagram, a work of art, or a piece of equipment. Parents may ask questions like: "Can you see any triangles in this design? How many are there? Are any of them isosceles? Is one of them in front of another one?"

4. When weak visual processing is interfering with the growth of skills in reading, writing, spelling or mathematics, parents can be helpful in identifying a child's processing strengths and helping the teacher and, perhaps, a tutor to use these strengths to enhance the weak skills. For example, if a child with weak visual processing is having trouble spelling but has very strong language function, that child could be helped by concentrating on word derivations and language rules and how they affect spelling.

5. Children with weak visual processing should be examined thoroughly by an ophthalmologist at least once. She or he may recommend periodic follow-up visits to monitor the child's visual acuity and other visual functions.

Managing Weak Visual Processing in School

Children with weak visual processing may need special provisions made for work in art, science, industrial arts, and mathematics. Their teachers also should be alert for any possible effects on reading, writing, and spelling.

1. Teachers should be aware of those aspects of learning in their subjects that require sophisticated visual processing. This will help them identify students who have trouble. For example, there may be certain students who are likely to have a hard time learning about astronomy through charts or maps of the solar system.

2. Teachers can help these students by constantly providing strong verbal reinforcement for nonverbal material and by reminding them to provide this for themselves. Children learning to form letters in the early grades, for example, can be guided through the process verbally: "First go up, then across, then down."

3. Art therapy often benefits children with weak visual processing. Creating artistic products may actually enhance their visualization skills. Since some of their products may not be as well executed as those of their peers, these often self-conscious students need privacy and encouragement, at least initially, to open up and to create.

4. Teachers can provide children with opportunities to describe what they are observing. For example, students could be told that they will be called upon in class tomorrow to use their good language skills to talk about trapezoids, parallelograms, and other four-sided figures. For children with weak visual processing skills who also have good language production skills, this can be especially helpful because they can use one of their strengths to improve one of their weaknesses.

SLOW DATA PROCESSING

Achievement in school depends greatly upon being able to keep pace with the rapid presentation of information. During the early elementary grades, new facts and procedures are usually presented at a slow pace and with considerable repetition. Gradually, presentation rates increase. By high school, adolescents must be able to process instantaneously in order to take good notes, solve geometry problems on a test, and figure out expeditiously what is expected on a homework assignment. The instant processing of entirely new material is demanded with much

COURTNEY

Courtney is an eleven-year-old girl who is finding school increasingly difficult. Her teacher has observed that Courtney has trouble keeping up with the rest of the class during most discussions. She reads well but very slowly. She is often confused when new material is explained in class. At such times she appears to tune out and give up on even trying to understand. She requires repetition of instructions in order to process and carry them out. Courtney likes it when her mother explains and reviews lessons at home. According to Courtney, "Mom goes over the stuff more slowly so I can understand."

greater frequency during the school years than during the career years of an adult! Speed is essential for school success. Students must be quick to understand questions on a quiz. They must be able to respond rapidly to comprehension questions posed during a class discussion. They need to grasp numbers, charts, pictures, and other forms of nonverbal material with speed as well. If comprehension is too slow at a particular moment, whatever follows may not be processed at all.

Forms of Slow Data Processing

There are many students who have difficulty processing material fast enough while they listen, read, or observe. Courtney manifests this pattern. Students like her may find themselves trying to understand one statement that the teacher has made. In the meantime, she or he has communicated several additional ideas which they missed. Consequently, they acquire an incomplete understanding of the subject matter. If this occurs regularly, it is not unusual for these students to show signs of weak attention control. As they struggle to keep up, they may experience overwhelming mental fatigue and a loss of focus. This is sometimes a problem for Courtney. It is important to determine if children's slow processing is a general characteristic of all of their learning (as with Courtney) or whether the slow processing is confined to certain types of information.

Slow processing of information may be connected to a specific kind of format. Some children may be slow when processing language, others when processing nonverbal material. Slow processing can also occur in children who have trouble accessing memory fast enough. When they encounter a new idea or fact, they are not sufficiently quick at activating what they knew before that will help make sense of the new information, nor are they able to instantly *recognize* familiar patterns. In general, these children usually can process with accuracy but not at a sufficient rate.

Managing Slow Data Processing at Home

Very often slow processing children become discouraged and anxious in school. Here are some suggestions for parents when assisting these children.

1. Parents need to understand that doing homework and studying can be very tiring and frustrating for a child who processes data slowly. Because it takes them more time to complete homework, they should be encouraged to take frequent breaks.

2. There should be a strong emphasis on the review of material, especially in those subjects that are causing difficulty. Students may not have assimilated important concepts, vocabulary, and procedures because they were initially presented too rapidly. Parents need to detect and repair these "holes" in knowledge and understanding.

3. It is possible for students to improve their rate of processing. Parents should help them do this gradually and in a relaxed manner. They can give children a time limit for reading a chapter, for studying a diagram, or for demonstrating a correctly solved mathematical problem. Later they can be tested on the material.

4. Parents can teach these children scanning and skimming techniques while reading as well as ways to cover the material in stages, for example, first scanning, then careful reading, then quick reviewing.

5. In day-to-day living, parents will help these children by repeating directions and explanations. Family conversations may need to be slowed to ensure that children who process slowly are able to participate meaningfully.

Managing Slow Data Processing in School

Schools can do several things to alleviate the inevitable anxiety experienced by students who are unable to keep pace with the flow of information. Just knowing that a teacher is sympathetic can sustain or restore a student's motivation to persist at understanding.

1. Teachers should watch for possible disorientation in children who are slow processors. The student may appear confused and somewhat "spacey" when she or he is unable to keep pace with the information. On these occasions repeating the information may be helpful.

2. Because note taking and copying may be especially difficult for these students, teachers can provide them with handout materials which can be studied at a comfortable pace.

3. Students with slow processing need either more time or fewer questions on tests. Teachers may ask these children to do the latter and then require that they complete the remaining problems as homework. They should be allowed to take standardized tests without being timed.

4. A teacher should make a conscious effort to slow the rate at which she or he presents material when there is a student with slow processing in class. A slower pace is unlikely to harm or bore the other students.

5. When there is an important lesson or review session, teachers may suggest that a student use a tape recorder in class. This will allow him or her a second opportunity to process the information and to do so at his or her preferred rate.

6. In order to save face, students with slow data processing may try to look as if they are keeping up. But when they get home at night, they may have no idea about the assignment or what tomorrow's quiz will cover. Teachers should try to make sure that they really do understand what is expected of them before they leave. One way to do this is to have students maintain an assignment pad where they record what they are to do. Teachers should check these to decide if students have understood.

7. To avoid embarrassing students with slow data processing, teachers can refrain from calling on them to respond to complex questions rapidly. Instead they can warn students that they will be called on to discuss a particular issue.

SMALL CHUNK-SIZE CAPACITY

As the school years move onward, there is an assumption that children will be capable of handling an increasingly large volume or chunk of information at one time. They need to develop in their capacities to take in and work with these steadily growing amounts of

---

FAITH

Faith is a ten-year-old girl who is enduring many academic delays. She has particular problems with spelling. Her errors are characterized by omissions of critical word parts. When she writes, she leaves out words in the middle of sentences. Faith's teachers have noted that she has trouble following extensive directions. She requires frequent repetition, especially if directions entail the processing and retention of multiple steps. Faith's parents report that she does very well if she is given one thing to do at a time. Her teachers have made the same observation. She seems overwhelmed when confronting large volumes of information or the need for substantial output.

---

data. The challenges children face in relation to large chunk sizes are delineated below:

- Being able to perceive visually and through language the growing amounts of information they are receiving, including highly detailed graphic displays as well as longer, more complex sentences
- Being able to understand longer sequences of data in the form of serial instructions and multistep processes and explanations
- Being able to hold more data simultaneously in active working memory and/or short-term memory in order to understand longer reading assignments or lengthy oral explanations
- Being able to condense, paraphrase, distill, or find the main points within progressively larger amounts of data
- Being able to compare and contrast greater quantities of information
- Being able to apply acquired skills (i.e., reading, writing, math, spelling) when working with long spelling words, extended reading passages, and other large volume contexts

Forms of Small Chunk-Size Capacity

As the amount of information a child needs to process in a short period increases, some children, like Faith, simply cannot keep pace. We have already considered children who have trouble in one way with the quantity of what they are processing—those with limited short-term and active working memories. However, there exists a group of students who have difficulty with the quantity of material "across the board." They have problems in all or most of the ways we have just listed. This broad impact is observable in Faith's case.

Often, affected children seem to be viewing the world of ideas through a keyhole. They are able to perceive and integrate only a small portion of that which they are exposed to. Therefore, in what seems to be a random manner, they process pieces of information rather than the whole. Not surprisingly, the "big picture" eludes them. Their comprehension is mostly incomplete. What they learn has a fragmented quality, conspicuously lacking in cohesion.

Children with small chunk-size capacity are likely to reveal many of the following traits:

- They are slow at learning to decode multisyllabic words for reading, although their recognition of shorter words is relatively well automatized.
- They commit spelling errors characterized by the omission of word parts, often medial sections.
- They show a disparity between their understanding of small amounts of information (e.g., word meanings) and their comprehension of larger amounts (e.g., a book chapter).
- They have difficulty with multistep instructions and/or long explanations.
- In the middle of trying to understand an extensive mathematical process, they may become disoriented.
- They may show very inconsistent and unpredictable recall of factual material they've read or heard.
- They may refuse to read lengthy text.
- In the presence of large quantities of information, their attention controls weaken noticeably.

Children with small chunk-size capacity may ultimately catch up with the demands in school, but they need sensitive help. Without it, they can easily become very discouraged and lose motivation.

Managing Small Chunk-Size Capacity at Home

Parents need to anticipate when a particular academic activity is likely to exceed a child's chunk-size capacity. Then they can take specific measures to help the child break down the material to manageable amounts.

1. Parents should comment openly and sympathetically about how long a reading passage or other assignment seems to be. Such empathic comments can reduce the frustration and anxiety these children frequently feel when they confront the large chunks.

2. These youngsters may need frequent breaks while doing homework. They should be helped to schedule these breaks around specific amounts of work. For example, instead of persevering through twelve math problems, a child should be told to take a break after every four problems.

3. Parents can help divide reading assignments for these children by having them read several paragraphs or a section rather than an entire chapter. Students should think about and/or summarize each section individually after reading it.

4. Parents can give these children practice with note taking, paraphrasing, and underlining skills, all of which serve to break down the chunk size of material in texts.

5. Since the decoding and encoding (spelling) of multisyllabic words is often difficult for these students, parents can provide extra drill to make these words automatic. It is sometimes helpful for students to try to spell or read each word twice. Using a reading list, the first attempt should be recorded on tape. Children, then, can review the taped words to see if they are missing any sounds. If so the word can be restated. For spelling, children simply write words down and then check carefully for missing parts. For both reading and spelling, these children may benefit from practicing with lists of long words that contain missing parts which they are expected to fill in.

6. Parents can help children learn to pull together relevant information from their reading or experiences by having them describe in their own words the content of a story, the steps in a process, the explanation for an historical event or scientific phenomenon or, in general, the important material learned in school that day. This activity will help both parents and children to see where knowledge gaps exist.

Managing Small Chunk-Size Capacity in School

Within a classroom setting, children with small chunk-size capacity can feel disoriented and confused, as they try to extract bits and pieces of data from a seemingly gargantuan body of knowledge. It is vitally important to be sympathetic and flexible in dealing with them.

1. Whenever possible, teachers should present instructions or explanations in a concise manner and repeat them if necessary.

2. Teachers should try to be familiar enough with students with this problem to know how they look or act when feeling overwhelmed by the volume of material in class. They can then help or reassure these students.

4. Whenever it is feasible teachers should reinforce visually what they have presented verbally. Diagrams and demonstration models used as supplements to verbal explanations may help these students process information that otherwise would be unmanageable for them.

5. Teachers, like parents, can help students break their processing down into smaller units or stages.

6. These students are helped significantly when teachers stress what is most important about an explanation or lecture. For example, after talking about a topic, a teacher can say, "These are the three points that you really should remember. If you learn these things, you will be able to figure out the rest."

7. Whenever possible a teacher should make sure that these children understand a piece of information well before expanding or elaborating upon it.

8. Children with chunk-size limitations, like those with slow processing, may benefit from having a tape recorder in class. When the material about to be presented is extensive, they can turn on the recorder. Later at home they can play back the recording and work on assimilating the new information.

9. Teachers should try to determine if there is any mode in which an affected student does not have trouble processing large amounts of information. For example, perhaps the teacher sees that a student can handle more information in a gestalt or configuration, such as a diagram, than she or he can in a sequence. That knowledge can help a teacher devise the best ways to present information to that student.

10. When small chunk-size capacity interferes with the development of reading and/or spelling skills, teachers should work along with parents, using the techniques described under home management (page 113, item #5).

MYRA

Myra, a seventeen-year-old adolescent, is a real enigma to her teachers. She is described as a highly imaginative child who writes superb book reports and short stories. She performs very well in history class and in biology. She has had more difficulty in classes that stress mathematical reasoning. Myra's teachers agree that hers is a highly "divergent" mind. She often misses relevant fine detail and likes to infuse her own original ideas into whatever she reads or thinks about. Recently Myra was shocked to discover how poorly she had done on her college entrance examinations. There was a marked disparity between the quality of her grades in English classes and her scores on reading comprehension. Myra's parents point out that she is a child who has never done well on multiple-choice tests. She seems to need more "mental leeway" than is offered on such examinations.

EXCESSIVE TOP-DOWN OR BOTTOM-UP PROCESSING

Many studies of learning and understanding have explored two contrasting approaches to processing information, described as top-down and bottom-up. Top-down processing occurs when an individual confronts some spoken or written information and attributes meaning that comes largely from his or her own values, associations, perspectives, and personal experiences. Bottom-up processing, on the other hand, sticks to the facts or data in a tightly confined and literal manner. The listener, viewer, or reader adds little if anything to that which is presented.

There are times in school when one approach rather than the other is better. For example, when answering a multiple-choice question on a mathematics achievement test, bottom-up processing is definitely preferable. That is not the time to infuse personal values and creative thoughts! However, when interpreting a poem, a short story, or a painting, personal points of view, some imaginative thinking, and associations with life experience will very much enrich interpretation. It is very important to know how and when to use a particular form of processing in school. Some students are conspicuously unable to do this and depend on one or the other form excessively.

Forms of Excessive Top-Down or Bottom-Up Processing

Children who display a pattern of extreme top-down processing are likely to scintillate with original ideas and insights, but this approach to understanding can create some problems in school as we have seen in the case of Myra. Students like her are apt to show at least some of the following tendencies:

- These children usually perform better in subject areas that allow for or encourage creative thinking and free association. In particular, they are likely to make innovative contributions when there is more than one possible correct answer to a question.
- They are most likely to succeed with teachers who encourage innovative thinking and the expression of personal perceptions and values.
- They are susceptible to problems in classes that demand great precision, attention to fine detail, and highly convergent, or precise, thinking.
- They do not usually do well on multiple-choice tests.
- They may be more interested in generating their own ideas than in studying facts.
- They may have trouble grasping procedures or processes in mathematics and science.
- They may be far better at understanding and remembering the concepts in history than they are at memorizing specific events and their dates.
- They are apt to be so highly intuitive in their thinking and in their interpretations of what they read or hear that they may have trouble justifying their understandings to others.
- They may or may not have trouble with attention control. While children with attentional dysfunction often may show this pattern of processing information, it is important to emphasize that it also appears in children with no obvious attentional dysfunction. Where weak attentional control and excessive top-down processing coexist, it is often in the form of the free flight of ideas (page 24).
- They may wish to engage in imaginative play long after their peers have stopped doing so.

Students who use bottom-up processing excessively are less apt to experience any obvious academic difficulty. The kind of material studied in school often lends itself to this form of processing, thus enabling children with this comprehension style to achieve good grades in most if not all areas. They are likely to show some of the following tendencies:

- They often are able to analyze and memorize information without difficulty.
- They perform well on multiple-choice or short answer tests, although they may be less successful on essay or oral examinations.
- They are likely to enjoy and succeed in mathematics and science classes.
- They may not be as successful in classes demanding creativity. They can have trouble selecting topics, brainstorming, and making up original stories. They may have difficulty generating original ideas or relating new knowledge to personal life experiences.
- They are less inclined to seek opportunities for imaginative play.

Managing Excessive Top-Down or Bottom-Up Processing at Home

Parents need to be aware of a child's tendency to be excessively top-down or bottom-up in processing. They can engage in conversations with the child regarding when one or the other of these forms works best at home and in school.

1. Parents can help children separate those aspects of a task that lend themselves primarily to top-down processing and those components for which bottom-up processing works best. For example, sometimes in helping a child read a story and prepare a book report, the parents might encourage the child to describe the facts of the story. Then the child can offer his or her interpretations and link the story to personal associations and experiences.

2. Parents can help give direction and structure to children who use top-down patterns excessively. These children need to know when they'd better "stick to the facts." Gentle reminders during mathematics homework or while studying for a science test that "this is no time to be dreaming up new inventions or creating far-out interpretations" can be helpful.

3. Parents should provide productive outlets for the creative energies of top-down processors. These children need to be rewarded for creative thinking channeled through art work, music, writing, inventing, or building things. Their original thinking should be directed but not stifled. Parents can document their creative output as part of an ongoing portfolio of accomplishments. Also, these children can benefit from opportunities for imaginative play which can sometimes be accomplished through participation in a drama group.

4. If a student with top-down processing performs poorly on standardized multiple-choice tests, parents need to consider the possibility that such assessments fail to tap the child's true ability. They may wish to advocate for alternative forms of assessment. For example, if such a student performs disappointingly on college entrance examinations, the parent may wish to obtain a letter from the school or from a clinician who has seen the child stating that the testing does not reflect his or her ability and that the scores should not be given great weight in decision making.

5. Children with extreme bottom-up processing may need help selecting topics and coming up with original ideas for reports and/or projects. Parents can give them practice with brainstorming and with deriving their own personal interpretations or opinions about issues. They need to be discouraged from using rote memory while studying.

6. Parents should involve these children in activities that require them to create and to innovate. If all of their pursuits involve imitation, memorization, and close compliance with instructions, they may succeed in school without being able to generate new ideas and products that are uniquely their own.

Managing Excessive Top-Down or Bottom-Up Processing in School

Teachers usually can identify these extremes of either comprehension style in the classroom. They are also likely to observe that some of their most successful students are remarkably agile in shifting as needed from top-down to bottom-up processing and in achieving optimal blends of the two approaches during tasks. The extent to which extreme tendencies or an inability to shift and blend the two creates learning difficulties depends on the subject matter and the teacher's personal teaching style. In some cases, substantial accommodations may be needed.

1. A student who depends almost exclusively on top-down processing may need opportunities to make use of this approach in class. For example, in mathematics, a student might be asked to write a story about multiplication or create some funny or highly imaginative word problems. He or she might even receive extra credit for submitting original art work or essays or word problems relating to what is being studied.

2. Students who use excessive top-down processing may need help in teasing out factual data from reading materials. The kind of approach suggested for use at home (page 117) can be reinforced in school

by helping these children to separate understanding from personal interpretation and intuition. For these students, a teacher might suggest a first reading during which they simply underline or list the critical factual data. On a second reading they can go back and write comments (perhaps in a different color) in the margins or add their own ideas or perspectives before writing or talking about the material. They are likely to need continuing help in separating what's actually there on the page from what their interpretations might be.

3. Children who process most information with a bottom-up style need encouragement to generate original ideas and interpretations, even when they are basically succeeding academically. Teachers should help these students understand that imitating and repeating is not really complete learning.

4. Teachers can help bottom-up processors find some medium in which they can experiment with more original thinking within an academic setting. This may take the form of art work, craft activities, musical composition, or some other pursuit in which compliance and imitation are not the sole ingredients required for mastery and satisfaction.

5. In collaborative learning situations, teachers should seek to team excessive bottom-up processors with their opposites. On some occasions, they each should pursue their usual inclinations, but at times it can be helpful to ask the top-down processor to do the bottom-up work and vice versa.

The Demystification of Chronic Misunderstanding

It may seem oddly circular to be helping children understand their problems with understanding, especially since they may not sufficiently understand after such explanations. Nevertheless, one can proceed toward helping them build greater personal insight.

1. It is important to acknowledge that everyone, including these children have things they can understand easily and things that seem too hard to figure out. They should be encouraged to discuss both of these aspects of their school experience. They need to see that their kind of misunderstanding does not mean they are stupid.

2. It is important to describe to the child the nature of his or her inadequate understanding. For example, if a child has difficulty processing language, one might point out: "You seem to have your most trouble

understanding language—words and sentences. You're much better at knowing how things work or figuring why your friend is sad."

3. There should be a review of the kinds of situations in which the particular misunderstanding causes the most problems (e.g., on tests, during class discussions, when trying to understand what the assignment is).

4. Students should be helped to see that their problems with understanding information are likely to improve as they get older. They also should know that they will be able to use their strengths more when they grow up. It is good to stress that the world needs many different kinds of minds. For example, a child with excessive top-down processing might be assured that the world needs citizens with both extremes of processing, and both can be equally successful and happy as adults (and hopefully while growing up too).

5. Students should consider and talk about how they can use their strengths to improve understanding.

6. It is important to discuss with these students what they can do in school when they don't understand. The adult carrying out this discussion should be sensitive to how embarrassing it can be to ask questions in a class where one may feel overwhelmed and inadequate and to how important the need for some privacy and safety is.

Recognizing Comprehension Strengths

Every child possesses comprehension strengths. Often these pockets of understanding are crying out for detection, but frequently their potential is ignored. These strengths, which may be in nonacademic areas, can be especially valuable for the development of academic skills. It has been shown that one of the best ways to learn how to read is by reading in areas that one knows a lot about.

Comprehension strengths can also be used to help children develop and employ expertise which can kindle enthusiasm for learning, at the same time that it can provide practice in good organizational skills and strategies. Such tactics are most easily incorporated within contexts of good understanding of the subject matter. Assembling a collection of football cards by team, division, and league, cataloguing a doll collection, or keeping win/loss statistics for a school team are examples.

No child can be understood without a careful analysis of that which the child understands well. Many clues about a child's strengths and potential strengths can be discovered as we attempt to determine what and how she or he understands.

It is not sufficient merely to understand in school. Somehow students must keep on demonstrating that they comprehend and that they can think and create independently. They do so by creating products, such as written reports, spoken responses, or test papers. They must concentrate, remember, and understand as they develop different modes of achieving results. This ability to turn out worthy products is the subject of the next chapter.

CHAPTER FIVE

Phenomena Related to
Deficient Output

S TUDENTS must produce clear evidence of their competency. Such evidence takes the form of effective output or visible results that demonstrate their knowledge and skill. Children often need these tangible products to convince adults of their ever-growing ability. Equally, children need these forms of successful output to satisfy themselves that they are capable. They can demonstrate their competency through their verbal communications, their motor performances, their ways of organizing their efforts, and the approaches and strategies they deploy for problem solving.

Successful output perpetuates motivation, feelings of overall effectiveness, and stable self-esteem. When the work produced is substandard, on the other hand, it becomes a source of gnawing humiliation. Every child needs to be able to create at least some products worthy of public display. Every child has to have concrete evidence that at least a portion of his or her output is competitive in quality with that of classmates. It should not be surprising that low-quality or inadequate output during the school years can exact a heavy emotional and motivational toll from a developing child.

In this chapter we examine principally four forms of output: language production, motor performance, organizational behavior, and problem solving. We will also consider certain potentially rewarding forms of output that may sometimes be overlooked.

WEAK LANGUAGE PRODUCTION

Language production involves many functions similar to those delineated in our discussion of language processing. As with the processing of verbal material, language production requires facility with the sound system (phonology), with words (semantics), with sentences (syntax), and with paragraphs and passages (discourse). Students need to be capable of creating ideas or responses and then making efficient use of these language levels as they communicate their thoughts. As with language processing, through their school years children are expected to communicate verbally with increasing speed and automaticity, in ever-growing "chunks," with greater density of ideas, and frequently with more abstract conceptual content.

Language production is an integral part of most school activities. It is critical for being an active participant in the learning process. Much solid learning involves the ability to elaborate verbally, to extend and relate ideas to each other, as well as to categorize and to infuse one's own personal experiences and interpretations into what one is studying. Language production is also essential for relating to others, for writing, and even for having vicarious experiences (as one talks one's way through fantasies). Because it enriches understanding, remembering, and thinking, it is not surprising, that children who are adept at language production are often highly successful in meeting expectations in many aspects of school and daily life.

Forms of Weak Language Production

The process of *encoding* ideas into spoken words needs to occur with tremendous speed, accuracy, and efficiency in school. For some children such oral expression is a labored and unrewarding activity. This is clearly evident in Frank's case (page 124). Dysfluency, or the inability of individuals to express themselves well in language, may be found in a wide range of patterns. The following are often signs that a child is struggling in this domain:

- Hesitation and labored speech. While trying to explain something, these students are apt to falter, make use of delay words (like "whatchamacallit," "umm," and "uhhh"), and in general work too hard to put forth their ideas orally. Sometimes such hesitancy may reflect a *word retrieval* dysfunction. Such children may have trouble finding the right vocabulary quickly when speaking or may have difficulty formulating sentences and organizing narrative fast enough. This is a serious problem for Frank.
- Low ideational density. Many of these students take a long time and use a lot of words to say relatively little. They may take five sentences to state what someone else could express in just one.

FRANK

Frank is a fourteen-year-old boy with strengths in a number of areas. He is a very good mathematician and he is excellent at fixing and building things. In school, Frank is conspicuously quiet. During classes, he has difficulty expressing his ideas quickly and accurately. In fact, he lives in constant fear of being called on in class. Frank was somewhat late in learning to speak. He struggled with articulation problems and received speech therapy for two years as a preschooler. At present, it is hard for him to find the exact words he needs and to formulate good grammatical sentences. Frank's written output is often ungrammatical and notably disorganized. He was discouraged from taking a foreign language, but he did so because he wanted very much to study Spanish. Frank is currently failing that subject.

- A lack of cohesive ties. Some students do not connect sentences together very well, so that it sounds as if they are conveying a list rather than a coherent narrative. There is a noticeable lack of connecting words (like "then," "next," "so," and "when"). There may also be a tendency to repeat nouns too often rather than making use of pronouns. They may prefer to use two separate sentences rather than constructing a sentence containing a conjunction.
- Overuse of high frequency vocabulary. They may employ only very common words.
- Weak revision skills. They may have trouble clarifying or revising something they just said.
- Inability to take another's perspective. These children may find it hard to take the perspective of the listener in order to understand what that person needs to know. For example, they might say to a new acquaintance, "I went to the movies with Joe on Saturday" without considering that the listener has no idea who Joe is. The effective speaker would say, "My cousin Joe and I went to the movies on Saturday."
- Trouble organizing ideas in the best order. It may be difficult for them to present their ideas in the most coherent sequence. As a result, the punch line in a joke is revealed too soon or the events in

a story are presented out of order. Such disorganization is seen in Frank's written output.

- Poor grammatical construction. As is true with Frank, they may commit too many spoken grammatical errors for their ages and cultural backgrounds. Also, they may overindulge in simple sentences to avoid grammatical complexity in their speech.

- Underdeveloped summarization skills. It may be hard for these students to summarize personal experiences, reading assignments, or school-related subject matter. Their descriptions may be run-on, poorly organized, and infused with nonsalient information.

- A significant difference between everyday language production and literate communication at school. Many of these children can express their thoughts adequately at home and with their friends but are unable to keep pace with the more formal and analytic language production expectations of school.

- Problems organizing discourse. These children may find it very hard to narrate, to expound upon ideas, or to tell stories because they find it difficult to organize their thoughts in language. Some of them have problems organizing nonverbal activities as well. They may find it hard to organize a project or a recreational activity. They may require that someone else help them structure what they want to say or do. For example, in writing a report they may need help in setting out the points to be made in each paragraph because they are unable to impose such structure independently.

It should be evident that children with weak language production are destined to have trouble participating actively in many subject areas during the school day, and their difficulties may be complicated by some commonly associated factors which are summarized below.

A nonelaborative style. Many of these children fail to extend or elaborate on anything in school. Typically, such a child when arriving home responds to the question, "What did you do in school today?" with a concise "Stuff." "Wasn't there anything special?", the parent continues. "No," answers the child. "Didn't you have social studies?" "Yeah." "What did you learn about?" "Nothing." "Nothing, nothing at all?" "A war." "Which war?" "Two."

Sometimes it is hard to decide whether students have become nonelaborative because they have difficulty producing language or whether they are showing expressive language dysfluency because they seldom elaborate on anything. The best way to become verbally fluent is to have experience elaborating verbally! Some students who fail to elaborate exhibit a pattern of passive processing too (page 23). They may also have trouble elaborating information for long-term memory consolidation, since as we have seen (chapter 3), knowledge must be extended to be stored and easily accessed.

Performance anxiety. Some students with expressive language dysfluency become very anxious. They spend their school day living in fear of being called upon in class. They worry that their utterances will sound non-sensical to their peers and teachers. As one student said, "I have a lot of good ideas, but when I try to say them, they come out sounding stupid, and I get real embarrassed."

Aggressive behavior. It is not unusual for students with expressive language dysfluency to show aggression. In its most extreme form, this dys-function has been shown to be a very common finding among adolescents jailed for violent crimes.

Speech articulation problems. The pronunciation of certain words, especially long ones, can be difficult and elusive for some of these students. Such articulation weaknesses can add to the labor and embarrass-ment of expression in the classroom. There are many different kinds of speech problems, and they call for different therapeutic strategies.

Foreign language disabilities. It is common for students with weak language production to have problems learning a second language. The pronunciation, semantics, morphology, and grammatical rules and con-struction of a new language may cause considerable frustration for them, especially when they have not completely internalized these components of their native language.

Trouble with written language. Students with oral expressive weak-nesses often write poorly. Transmitting ideas in language on paper may be a very slow and tedious undertaking for them. Their writing may feature simple or poorly constructed sentences and very limited vocabu-lary. Sometimes they simplify their ideas as well. We will discuss these and other forms of delayed written output in chapter 6.

Social problems. Some children with weak language production may have difficulty making prompt and appropriate use of language in social settings and sometimes, as a result, develop aggressive or withdrawn behaviors. This phenomenon is discussed further in chapter 7.

Components of weak language production are identified in figure 5.1.

Possible Components of
Weak Language Production

PHONOLOGY
- **Trouble Producing the Sounds of Language**

SEMANTICS
- **Not Knowing How to Use Word Meanings Effectively**

MORPHOLOGY
- **Inability to Modify Words to Convey Precise Meanings**

SYNTAX
- **Difficulty Making Good Use of Grammar and Word Order**

DISCOURSE
- **Problems Communicating Beyond the Level of Sentences**

METALINGUISTICS
- **Being Unable to Think About How Language Works**

PRAGMATICS
- **Poor Use of Language in Social Contexts**

Fig. 5.1. This figure shows common components of weak language production, which parallel the common components of weak language processing (page 91).

Managing Weak Language Production at Home

Children can be helped to be increasingly fluent through conversation at home. Such communication can be "safer" than oral expression in a classroom, so a dysfluent child may feel less inhibited while developing more effective language production. The following suggestions should be helpful:

1. It is important for these children to learn the meaning of the word *elaboration*. They can then be encouraged to develop their verbal responses at the dinner table, in the car, and at other times when extended conversation can take place. Periodically, the child may need to be reminded of how important it is to "build up your elaboration muscles!"

2. Children can practice summarizing. Parents should encourage them to describe their personal experiences from time to time and can make use of interview techniques to help them with verbal expression. Concerning a surprise party she attended, a child might be asked, "How did the birthday girl look when she walked in? How do you think she felt? How would you feel?" Single word or simple sentence responses should be discouraged.

3. Children can improve their expressive language fluency most effectively by talking about things they know a lot about. They should be encouraged, therefore, to discuss subject matter that is of great and long-standing interest to them. When children have no such interests, parents should try to help them acquire one or more areas of intellectual focus that can be used to foster communication (and many other) skills.

4. Often children can be helped to express themselves by talking about a visual stimulus. A child can be shown a picture from a newspaper or magazine and asked to describe or explain it and also to elaborate on what is going on in the illustration.

5. Parents should be careful not to embarrass these children. For example, in front of friends or relatives, they should not ask questions that require long or complicated answers. They should also avoid correcting grammatical or other speech errors in public. However, in a non-threatening and uncritical manner they can correct such mistakes in private.

6. It is important to discourage children from giving very brief answers to questions that arise in everyday life at home. In a supportive way, a parent should say, "Can you tell us some more about that?"

7. Parents must become good listeners. By showing a sincere interest in their child's experiences, interests, knowledge, and opinions, they can make language expression a rewarding form of output.

8. In the presence of one or more highly verbal (perhaps even verbose) siblings, a dysfluent child may remain mute. Parents should be sure such a child is getting a chance to speak up either while with the siblings or at a later time alone.

9. There are many activities at home that can be undertaken to enhance language production. These include various games or puzzles to strengthen vocabulary and word retrieval (e.g., Scrabble, crossword puzzles), reading aloud, writing activities (such as a journal or family newsletter), and opportunities to teach a younger sibling.

10. Some children with weak language production can benefit from speech and language therapy. Such intervention might include regular visits to a professional as well as further advice on management at home and in school.

Managing Weak Language Production in School

Weaknesses of language production are often most conspicuous in the classroom. As we have noted, some children are far more fluent at home where the language demands are less stringent. This may result from the fact that communication at home is highly redundant, full of context clues, and relatively limited in its demands on semantics and syntax. Language expression at school is far more exacting. Teachers are in a unique position to monitor and manage language production difficulties.

1. Teachers can warn a child in advance that he or she will be called upon (e.g., "I will ask you tomorrow to tell us about the dangers of pesticides"). The additional time can help a child prepare and in this way reduce anxiety.

2. When it is not practical to provide such advance notice, a classroom teacher should sometimes avoid calling on a child with expressive language difficulty, except for answers that can be provided without substantial elaboration or verbal complexity (e.g., yes or no responses).

3. These children should know that their teachers are aware of how hard it is for them to explain complicated ideas in class.

4. Children who have trouble expressing themselves need to have other nonlinguistic modes of expression with which to experience suc-

cess in school (and at home). Such potential outlets are described in subsequent sections of this chapter.

5. These children need to have opportunities to develop their expressive language fluency and confidence within school. This can be done through parts in plays, oral reports (with adequate preparation time), storytelling or teaching activities with younger students, and occasions for relating personal experiences and special knowledge. As at home, these children in school should be encouraged to elaborate on any areas of personal expertise or strong interest.

6. Many of these children should delay foreign language learning until late in high school and, perhaps, have any requirements for it waived completely. This is especially the case if their language weaknesses are severe and/or accompanied by memory problems.

7. To encourage greater cohesion in spoken discourse, children can practice combining two sentences into one (e.g., "That dog behaved well today. He's usually quite wild"). They can also be helped to make oral presentations based on a list of specific points they need to cover in the correct order. The teacher can provide such a list or a child can create it.

8. It is often good to give these children opportunities to discuss and interpret cartoons or to retell stories. They also can develop stories of their own to share with the class. They should rehearse these stories at home by reciting them over a tape recorder.

9. Students with weak language production should be encouraged to write. Writing activities can enhance language expression, and they allow children to control the rate more than is possible during oral communication. Keeping a journal, reporting for a newspaper, and writing stories, poems, or plays can all facilitate language expression. They are likely to benefit from using lists of ideas or subheadings provided in advance to guide the organization of their writings.

DISAPPOINTING MOTOR PERFORMANCE

The motoric performance of a child is perhaps the most visible of innate abilities. Consequently, children are apt to be highly conscious of their various motor skills and the potential and actual effects of such performance on how they are judged by others. Children crave motor gratification as they grow up. They need to feel that their bodies are somehow effective in space. Such feelings contribute substantially to the development of a positive body image and self-concept. It is disheartening to have physical inabilities that perpetually bring embarrassment and incite ridicule or criticism. An awkward child, who is chronically deprived of motor gratification is at risk for a significant decline in self-esteem.

It is possible to delineate three major forms of motor productivity: gross motor output, fine motor output, and graphomotor output. Gross motor output entails the use of large muscles for participating in athletic events and accomplishing a range of chores at home. Fine motor output often requires the processing of visually presented information that guides the fingers during an activity (such as drawing, tying shoelaces, sculpting, building models, or repairing a motor). Graphomotor output also involves the fingers but is limited to the act of writing. It is important to stress that the motor skills for effective written output (page 185) are rather different from those needed to mend a hem or to use a pair of scissors. A child may be excellent at fixing things but have an illegible or labored handwriting. Individual students may experience difficulty with one, two, or all three of these forms of motor output. In the sections that follow, we will explore the phenomenology of disappointing motor performance affecting each of these three forms of output.

Gross Motor Dysfunction

Gross motor ability is needed to succeed in athletic activities. Such skill has many different subcomponents. To perform adequately in sports, an individual must be able to form judgments regarding various kinds of incoming data and respond quickly with appropriate and accurate muscle movements. She or he must also make use of ongoing sensory feedback

---

BESS

Bess is a very good student. At age seven she is reading on a sixth-grade level. She is also excellent at spelling and in mathematics. Bess loves to write poetry, and she is a good artist. However, Bess has had tremendous difficulty keeping pace with her peers in various athletic pursuits. She is very clumsy on the playground. She is slow at running and is totally unable to jump rope. In physical education class, her classmates sometimes have ridiculed her. She has become increasingly withdrawn. Her parents have observed that Bess much prefers to play by herself.

while in the midst of a motor activity. Gross motor competency also requires good motor memory, that is, the ability to recall the muscular steps used in the past for successful performance. Additionally, the vast numbers of muscles and muscle groups must be properly and rapidly deployed, so that the right muscles are accomplishing the appropriate, necessary steps at the right time. For some children these processes are nearly instinctive. They become easily automatized (page 71) and applied with speed and with precision. For others, they are forever elusive.

Forms of Gross Motor Dysfunction

There are children who experience daily humiliation on the playground and in physical education classes because of their inability to use large muscle groups skillfully. This plight has a serious effect on Bess whose gross motor dysfunction engenders ridicule from peers. Children like her are apt to become anxious on days when there is a gym class. They may be reluctant to be with peers who like sports. They may shy from events or opportunities that have an athletic component (e.g., summer camp). They become understandably upset at perpetually being chosen last for teams and being subjected to harsh criticism or verbal abuse during games. Their plight is not easy. Their body image and feelings of effectiveness may well deteriorate.

There are many forms of gross motor dysfunction. Table 5.1 summarizes some of these.

The weaknesses delineated in table 5.1 can occur in different combinations and degrees of severity in an individual student. Unfortunately, very few children with gross motor incoordination have much understanding of their specific dysfunctions. Such insight can help them seek pathways toward motor gratification.

Fine Motor Dysfunction

A student's fine motor ability permits him or her to make good use of the fingers to accomplish tasks. The subcomponents of fine motor function are essentially the same as those described for gross motor output. Fine motor dexterity can facilitate fixing or constructing things (such as model cars), preparing food, playing a musical instrument, and creating works of art. While gross motor activities usually require speed, one clear advantage of fine motor pursuits is that many of them can be accomplished at a moderate pace. Consequently, fine motor activities may allow children who work at a lower speed to experience successful output.

Fine motor success may provide developmental salvation for chil-

Table 5.1: Forms of Gross Motor Dysfunction

DYSFUNCTION	DESCRIPTION
Poor sense of body position	Trouble perceiving the location of the body in a static position; possible problems with balance
Weak kinesthetic sense	Trouble keeping track of body movements while in the middle of a motor activity (e.g., while jumping, hopping, or dribbling)
Inaccuracy of visual-spatial processing	Trouble perceiving, timing, and predicting in the spatial domain (e.g., problems judging trajectories for catching, throwing, or hitting a ball)
Ineffective verbal-motor integration	Trouble translating verbal inputs into desired motor responses (e.g., difficulty following instructions from a tennis coach or a dance teacher)
Poor motor planning	Trouble previewing outcomes and selecting motor strategies to meet a motor challenge (e.g., how fast to run to catch a ball)
Motor memory weaknesses	Trouble recalling accurately and quickly the sequences of muscle movements needed for a specific skill
Incoordination of muscle groups	Trouble "assigning" muscles to specific task roles and/or poor synchronization (selective facilitation and inhibition) of muscles during activities
Poor monitoring	Trouble evaluating how effectively muscle performance is proceeding during activities
Tone control weaknesses	Trouble developing appropriate muscle tone and strength

dren experiencing disappointing academic performance. An early interest in playing with Legos, sculpting with clay, or drawing cartoons may be an indication that a child is capable of rich fine motor gratification. Such signals should be taken seriously.

Forms of Fine Motor Dysfunction

Students who have trouble carrying out precise work with their fingers may show some of the following characteristics:

- They may have trouble acquiring basic self-help skills, such as dressing themselves or tying shoelaces.
- They may perform poorly at art and craft activities. Tracing, drawing, and using scissors may present difficulty.
- These children may be very self-conscious when they and classmates are engaged in art work. Their behavior may become disruptive or oppositional at such times.
- There may seem to be a lack of insight when it comes to motor problem-solving activities, such as using tools, replacing a light bulb, or fixing a broken toy. They may tend to keep doing these things the hard way.
- They sometimes display inappropriate rapid pacing of fine motor challenges (preferring to "get them over with").
- They may become frustrated trying to learn to play a musical instrument.
- They may appear to have poor table manners as a result of their clumsiness with eating utensils.

Fine motor dysfunctions deprive these children of important outlets for creative thought and energy. While a lack of fine motor gratification is not incapacitating, it can become an especially serious problem in children who may be experiencing multiple or other forms of failure in their lives.

Graphomotor Dysfunction

There are many children who endure high levels of frustration in school because of serious problems with written output. In some cases these children have substantial motor dysfunctions such that their fingers are just unable to keep pace with the flow of ideas. The result is writing that is laborious, frequently illegible, and poor in content. As we have noted, in some cases, graphomotor dysfunction is part of a broader cluster of motor dysfunctions, while in others, the motor aspects of writing are impaired but other motor skills are left intact or are highly developed.

We will describe graphomotor dysfunctions and their management in detail when we discuss writing in chapter 6.

Managing Disappointing Motor Performance at Home

Children with disappointing motor performance need parents who understand the possible impacts of these dysfunctions so that they can protect and help these youngsters.

1. Parents should not coerce or force children with gross motor dysfunctions to participate in competitive sports. These children very much need protection from public humiliation.

2. With the child's active participation, parents should try to find one sport at which that youngster can succeed. Knowledge of the child's specific form of gross motor dysfunction ought to inform the selection process. For example, if a child has trouble processing visual-spatial information during motor activities, she or he will probably receive little gratification from ball sports but instead can concentrate on gymnastics, karate, wrestling, or swimming.

3. While developing initial skills in a sport, a child can benefit from one-to-one help (perhaps from a relative) with a safe level of privacy.

4. Children who have problems with fine motor output may be able to find some specific mode of artistic or musical expression which gives them satisfaction. This can be highly therapeutic, especially if they are struggling academically.

5. Parents should never ridicule a child for being clumsy with either whole body movements or fine motor tasks. Constant criticism for being sloppy at the dinner table or spilling things may seriously erode a child's self-esteem and subject him or her to steady ridicule from siblings.

6. Parents need to help children with motor problems to perceive motor activities as forms of entertainment and gratification rather than all important emblems of their overall competency. This can be difficult to do in a culture that emphasizes just the opposite. Whenever possible personal improvement should be stressed over competition with others.

7. Work on computers, especially with computer graphic software, may help some children create products that reflect motor mastery.

8. Allowing a child to develop motor proficiencies that differ from those of siblings is a good idea because it helps that child avoid being compared negatively.

9. Some communities offer programs of art, music, or dance that can help these children build skills and confidence. Camping and other outdoor activities that encourage collaboration as well as the mastery of certain motor skills can also be very beneficial.

Managing Disappointing Motor Performance in School

Students with motor dysfunctions often experience great stress at school because of their weaknesses. Good management of such children involves minimizing the effects of their problems while also trying to detect and nurture any latent motor assets.

1. Physical education teachers must avoid publicly criticizing or embarrassing students with disappointing motor performance.

2. When a child fails to or is hesitant to dress for physical education, it is important to try to understand what this student is trying to cover up and then provide some sensitive counseling if necessary.

3. Physical education teachers should restrain any temptation they might have to show lopsided preference for the best athletes. They need to attend as well to those who struggle with motor activities. It is important to recognize that heaping too much praise on excellent athletes may not be in the best interests of these young stars. Children who derive too much satisfaction from their motor performance may have difficulty adjusting to more normal levels of gratification later on in life.

4. Adaptive physical education programs can enhance the motor experience for some children. These are remedial programs aimed at improving the gross motor skills of these students. They include a variety of exercises and activities that are noncompetitive and are designed to enhance specific aspects of motor function (e.g., body position sense and balance).

5. For students who are interested in sports but have significant delays in gross motor ability, teachers can find useful roles related to athletics, such as managers, assistant coaches, sports reporters, and statisticians.

6. Teachers of music, woodworking, art, and other such areas may exert a very positive influence on the lives of children with disappointing motor performance. If a teacher can emerge as a mentor and a supporter of the child, great things can be accomplished. This is especially critical in the case of a child who is deprived motorically and is having

trouble in academic subjects. Finding a successful mode of motor output for that student can be dramatically therapeutic.

7. Teachers can help children who are developing a fine motor skill to document their progress. Students should accumulate a dated portfolio of all of their work. Their products also need to be displayed proudly in school (and at home).

8. Occupational or physical therapy may benefit children whose motor problems are substantial. If such services are available in a school, children may work in a group setting, sometimes called activity groups.

PERSISTENT ORGANIZATIONAL FAILURE

Effective organizational behaviors can make the difference between competent and inefficient school performance. School is much easier for children who know how to organize time and materials. Their organizational tactics make up patterns of behavior that simplify demands. Many students have internalized these. Such habits and practices are a valuable byproduct of their learning and can be a vital asset throughout their education and career.

Good organizational behaviors require some of the attention controls we discussed in chapter 2, especially previewing, pacing and self-monitoring. They also demand memory for sequences, for procedures, and for other matters. For example, organizing materials for school in

---

SCOTT

Scott is a sixteen-year-old boy with a multitude of strengths. He is highly inventive and certainly motivated to succeed. Yet Scott's day-to-day productivity is very problematic. His work is constantly left for the last minute. He never seems to know what to do when. His parents have observed that Scott has real trouble allocating time. He has no sense of how long something will take. He is perpetually late for activities. One of his teachers recently commented that Scott is in a "time warp." When Scott approaches projects or extended tasks of any kind, he has no idea what to do first, what to do second, or what to do third. He simply lacks any stepwise approaches. Scott himself admits, "I am totally and hopelessly disorganized."

part requires recalling where things are. Typically disorganized people are described as "absent minded" which often refers to the fact that they forget objects, appointments, and demands made on them.

Children can often be taught how to get organized. However, there is considerable variation in the degree to which they can actually generalize or apply organizational skills in everyday life situations. All individuals show signs of disorganization under certain circumstances, but for some children such disorganization is widespread and perpetual.

Forms of Persistent Organizational Failure

Organizational problems are common and aggravating among students whose performance in school is disappointing. Often they must withstand a barrage of criticism for their seemingly careless ways. Yet, even the most motivated of these children may find it hard to alter their patterns of disorganization. Four frequently encountered forms of organizational difficulty are material-spatial, temporal-sequential, transitional, and prospective retrieval.

Material-Spatial Disorganization

Children with material-spatial disorganization are plagued by their seeming inability to deal effectively with the various equipment needed to be efficient in school. It is simply too hard for them to have in their possession the things they need when they need them! Some of the frequent manifestations of material-spatial disorganization are summarized below.

- A tendency to keep losing things (including trouble associating in memory an object and the site in which it was last observed)
- Trouble remembering what to take to or bring home from school
- Difficulty knowing where to put things consistently (including trouble developing systems for filing or for space allocation)
- A habit of creating nearly insurmountable "messes" on desks, in lockers, in closets, in dressers, etc.
- Problems organizing a notebook or maintaining an assignment pad

A child with material-spatial disorganization may spend inordinate time searching for a pencil, seeking paper, and creating a clean desk or table surface upon which to do work. She or he may accomplish a writing assignment only to leave it home or on the bus the next morning.

Many students with material-spatial disorganization harbor other difficulties in the spatial domain. They may have a history of left-right confusion, poor sense of direction, weak facial recognition, and difficulty processing or discriminating visual symbols.

Temporal-Sequential Disorganization

Other students display enormous confusion when it comes to time and sequence. Such confusion is conspicuous in the case of Scott (described earlier) who appears to be in a perpetual "time warp." Children like Scott do not fully understand time. They have difficulty with the ordering of things in time. This creates problems in school when they need to process and store information in such order or when they must develop their own sequences of activities, of events, and of steps in a process. The list below summarizes some of the common signs of temporal-sequential disorganization.

- Trouble allocating time
- Difficulty estimating how long something will take
- Problems knowing the order in which to do something
- A tendency to be late and to procrastinate
- A pattern of constantly losing track of time

As Scott demonstrates clearly, for these children time management is an elusive skill. They are often limited in their ability to plan and use time efficiently. They are also susceptible to other sequencing weaknesses, including trouble remembering things in the correct order (page 58), problems learning the days of the week and the months of the year, delays mastering multistep mathematical and/or motor procedures and difficulty following multistep directions or explanations. Some of these children seem limited in their ability to tell a story or narrate a series of events in the correct order. This makes their expressive language seem incoherent at times, and their writing may lack a logical ordering of ideas.

Parents and teachers of children with temporal-sequential disorganization may feel exasperated at how little they seem to accomplish during a specific time period. The students themselves often are overwhelmed by a workload that they are unable to break down into a series of manageable sequential steps.

Transitional Disorganization

Some children experience their greatest organizational confusion during key transitional times. It is hard for them to "shift gears," to prepare adequately for that which is coming next. A child may rush through transitions between activities. Some children seem to alternate between taking too long for transitions and being too abrupt. The student may be slow or unable to adjust appropriately to a new setting and/or a new set of expectations. The following list describes some common manifestations of transitional disorganization:

- A tendency to rush frenetically from one activity to another
- Failure to take the right books or other materials home (often because of a too hasty departure from school)
- Difficulty settling down and beginning work efficiently after changing classes, returning from lunch, or arriving at school in the morning
- Diminished understanding of, preparation for, and compliance with daily routines (often as a result of trouble with switching effectively from one routine to the next)
- Slowness with certain routines at home, such as dressing in the morning, getting ready to leave for a family outing, coming in for a meal, switching from play to work

Often children who have difficulty with transitions also show attentional dysfunction (chapter 2). They may exhibit some of the traits we discussed earlier, such as being highly impulsive and notably lacking in planned behaviors. The moment a bell sounds they may dash out of class as if they are competing to get to the next one as rapidly as possible. In their extreme haste, they are likely to leave a trail of pencils, papers, and other belongings or they may end up at the wrong site. In other cases, these children may become distracted during transitions. They may daydream or lose track while shifting from one place or one task to another. Alternatively some of them may *perseverate* or focus too long and too hard on one activity and then find it hard to "switch gears."

Prospective Retrieval Disorganization

Prospective retrieval refers to the ability to remember to do something. Children may be told (or asked) to carry out a task or assignment at a later time. The ability to recall and undertake at the proper time exactly what was expected comprises an important organizational skill. Prospective retrieval also involves the ability to remember things that the children themselves decide to do later (e.g., "When I get home from school, I'll call my grandmother"). There are children who are perceived as disorganized because they keep on forgetting to do what they had intended to do! Some manifestations of this pattern are listed below.

- A tendency to forget assignments
- Poor or incomplete performance on errands
- Unreliability with daily responsibilities (such as feeding the dog or remembering to take sneakers to school)
- Trouble following through on promises

Often these children are thought of as highly irresponsible. Their inadequate "follow through" makes them appear undependable. Adults, however, need to recognize how difficult it is for many of these children to maintain in memory and later carry out their intentions.

Managing Persistent Organizational Failure at Home

Part of the management of organizational problems needs to occur in the home setting. This can be complicated because it is not unusual for disorganized children to have somewhat disorganized parents! A child with organizational difficulties is not likely to become organized in a home where space and time and transitions are haphazard and unpredictable. Parents, therefore, need to become better organized as a step toward enabling their children to do so. The difficulty of accomplishing this should not be underestimated. The challenge is likely to be enormous in homes where both parents work, in single parent households, in large families where there are several children with many differing needs, and in settings where the adults are experiencing major personal problems or stresses. Nevertheless, disorganized children can be helped by even modest efforts to impart some order and predictability when and where it is needed at home. Here are some suggestions for accomplishing this.

1. Parents can emphasize efficient time management. Every Sunday evening a parent should meet with the child to plan and record work and activities for the coming week. The child should have a desk calendar or computer software for scheduling work and recreation. It can be helpful to discuss how long each pursuit is likely to take. Breaks should be scheduled, but weekend leisure time should not be included. A child needs some spontaneous unscheduled stretches. Before going to bed each night, the child should check off his or her accomplishments and document how much time they consumed. This checking off can provide satisfaction, while the documentation of how long activities took may guide the child in future planning. One system for improving time management is illustrated in figure 5.2. Using the Time and Accomplishment Record, students estimate and allocate time for various activities (e.g., studying for a math test, practicing the guitar). After

TIME AND ACCOMPLISHMENT RECORD

Name_____ Week_____ Sheet Number_____

	MON.	TUES.	WED.	THUR.	FRI.	SAT.	SUN.
Activity:							
• Planned Time	____	____	____	____	____	____	____
• Time Taken	____	____	____	____	____	____	____
• Completed	☐	☐	☐	☐	☐	☐	☐
• How I Did	1 2 3 4	1 2 3 4	1 2 3 4	1 2 3 4	1 2 3 4	1 2 3 4	1 2 3 4
Activity:							
• Planned Time	____	____	____	____	____	____	____
• Time Taken	____	____	____	____	____	____	____
• Completed	☐	☐	☐	☐	☐	☐	☐
• How I Did	1 2 3 4	1 2 3 4	1 2 3 4	1 2 3 4	1 2 3 4	1 2 3 4	1 2 3 4
Activity:							
• Planned Time	____	____	____	____	____	____	____
• Time Taken	____	____	____	____	____	____	____
• Completed	☐	☐	☐	☐	☐	☐	☐
• How I Did	1 2 3 4	1 2 3 4	1 2 3 4	1 2 3 4	1 2 3 4	1 2 3 4	1 2 3 4

How I Did: 1 = I Did Poorly; 2 = I Did O.K.; 3 = I Did Well; 4 = I Did Very Well

Fig. 5.2. This grid can be used by students to help them organize time more effectively. It is meant to be filled out each week, perhaps with the help of a parent or teacher. Children can check off various tasks or steps as they are completed.

completing the activity they document how long it took and they rate the quality of their effort. This kind of documentation can improve time awareness, organization, and overall self-monitoring.

2. A consistent period set aside each weekday evening for cognitive work can benefit these children. There should be as few distractions as possible during that time. Television, telephone calls, and other diversions should be eliminated during the work hour. Ideally, other family members will be engaged in quiet intellectual work, such as reading. If possible the work hour should occur at the same time each evening. Consistency is especially important for children with temporal-sequential organizational problems and attentional dysfunction.

3. Parents should help children to set up a well-organized study or work space at home. They need to think about its location carefully, trying to find a setting that is as free of distractions as possible. For this reason a child's bedroom may not be a good choice. Once selected, the space should have a desk or table. Drawers should be well labeled with designated space for writing utensils, paper, ruler, stapler, paper clips, etc. One drawer should have color-coded folders for different subjects in school. The child can save papers in these folders. There can also be specific folders for work in progress and for articles related to the child's other activities and hobbies.

4. This work space should always be kept organized, even if a parent must maintain it for the student. Sometimes a mother or father may need to straighten out or reorganize children's work spaces for them. It is often good to do this while the child is present. It would be excellent if children would undertake this responsibility themselves, but for many it is an agonizing chore. Parents should never make children feel guilty or inadequate because they have to keep organizing space for them. The aim is to get children accustomed or even addicted to working in a neat and organized manner. Ultimately, as they grow older, this habit should become strong enough to give these children the motivation to take on the organizational challenge.

5. Children with organizational problems may need help maintaining a notebook and making good use of an assignment pad. Parents should feel comfortable in assisting a son or daughter to carry out these routines in an orderly manner. Students with material-spatial problems often feel exasperated and embarrassed over the disheveled state of their notebooks. A parent can help to put things in the right order, repair damaged notebook paper holes, and discard unneeded materials.

6. Children who have trouble with transitional organization need to have their parents talk explicitly to them about transitions. A parent can say, "Let's have a speedy transition this morning" or "Now let's slow down during this transition and figure out exactly what we need to take with us." Sometimes a parent needs to assign a reasonable amount of time for a transition, so that it does not transpire too quickly or too slowly. If children enjoy it, parents can devise a scoring system and use a graph or chart on the wall to document how well they succeed at critical daily transition points (e.g., getting out of bed, arriving at the bus stop). There can be rewards for days on which the child displays organized transitional behaviors.

7. Lists of what they need to do often help children with prospective retrieval disorganization. These children should understand the serious trouble they have remembering to do things. They should be helped to see the problems associated with being considered an "unreliable person." They can keep a "reliability" notebook with lists of things to do. It may be possible to combine the reliability notebook with the student's assignment pad for school, so that the lists contain academic as well as other responsibilities. Children should cross out or check off items after completion. Looking back over the notepad from time to time helps them to see how much they have accomplished of what they said they would do and, in this way, to see how reliable they have become. Children can get practice, for example, by assisting a parent to compile a list of things that need to get done before going away on a trip.

Managing Persistent Organizational Failure in School

Schools also have an important role to play in fostering good organizational habits in children. Teachers, especially in the early grades, should not let students become accustomed to being disorganized. The longer children are disorganized, the harder it is to get them organized. As they proceed through school, the requirement for organization grows and intensifies. A student with organizational problems may feel overwhelmed in secondary school. The following suggestions for teachers may help them to assist children with organizational problems.

1. Students should not be publicly embarrassed for their organizational problems. Thus, it is inappropriate to humiliate in front of classmates a student who is often late to class or to school or who forgets assignments. Shame does not organize a student very well and, in fact,

may lead to behavioral difficulties, anxiety, and a loss of motivation. More private kinds of feedback and accountability need to be established.

2. Teachers can remind these students what to take home from school to complete assignments (or for other purposes).

3. Teachers should monitor the condition of the notebook and assignment pad of a child with organizational problems so that these materials don't deteriorate to a point where they are useless and exasperating to the student.

4. Just as at home, a student's desk and locker need to be organized. Color-coded folders in school might match those used at home.

5. For some students there needs to be excellent communication between home and school regarding assignments. A teacher may need to check a child's assignment pad each afternoon. The student should review the pad with a parent, so that the mother or father can derive a sense of what is expected and of whether the child is recording assignments properly. Another alternative is to make use of the What Needs to Get Done form (fig. 5.3). This form is checked each day by the teacher, parent, and student to ensure that expectations are being met.

6. In class teachers can emphasize time management, talk about budgeting time, and give students considerable notice regarding tests, due dates for reports, and other deadlines. They can help students plan their time—deciding what they will do when and how much time they expect to devote to specific activities or stages of work.

7. Children with organizational problems can benefit from any courses or units in school that stress good study habits. Many of them need considerable help to develop consistently effective skills for preparing for tests, organizing reports, and completing various projects.

8. Sometimes disorganized children become much more organized when they are doing something they enjoy and are good at. They may do an excellent job of compiling a science project, putting on a school play, building a go-cart, or painting a mural. A teacher can incorporate such activities into classroom work as a way of reinforcing good organizational skills which might have the potential of spreading to other areas.

9. Teachers can make sure that children with organizational problems have opportunities to participate in collaborative activities with

WHAT NEEDS TO GET DONE

Student's Name_____ Date_____

Teacher's Section				Student's and Parent's Section		
Teacher or Subject	Assignment or What Needs to Be Studied	Time It Should Take	Date It Should Be Finished	Completed: Parent's Signature	Completed: Student's Signature	Time Spent

Teacher's Comments:

Parent's Comments:

Student's Comments:

Fig. 5.3. This form, which is often helpful for students with organizational difficulty, can be sent home each day to make it easier for them to know what is expected and to be sure that homework is being completed.

well-organized peers. The methods and approaches of the latter may exert some lasting influence.

10. These children can benefit significantly from having to undertake long-term projects in school. These projects can relate to science, art, creative writing, or other forms of content. They can be individual or collaborative. Such activities can be designed in a way that students have to demonstrate good planning and time allocation along with the effective organization of the materials they need to complete the project. There should be ongoing discussion of the organizational techniques that are being used.

PROBLEMATIC PROBLEM SOLVING AND STRATEGY USE

When a child is systematic and strategic in problem solving, a multitude of academic accomplishments are likely to follow. Problem-solving skills and the effective strategies that they encompass must be deployed at every grade level and throughout the school day. Seven major types of problem-solving challenges are required of students, and these are summarized in table 5.2.

ELLIE

Ellie is a twelve-year-old girl who appears to be struggling in certain academic areas. Mathematics has been particularly troublesome for her. Her teacher has reported that Ellie shows no flexibility when she tries to solve a problem. Once she decides what she is going to do, she follows it rigidly, without any self-correction and without considering a different approach when the current one is not working. Her mother has observed that when Ellie writes a report, she just likes to start writing without any real planning or systematic thinking about what she will write and in what order she will need to express her ideas. Both her teachers and parents have noticed that Ellie has difficulty resolving conflicts with her friends. When things are not going well, she almost always resorts to verbal aggression. She appears unable to think of other alternatives.

These diverse problem-solving situations confront students throughout the school day. They have in common the fact that they cannot be dealt with in a single step. Nor can they be resolved automatically. Additionally, all of these situations allow for more than one possible solution or approach, so that the choice of methods is important. Problem solving is a thoughtful stepwise process that consumes time and demands the use of effective strategies. Although there is likely to be some variation in problem-solving tactics, depending upon the precise nature of the challenge, a series of necessary components can be described. These components are listed below. Their exact order during problem solving may vary.

Knowing a problem when you see one.

A child must recognize when a particular situation, imposed expectation, or challenge is a problem that calls for a solution rather than an automatic response.

Defining exactly what the problem is or what the question is asking.

This step entails clarifying. Students may need to make sure that they really understand the problem or question. Alternatively, they may need to develop their own questions about a situation, a story, or a topic.

Determining what information or skill will be needed to solve the problem.

Some vital information may exist within the problem itself (as in a word problem or a newspaper editorial). In this case it becomes important to decide what material in the problem is relevant and what is incorrect or unnecessary. This process often involves keen saliency determination (chapter 2). Sometimes outside information will need to be sought.

Deciding if you are capable of solving the problem.

A problem solver must decide whether a problem can be solved at all and, if so, whether he or she has the capacity to do so. Children's attributions about problem solving become important at this step, as they wonder: "Am I smart enough? Do I know enough? Will it come out correct or looking good? Is this too much work for me?"

Seeking familiar patterns.

Problem solving is facilitated through precedent. Good problem solvers try to determine if a problem reflects a familiar pattern. The pattern may not be immediately apparent, but it becomes evident with continued probing. Children with strong pattern-recognition memory (chapter 3) may be especially good at this aspect of problem solving. Children need to search long-term memory for prior knowledge, learned rules, or relevant skills that have worked well for them in the past when they have encountered that pattern.

Table 5.2: Examples of Problem-Solving Challenges for School Children

PROBLEM-SOLVING CHALLENGE	EXAMPLES
Mathematics	• Determining the best solution for a word problem • Performing a geometric proof • Representing a problem in an equation
Issues	• Resolving complicated dilemmas (e.g., the economic needs of countries vs. conservation of natural resources) • Evaluating opinions or views of others
Projects and Reports	• Selecting subjects or topics for reports or projects • Figuring out the best way to present ideas in an essay • Creating a work of art or a piece of music in a particular medium
Critical Thinking	• Evaluating a writer's perspective • Representing a particular point of view during a class discussion • Deciding what one likes and dislikes about a peer • Determining whether to believe an advertisement
Interpretations	• Deciding what a poem is about • Figuring out how something works (e.g., a light bulb) • Troubleshooting (e.g., finding out why the computer isn't operating properly)
Study Challenges	• Determining how to understand something that's hard to understand (e.g., using research skills to seek relevant information to clarify a question) • Knowing how to study for a math quiz • Figuring out the best way to learn a list of new vocabulary words
Personal Needs	• Resolving a conflict with a peer • Making difficult personal decisions • Solving personal problems and/or contending with stress • Deciding how to improve (e.g., in spelling or in soccer)

Thinking strategically.

A student confronting a problem needs to ask what is the best (or perhaps easiest) way to solve it. Effective problem solvers are methodologists; they consciously seek strategies rather than acting on the first approach that comes to mind.

Thinking up alternative strategies for the solution of the problem.

The best problem solvers consider several alternative strategies. They think: "This looks like the best way, so why don't I try it. If that doesn't work, I can always do this, and if this fails I can try that other idea." Having multiple alternative strategies is especially important for dealing with daily stresses. Such strategies are often referred to as "coping skills." People who have good "coping skills" can minimize the effects of stress in their lives.

Estimating or previewing outcomes.

Problem solving can be enhanced by projecting likely results. This process is often referred to as estimating or previewing. It was mentioned as an important part of production control in chapter 2. A strong problem solver is likely to ponder the "what ifs," that is, "What if I say it this way, how will it sound? What if I do this, what will happen? If I solve this word problem like this, roughly, what do I think the answer will be?" Subsequently, previewing skills allow students to determine whether or not they are on track. If their results are very different from their previews, they may need to go back and determine where they went astray.

Initiating and monitoring the problem-solving activity.

As children initiate the actual problem-solving process, they must try to stick with their strategies until they see if they are working. At the same time they need to remain flexible and prepared to use alternative strategies if and when the initial "best bet" strategy is ineffective. At all times, they need to keep sight of the original question or problem. They must also allocate sufficient time, pace themselves, and continue to monitor what they are doing while they are doing it.

Using a stepwise approach.

A child needs to think of problem solving as a sequence of steps rather than something you do all at once. He or she needs to have a sense of what needs to be done first, then what should follow in a logical order.

Encouraging oneself.

In the course of their problem solving, students need to cheer themselves on. It is helpful if they whisper encouraging and optimistic thoughts to themselves (e.g., "You can do this. You can solve this problem. Don't give up, just hang in there.").

Evaluating the solution.

Monitoring the outcome is a critical part of problem solving. Students must be able to determine if the solution or product really answers the question. The problem solver should ask: "Does this look right? Did this come out right? Can I make it better?"

Refining the solution.

The refinement of a solution or a product may entail only the alteration of some small detail (as in proofreading a report) or, alternatively, it may mean an overhaul of the entire plan. Students who have multiple alternative strategies for problem solving have the convenient option of making use of an entirely new tactic when their initial choice falls short.

Generalizing to other situations.

Generalization is the rather elusive process through which students are able to make use of their solutions to current problems to solve future problems. They can retain a method that has worked well for them and use it to solve problems that are similar to if not exactly the same as the initial one. In other words, they learn from their problem-solving experience.

Forms of Problematic Problem Solving and Deficient Strategy Use

Although there is wide diversity among them, children with problematic problem solving and deficient strategy use are likely to reveal varying degrees of the following tendencies, a number of which are illustrated in the case of Ellie (cited at the opening of this section):

- They may fail to make use of stepwise approaches. This causes them to try to do things all at once without thinking through what should be done first, second, then third, etc.
- They may not fully understand or appreciate in depth the question or challenge at hand. Consequently, inadequate or incomplete solutions may proceed from superficial processing of the question.
- They may work too quickly and without planning. Their impulsive approach may impede the quality of their problem solving and, ironically, in trying to work so fast, they are apt to do many things the hard way! In omitting the planning stage, these children frequently proceed using trial and error or "the first thing that comes into their heads." Such students are nonmethodologists.
- They may work too slowly and without planning. These students are also nonmethodologists, and their lack of strategies creates inefficiencies that cause them to proceed in a labored and slow manner.

- They may not recognize familiar underlying patterns within a problem. This pattern-recognition weakness (chapter 3) can prevent them from applying strategies that have worked well for them in the past. Consequently, they may fail to generalize from strategies they have used successfully.
- They may fail to think about alternative strategies. As a result, they are apt to be rigid in their problem solving. They may use a particular approach and have no options but to continue even though that approach is not achieving desired results. Such inflexibility can be extremely frustrating for these students and for the adults trying to help them. Another aspect of this failure is that they often have diminished coping skills (page 222).
- They may have trouble understanding and applying rules. Many problems can be solved or their solutions facilitated by invoking one or more previously encountered and applied rules. Such rules, as we have noted earlier in this book, usually take the form of "if . . . then" (page 69). There are, of course, spelling rules, grammatical rules, mathematical rules, and scientific rules. Poor problem solvers may have trouble recognizing a familiar challenge (see above) and then coming up with a rule that applies to that context. They may also have difficulty developing their own rules even after repeated exposure to a particular type of problem.
- They may lack automaticity and therefore experience trouble with problem solving. If they need to use their supply of mental effort or active working memory capacity on aspects of a problem that should be automatic, they will have little left for developing and maintaining good strategies. For example, a student who must work hard to recall multiplication facts may have trouble coming up with a clever strategy to solve a word problem.
- They may have problems with particular forms of reasoning. Some children have trouble reasoning analogically. They cannot use analogies well enough to assist in problem solving. An example might be: "Holly bushes are not supposed to lose their leaves through the winter. Since this looks to me like a holly shrub, it should stay green over Christmas." Other children have trouble with proportional reasoning, finding it hard to use equations, to understand ratios, to convert from ounces to quarts, or to change fractions into decimals or percentages.
- They may fail to self-monitor (page 38) as they solve a problem or evaluate the results. They are likely to stray from the problem or the plan in midstream.

- They are apt to be reluctant revisers. They may detest proofreading and self-correction. They may have trouble refining their solutions.
- They may have negative attributions about problem solving. These students, believing solutions are somehow beyond them, may rush through tasks. Instead of encouraging themselves, they may think or whisper negative feelings, such as "This is too hard. There's no way I can do this. Boy, am I stupid." This self-deprecation can actually interfere with problem solving by making a child give up too easily or settle for an inadequate effort.

Problem-solving skills may be uneven. A child may be excellent at tackling problems in mathematics but have great difficulty utilizing problem-solving skills to interpret a poem. Another student may have pervasive difficulties with problem solving in school but be impressively strategic in fixing tractors or helping friends solve their personal problems.

A number of observable phenomena that we have described earlier can interfere with the effective application of problem-solving skills. For example, children with weak attention controls may find it hard to slow down and refine a question, select strategies, and self-monitor carefully. A student with weak language processing may have difficulty interpreting questions or analyzing word problems. Some children with temporal-sequential disorganization have difficulty performing tasks in a stepwise fashion. Students with insufficient active working memory may not be able to hold in their minds and coalesce all of the components needed for systematic problem solving. In addition, as we have pointed out, poor automatization of individual task components may thwart problem solving.

It is important for parents and teachers to note whether a child's problematic problem solving and deficient strategy use are closely associated with other problems (like weak attention control) and whether they are confined to specific areas of content (like scientific subjects). Once these specific forms are isolated, they may need to be addressed within the context of a specific subject area or as part of the management of a neurodevelopmental dysfunction. For example, a child with weak language processing plus a problem with problem solving may need targeted help learning to interpret and clarify questions. Likewise, a student with poor problem-solving skills limited to mathematics may need to be helped to consciously apply stepwise approaches and specific reasoning processes, as well as to think about alternative strategies while solving mathematical problems.

Some children experience difficulty at the "junctions" between organizational and problem-solving skills. These are students who often experience difficulty organizing reports and projects. They succeed admirably when the expectations are made extremely clear and when tasks are carefully structured for them. But when they must start from scratch—pick a topic, develop ideas on their own, decide what information they need to use or acquire, sequence their thoughts, and demonstrate initiative within a self-imposed structure—they are simply at a loss! They are students who are notably adept at performing tasks that have a single component (e.g., remembering spelling words) but have serious trouble with tasks that require mobilizing, integrating, and synchronizing multiple simultaneous components (e.g., writing, project implementation, and certain mathematical operations). They are apt to be much better at answering specific questions about a paragraph they have read than at summarizing the material on their own, which requires considerable organizational skill.

Managing Problematic Problem Solving and Deficient Strategy Use at Home

Once a parent becomes aware of the general or specific gaps in a child's ability to solve problems and to use strategies, there is much that can be done.

1. A parent can help a child develop a plan before undertaking a task or an assignment. The Problem-Solving Planner (Appendix 1) is an example of a work sheet that can be used to plan and monitor problem solving. This planner is especially helpful to students when they can check off each step as they complete it. Ideally, this form should be used and monitored both at home and in school.

2. Parents should encourage stepwise approaches, especially in children who are impulsive and/or have difficulties with temporal-sequential organization. A parent can offer to look over the work after each step.

3. Often, there are many opportunities for practicing problem solving at home. For example, if a child is having a conflict with a sibling or a friend, a parent can work through some effective problem-solving steps with him or her. Questions—such as What is the real problem? What have you done in the past that's worked, and what hasn't worked? What are some other situations like this one? What are some possible strategies? What looks like the best one? How will you know if

it's working?—help to make the process explicit. Issues in the news and decisions at home (e.g., about fair discipline) also lend themselves to the application of systematic problem solving.

4. Parents can try to model good problem solving for a child. Thus, a parent might share with the child some problem that she or he is currently facing (at home or at work) and discuss the steps that are being used to deal with it.

5. Children should be praised for their problem-solving accomplishments. They should be encouraged to discuss how they did something that they did well. Such descriptions of stepwise problem solving can relate to an area in which a child demonstrates expertise and/or a strong interest.

Managing Problematic Problem Solving and Deficient Strategy Use in School

Weak problem-solving skills may be strengthened within the context of specific subject areas or disciplines. It is possible also to teach problem solving as a subject unto itself. Ideally, both approaches should be available to students who are struggling in this area.

1. Students should be taught what is meant by systematic problem-solving skills. They should conceptualize problem solving as a planned, well-paced, and carefully monitored stepwise process. They should be helped to understand the advantages of slowing down to accomplish tasks and of using good problem-solving tactics to answer complex questions.

2. The Problem-Solving Planner described for use at home and contained in Appendix 1 should also be utilized at times in school. Children can be assigned the task of developing a plan for a particular purpose. It should be evaluated and graded. Examples might include: "How I intend to study for this final examination" or "How I should decide whom to vote for in the next school election."

3. Children can benefit from opportunities to teach each other problem-solving strategies. They should describe systematically how they solve their problems. They can make use of areas where they seem to function well as problem solvers. Topics might include: "How I can figure out what's wrong with a bicycle and fix it," or "How I decide what to do when I want someone to be my friend," or "How I figure out what to get my mom for her birthday," or "How I draw original cartoons." In

offering these explanations, students should use problem-solving terminology (i.e., words like "my plan," "my alternative strategies," "my preview," etc.).

4. Children need to have opportunities to apply systematic problem-solving skills when discussing complex issues. Teachers should emphasize multiple alternative strategies (e.g., "What would you do about this if you were the president? What if that didn't work, what would you do? Then what could you do if that failed?").

5. If there is a particular component of problem solving that is especially difficult for an individual child, the teacher should develop tasks that stress and include that component only. If a child has trouble estimating outcomes, she or he should undertake tasks in which that is all that is required. If a child is weak at planning, he or she should submit hypothetical plans but not have to carry them out. In other words, the critical but weak link in problem solving is made into an end in itself.

6. If a problem-solving weakness is associated with another observable phenomenon (such as weak language processing and/or production, incomplete concept formation, or weak attentional controls), help with problem solving should be one part of the overall management of the other area(s) of difficulty. Thus, helping a child to be better at pacing can be facilitated through the teaching of good problem solving. The need to figure out the meanings of concepts or understand the language of a poem can be taught to the child as if it were a problem-solving challenge requiring the steps delineated earlier in this chapter (pages 148–51).

The Demystification of Deficient Output

Children with deficient output may often long for results in which they can take justifiable pride. Those with organizational problems may be labeled as lazy or lacking in motivation and a sense of responsibility. Students with motor problems may be told they are careless or clumsy. As they hear such attributions with great enough frequency, they come to believe them firmly. The following guidelines for demystification can help these students put their difficulties in a better perspective.

1. Parents and teachers should let these students know that there are some adults who realize how hard it is for them to be as productive as other students in school.

2. These children need to be helped to see specifically what is impeding their output. They should realize that some students have problems that make work much more work for them! It should be emphasized that these problems do not mean that they are "stupid."

3. If students have one or more organizational weaknesses, they need to recognize how their disorganization is making academic accomplishment so hard. They should be taught about their organizational problems. Adults can cite specific examples of how the problem is affecting these students. Students need to be able to distinguish between an organizational problem and what might be considered willful or sloppy carelessness. An organizational problem is just as legitimate as a problem learning to read or do math. Like those kinds of difficulties, organizational problems can be worked on and improved.

4. Students with language production problems should see the virtues of not being too talkative. They can be reassured that people respect good listeners. However, they also must acknowledge the benefits of being able to speak in a way that is at ease, somewhat fluent, and reasonably elaborative. Adults can encourage these children to talk about times and places where the language weakness has interfered (e.g., with friends, when called on in class, or when trying to write a story). Then they can discuss "safe ways" to develop stronger language production at home and in school.

5. Students with problem-solving problems need to learn the value of systematic, stepwise approaches to work output, test taking, and other pursuits. It is enlightening for them to recognize how their unsystematic approaches make school much harder.

6. Children need a chance to talk about the risks involved in creating works or performing in public when one does not feel good about the results. Adults need to show understanding of the dilemma the student faces: is it better to "shut down completely" or to risk being criticized or ridiculed for producing something that is inferior? They should not minimize or in anyway belittle this difficult decision-making process.

7. When children have motor dysfunctions, they need to understand specifically the nature of their difficulties. A knowledgeable adult should explain to them the precise nature of the motor deficit, for example, a problem getting muscles to work together or trouble using visual information while trying to catch a ball. Children should be reassured that as they get older, these motor weaknesses will become less and less impor-

tant in life. There should be discussion of whether or not the child wishes to spend time trying to improve in these motor pursuits.

8. When a child with output problems has retreated and either has stopped or drastically cut back on productivity (e.g., not handing in homework at all), it is important to stress the need for continuing output as an end in itself, even if the quality is disappointing. The student must realize that when one stops working for a long time, it becomes harder and harder to produce work again.

9. Demystification may need to address attribution issues directly. Students who have come to believe they are incapable of high-quality production must have their belief in their abilities restored.

Recognizing Strengths of Output

It is vitally important that children have the fruits of their labor acknowledged and reinforced. When a child is especially adept at a particular form of output, she or he should be praised and rewarded. A major goal for that child's education ought to be the ongoing enhancement of what she or he does well. Caring for animals, amassing a collection, scouting, and participating in a musical group are all examples of pursuits that can be perceived as output strengths.

Creativity represents an especially redeeming and important form of productivity. Every child should be helped to find areas in which she or he can discover an effective form of creative output. This needs to be a domain in which the student can allow his or her mind to diverge, to brainstorm, to be spontaneous, to innovate, and to be original. Sometimes students fear such intellectual excursions, as they are afraid they will be ostracized for having "weird" or unorthodox ideas. Therefore, creative thinking needs to be made safe and desirable. Parents and teachers need to discover a child's preferred medium for creative thinking. Acting, dancing, artistic endeavors, imaginary play, writing, and inventing are all examples of potentially gratifying processes generating praiseworthy products. Affording opportunities in these areas can uncover latent strengths in a struggling young child. In fact, it is important for all children to engage in creative brainstorming activities and not be overly programmed with highly structured school work and recreation that entail little or no original or inventive thinking.

Altruistic activities represent another very important form of laudable output. Various kinds of community service, such as volunteering in a day-care center, at a hospital, or in a nursing home, can provide successful forms of expression for a child who is in need of recognition.

The phenomena related to controlling attention, to remembering, to understanding, and to producing converge as students strive to acquire and apply basic academic skills in school. In the next chapter we will examine the plight of those students who lag and struggle to become skilled in the four traditional domains of reading, spelling, writing, and mathematics.

CHAPTER SIX

Phenomena Related to Delayed Skill Acquisition

T HE academic success of a student is often judged by his or her facility at acquiring and making good use of the basic skills or tools for learning. Traditionally, these skills have consisted of reading, spelling, writing, and mathematics. Children are expected to grasp, retain, and make use of these skills at predetermined rates or at specific grade and age levels. When they are slow to develop academic skills, students are destined for a stressful and sometimes highly frustrating academic experience. In the preceding chapters, we have discussed a wide range of observable phenomena, all of which exert direct impacts on skill acquisition. In the pages that follow, we will engage in some task analyses to portray the functions most needed for the learning of skills in reading, spelling, writing, and mathematics. We will also examine the forms of observable phenomena that frequently deter or delay skill building. Finally, we will expand on the implications of these phenomena for collaborative educational care.

SLOW READING DEVELOPMENT

Fascinating and important interactions take place between reading and a child's overall development. Learning to read demands the use of multiple developmental functions, such as language ability, visual processing, memory, and attention. At the same time, in the process of learning to read, a child actually strengthens these developmental functions. For example, language comprehension is likely to improve steadily as a child engages in reading. His or her visual processing efficiency is likely to become enhanced through practice in reading. Studying texts also sharpens selective attention while it offers experience in the efficient use

---

TERRI

Terri is a seven-year-old girl who has been receiving special help in reading. She has had great difficulty "breaking the code." Initially, she was exceedingly slow to equate sounds with visual symbols. She received some tutoring. Even with extensive drill, she had trouble acquiring and retaining sound-symbol associations. Recently she has improved, but her father notes that when Terri tries to read individual words, she will often forget the first sound in a word while she is sounding out the final one. She appears unable to hold together in memory the various sounds in a word. Because Terri has to work so hard to identify even single words, it is virtually impossible for her to understand much of what she is reading. She relies strongly on context clues, but sometimes this tactic fails to work for her. Terri is performing at a very high level in arithmetic. She is also excellent at sports and at dancing.

---

of memory. So it is that the acquisition and refinement of reading skills fosters the progressive strengthening of critical neurodevelopmental functions.

Reading: A Task Analysis

A proficient reader is one in whom multiple neurodevelopmental functions and relevant educational factors have worked together to promote the acquired ability to extract meaning efficiently from written language. These major functions and factors are described below.

Phonological awareness—the lucid processing and appreciation of language sounds. Children must be able to make fine distinctions between individual language sounds (page 83). They must recognize instantaneously and with minimal expenditure of effort the precise sounds that comprise their native language. Without such appreciation and recognition, they will have trouble assigning appropriate sounds to visually represented letter combinations.

Paired association memory—the formation in memory of a strong bond between a particular letter or group of letters and a language sound. This includes the ability to retain phonetically regular (and logical) associations as well as irregular (and perhaps not very logical or predictable) pairings. These paired associations were very troublesome for Terri in the case cited at the beginning of this section.

Visual processing and pattern recognition—the ability to appreciate the distinct visual characteristics of individual letters and whole words and to label them accurately. Ultimately, instant recognition of words and letter patterns will contribute to a child's *sight vocabulary*. Not only must a reader recognize familiar patterns, but she or he must be aware of words that are irregular, that do not fit an immediately recognizable visual pattern and must therefore be sounded out.

Active working memory—the capacity to take apart and/or put together the sounds within a word (sometimes called word analysis or word attack skill). This ability is likely to depend upon the adequacy of all of the above functions plus the capacity to hold the component sounds in active working memory (page 63) while reblending them. This process was frustrating for Terri.

Semantic facility—dependable and rapid access to the stored meanings of words, the brain's dictionary or so-called lexicon. Easy access to word knowledge greatly facilitates the decoding process. This access, in turn, may reflect the quality and extent of a child's semantic network (page 83) as well as the speed and precision of recognition and paired association memory.

Automatization—the simultaneous and automatic occurrence of all of the above operations, carried out with great speed and with little or no expenditure of mental effort. When too much time and labor are required to decode the individual words, few resources are left for understanding sentences, paragraphs, and passages. Delayed or incomplete automatization is a common cause of poor reading comprehension in the middle and upper grades.

Sentence comprehension—the ability to derive meaning from the structure of sentences. Good readers make use of multiple meaningful clues, including word order and grammar.

Discourse comprehension—the interpretation of reading beyond the sentence level (i.e., paragraphs, narratives, chapters, etc.). The understanding of large chunks of written language is dependent upon all of the above abilities plus others, including those enumerated below:

- Existence of prior knowledge relevant to the content of the discourse (i.e., having sufficient familiarity with the subject or related subjects before reading about it)

- Immediate access to that prior knowledge
- Capacity to retain, temporarily, facts or ideas read earlier in a passage while reading subsequent material in that passage
- Facility with conceptual and figurative language
- Ease of processing of cohesive language ties (conjunctions, prepositions, pronouns, ellipsis, anaphora, and other devices that enable language to cohere beyond the boundaries of sentences)
- Ability to recognize and use text structures to enhance meaning (e.g., narrative sequences, lists, comparisons and contrasts, problems and solutions, causal chains, descriptions, or arguments)
- Saliency determination (ability to identify levels of importance in text)
- Strong attention controls
- Practice and experience
- Interest in textual material and motivation to read
- Appropriate blends of top-down and bottom-up processing
- Pacing and appropriate regulation of reading style (knowing when to skim, when to scan, when to read for detail, when to read to remember)

A graphic task analysis of reading is portrayed in figure 6.1.

Forms of Slow Reading Development

Children with reading difficulties are likely to exhibit breakdowns in one or more of the above components required for reading development. Since reading is such a prominent element of the entire academic curriculum across all subject areas beginning in the earliest grades, children with delays in this skill are likely to experience feelings of deep inadequacy.

Many of the observable phenomena covered in *Educational Care* have significant impacts upon reading. As we shall see, problems with language, memory, visual processing, and other areas of function are often found in children with delayed reading skills. These difficulties may interact with environmental and emotional factors to produce serious reading deficiencies. The following are some of the sources and manifestations of reading difficulty that are commonly observed in children:

Preacademic underexposure. Some children from an early age are never sufficiently exposed to the written word. They fail to develop any attraction to reading or to perceive its relevance. They have little or no incentive to break the "reading code." They may have lacked the early experience of prereading behaviors, such as handling reading materials, being read to, pretending to read, and looking at pictures in books or

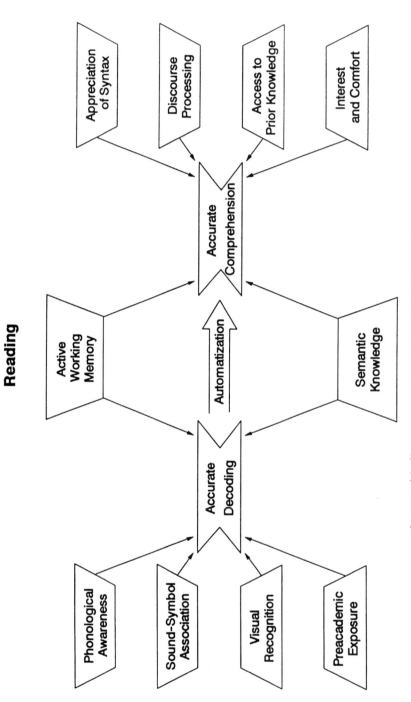

Fig. 6.1. This diagram presents a task analysis of the reading process.

164

magazines. In some cases these absent prereading behaviors may be associated with deficient early language development rather than a lack of exposure, as some children with language difficulties are apt to avoid the written word from an early age.

Ineffective word decoding. Many children with reading problems are very slow to acquire basic word decoding skills. Weak visual processing, faulty recognition and naming, poor phonological awareness, memory dysfunctions, as well as limited access to word meanings may operate singly or in combination to create barriers to the mastery of word decoding. The problem is often aggravated by a lack of practice, as a child becomes highly reluctant to pursue the frustrating process of decoding.

When a child is poor at decoding, it is important to try to detect exactly where and how the breakdown is occurring. Such determinations should be made by individuals who have experience in assessment and/or teaching of reading skills. The three common gaps (which may be found individually or in combination) are enumerated below.

Weak associations of sounds with symbols (poor phoneme-grapheme correspondences)—Such children may have deficient phonological awareness, weak visual processing, and/or trouble forming paired associations of this type in memory.

Difficulty segmenting and reblending the component sounds in a word—Some children appear to lack a strong enough awareness of how words are composed of constituent sound units. It is therefore hard for them to engage in processes for breaking words down into their individual sound components. In other cases, while sounding out the last portion of a multisyllabic word, a child may forget the first part, so that it becomes impossible to reblend all the sounds to capture the whole word. This phenomenon may be seen in children for whom the association of the individual symbols with sounds is taking too much effort as well as in some students who appear not to have sufficient active working memory to suspend in place initial sounds while working on subsequent ones. Some students with chunk-size limitations (page 110) may experience difficulty with the decoding of lengthy words.

Poor knowledge of or access to word meanings—Semantic and morphological gaps can render words much harder to recognize. Children with such shortcomings are likely to have trouble associating words with meanings.

At higher elementary grades, some students who were initially slow to attain accurate decoding may have acquired decoding skills, but their skills may not be sufficiently automatized. As a result, they use excessive effort to decode individual words during reading (especially oral reading). Their rate is likely to be slow, reading may seem like too much work, and insufficient mental effort remains for sophisticated sentence and discourse comprehension. Furthermore, these students rely too strongly on context clues, as they decode a few words and try to guess at overall meanings. This strategy only works some of the time and becomes increasingly less effective as texts become more sophisticated and remote from everyday experience.

Reduced reading comprehension. Many factors can limit a student's reading comprehension. The first and most common of these is poorly automatized word decoding. Further, any of the forms of weak language processing described in chapter 4 can obstruct the understanding of reading. Semantic gaps, poor understanding of syntax, and trouble drawing verbal inferences are common examples of linguistic breakdowns that impede reading comprehension. Students who are unable to relate prior knowledge effectively during reading are also susceptible to poor understanding. This limitation may occur either because students lack that prior knowledge or because they have weaknesses of memory that limit or slow down access to the needed facts or experiences. Some students reveal content-specific comprehension gaps; their limited knowledge or access within a particular subject area may obstruct comprehension. A poor grasp of the concepts within a content area may similarly prevent them from understanding the reading material. Additionally, students with limited active working memory are apt to lose track of a narrative flow or multistep explanation in a passage, thus making the text incoherent. Some children with weak attention controls miss critical textual details and have trouble regulating the rate of their reading. Others display the phenomenon of passive learning (page 23) and may not be engaged sufficiently in the reading process to activate relevant prior knowledge or experience. Finally, some readers with extreme top-down processing may tend to provide inaccurate (or highly divergent) interpretations of what they read.

Low levels of application and generalization. Some students have difficulty applying what they have read. In some cases this shortcoming stems from trouble summarizing written material. Affected students are likely to feel overwhelmed by discourse or any lengthy text. Others have trouble remembering what they have read long enough and with sufficient accuracy to make use of the material. Still others have difficulties with broadening the meaning of the text. Sometimes these are passive learners who rely heavily on rote memory and fail to generalize, elaborate, or ponder the personal relevance of what they are learning in school.

Inflexible reading style. As students proceed through school, they acquire a range of reading techniques (including scanning, skimming, and highlighting) that can be used under varying conditions and contexts. They also have to know when to be highly creative and personal during reading and when to adhere to the literal content. They must differentiate text structures as they read so that they approach narrative with a somewhat different reading style from that which is used to read a list or a geographic description. When students have trouble shifting into the right reading "gear" at the right time, when they read all materials in the same manner, they show reading inflexibility.

Inefficient reading. Some children read slowly and laboriously. This may simply reflect their lack of automaticity. It may also indicate poor attention control (especially problems with the maintenance of alertness) or it may be a lack of interest. Occasionally, a child's reading is inefficient because he or she *perseverates*, that is, becomes too obsessed with totally understanding and perhaps retaining too great a proportion of the material. This kind of reading may be part of a broader picture of slow processing and production in school.

Reading avoidance. There are students who simply hate to read. Many factors, including all of the kinds of reading difficulties we have just described may underlie their distaste. Because the process is so labored and the experience is so damaging to self-esteem, students with long-standing reading problems may read as little as possible. As a result their delayed reading skill becomes further complicated and aggravated by the chronic lack of reading experience and practice. Then they fall farther and farther behind and acquire an even higher level of antipathy toward reading. Reading avoidance may also be the result of cultural, peer, and family factors. When there are no identifiable reader role models in a child's life, the act of reading may fail to offer any potential romantic attraction. In some cases children have had such massive exposures to television or videos (media that gratify rapidly) that they lack the patience and reflective tempo often needed for written text.

Figure 6.2 summarizes the common findings in children with slow reading development.

Managing Slow Reading Development at Home

Without some collaborative support at home, a child's reading ability in school is unlikely to improve substantially. Parents can help children

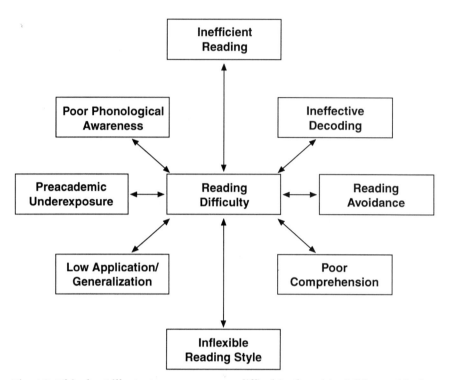

Fig. 6.2. This chart illustrates some common difficulties found in children with slow reading development.

appreciate the written word at the same time that they assist them to become more accurate, efficient, and flexible in their reading. The suggestions in both of the reading management sections have been divided into three sections, general management suggestions, help with decoding, and help with comprehension.

General Management Suggestions

1. Parents should try to create an atmosphere at home that encourages reading, so that children from a very young age are attracted to written words. Children with reading problems, in particular, need to see other family members reading and enjoying it. What family members have read about can be discussed at meals. Children should be encouraged to read about upcoming family activities. For example, if a family is taking a trip, children should be expected to read about the destination and formulate specific plans based on their reading.

2. Certain times each day should be set aside for reading in areas that are of great interest to the student. Parents can provide magazine subscriptions as well as visits to the library to facilitate this process.

3. One of the best ways to help children to read well is to have them read about topics they know a lot about. Therefore, parents should help children develop strong interests from an early age. Such interests can be used to bolster reading comprehension (as well as other skills). For example, a child who loves animals will acquire a certain amount of expertise by having certain pets. Over time this specialized knowledge will grow, and the child can improve reading skills by reading many books and articles on this subject. This approach also helps reduce reading avoidance and enables children to improve the application and generalization of what they read.

4. It is a good idea for younger students to take turns reading with a parent or to read in unison with the adult. This activity is often best accomplished at bedtime. Rereading books that have been enjoyed in the past enhances word recognition skills and helps children feel they are making progress.

5. For children in the early grades, parents can label objects around the house with their names.

6. Tactics used at home should be coordinated with techniques used in school. Often parents can reinforce the school's methods.

Help with Decoding

7. Children with word decoding problems need as much drill as possible. When they have problems with active working memory for the component sounds of words (page 162), parents should concentrate on the rapid recall of basic letter combinations on flash cards with less emphasis on rapid drilling using real words. Memory for the basic sound-symbol associations in such children may need to become fully automatic before they can become effective at segmentation, reblending, and whole word recognition.

8. Children can study words and pictures of what they represent together as they are learning to decode. Both parents and children can cut out pictures, paste them on cards, and label them with the appropriate words. Parents can also devise various games in which children match pictures with written words.

9. Parents should investigate current educational computer software to assist in the development of decoding skills. They can look for entertaining techniques and activities that also allow for regulation of the rate of presentation and of response in order to meet the needs of individual children.

Help with Comprehension

10. Older children can benefit from books on tape. They should read along as they listen. Parents may find these audio tapes in the library. Alternatively, a much larger selection is available by completing an application form and obtaining a certifying letter from a clinician. The tapes can be obtained in the United States from Recordings for the Blind, 20 Roszel Road, Princeton, New Jersey 08540. There are recordings of textbooks as well as literary works.

11. Parents should provide their children with frequent opportunities to read for a purpose and then show an interest in what they have discovered. Children can be asked to look up specific facts, to find out more about a particular topic, or to learn how something works.

12. Previewing with a child what is to be read and discussing what reading style or technique should be used is another way parents can help. They can ask questions like: Would it be a good idea to skim over it first? Should there be some specific questions to think about while reading this? Is this the kind of assignment where underlining or highlighting might be helpful? Would it be useful to make diagrams or charts while reading this text?

13. Parents should ask children with reading problems to try to summarize what they have read in a passage or chapter. Children can use a tape recorder for this or they can relate what they have read directly to a parent. A variation of this method is for a child to underline key ideas while reading and then read these highlighted thoughts into a tape recorder. Later the tape can be replayed, and the child can talk about the ideas with a parent. If it is not too intimidating to the child, parents can quiz him or her on the reading.

14. Secondary school students often need help in studying from textbooks. Parents can assist them in making diagrams or charts to summarize the material as well as help them in using word and conceptual maps and advance organizers (described in the school management section).

15. Some students insist that they get more out of reading if they listen to music. Even if parents have a different view, this is worth trying as an experiment.

Managing Slow Reading Development in School

A vast number of remedial reading curricula and methods have been devised to help children with slow reading development. Matching the method to the child's characteristics is of critical importance. Good resources that describe specific remedial methods are provided in the Suggested Readings at the end of the book.

General Management Suggestions

1. Reading difficulties at all grade levels need to be managed with the close consultation of a special educator or reading specialist.

2. The consultant and the regular classroom teacher should be aware of the child's cognitive strengths, weaknesses, preferred learning style, and their implications for the acquisition of reading skills.

3. Teachers need to be sensitive to the apprehensions these children may feel when asked to read aloud before their classmates. Such requests may need to be avoided.

4. Students with delayed reading skills usually require alternative means of acquiring information. They may learn best from diagrams, videotapes, audiocassettes, and hands-on demonstrations.

5. These children require more time to complete reading tasks. They may have to be given shorter reading assignments for in-class work. For standardized tests (including college entrance examinations) they may need permission to complete them untimed or with additional time.

Help with Decoding

6. The kinds of decoding drills described for management at home (page 169) are also appropriate for use within the classroom. In addition, multisensory reading activities, which have helped some children, can be used. These techniques stress facilitated entry into memory by having letter combinations and their represented sounds encoded in more than one sensory modality. For example, students look at a cluster of letters, say them, touch them, draw them on the board, and trace them in sand. Although the effectiveness of these methods is questioned

by some, many reading specialists believe that such approaches are especially helpful to children with underlying phonological weaknesses.

7. By late elementary and middle school, children who have not yet achieved sufficient automaticity of decoding are at serious risk academically. Even at that age, slow, labored readers require ongoing timed drill to establish basic sound-symbol associations independent of word identification. Teachers should identify those letter combinations that are especially elusive to a child in order to emphasize them in drill. Separate activities need to be used to stress word recognition and the reading of sentences.

8. Employing a word family approach may be effective for those children who are strong conceptualizers or who have good visual processing. They may benefit from mastering categories of words, such as all those that end in *ight*.

9. Many children enjoy and can learn from choral and echo reading. In the latter case, a teacher reads aloud several sentences, then the children read the same sentences while pointing to the words. In choral reading, everyone reads in unison.

10. Whole language approaches may also be helpful to some of these children, since they stress the personal relevance of reading and writing. Surrounding children with reading materials and immersing them in their use can be beneficial. On the other hand, some children with decoding problems may feel overwhelmed and intimidated when whole language techniques are used.

11. Schools need to develop eclectic approaches to children with decoding difficulties. They should not adopt a single curriculum or teaching method and believe it will be right for all of these students. Many children can benefit from combined approaches, such as whole language plus word family or a heavily phonological focus combined with a language experience or visual method.

Help with Comprehension

12. Children who have trouble reading discourse should always read with a pencil in their hands and underline and write comments in the margins. If they don't own their own textbooks (and therefore cannot write in them), they can use "Post-it" notes on each page to write down key words or phrases. At the end of a chapter, the child can

remove these, paste them on a big sheet of paper, and try to summarize the chapter by reading over them.

13. Teachers need to differentiate between students with poor comprehension and those with memory weaknesses affecting their reading. They can do so by asking a child to explain or elaborate on some points from a paragraph she or he has just read and then comparing this ability with performance on factual recall or tests. If memory is the major problem, a student will be able to do the former well but not the latter. Such a student will need to develop better memorization techniques. True comprehension difficulties can be dealt with in the ways described below.

14. Students often can improve comprehension through the use of advance organizers and various mapping techniques (figs. 6.3 and 6.4). These devices consist of charts or diagrams of the content of the text, and they can be used in a variety of manners. Students can keep a diagram of a paragraph or passage before them while reading. For example, using the list in figure 6.3, they might then read a passage on raccoons. Alternatively, they can be given a skeleton of a diagram and asked to fill it in during or after the reading of a passage. Using one or more of the formats shown in figure 6.4, children can condense paragraphs into diagrams. Finally, they can create their own diagrams from scratch. The use of these graphic materials can enhance comprehension,

Example of an Advance Organizer

What to be thinking about in chapter 14

- How raccoons are different from other animals in the woods
- How often they breed
- How they protect their young
- Who their enemies are
- What they eat

Fig. 6.3. The advance organizer can be used to assist students with memory or comprehension problems that affect reading. Children can refer to such a device as they read and can check off each item when they find it in a chapter.

Paragraph Graphics

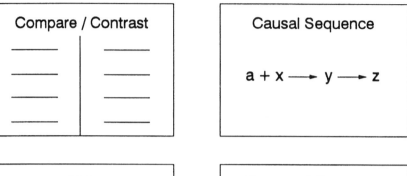

| Compare / Contrast | Causal Sequence |

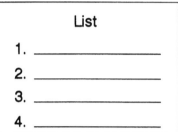

List

1. _____
2. _____
3. _____
4. _____

Temporal Sequence

1843 -

1846 -

1849 -

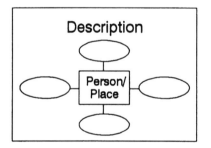

Description

Person/Place

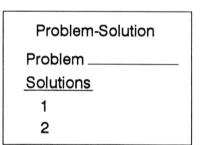

Problem-Solution

Problem _____
Solutions
  1
  2

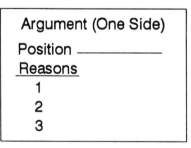

Argument (One Side)

Position _____
Reasons
  1
  2
  3

Fig. 6.4. Older students should learn to summarize on cards the content of paragraphs in texts. Each of the models above can be used with a specific kind of paragraph (e.g., a list, a compare and contrast, etc.).

improve awareness of text structures and how they work, and strengthen attention during reading.

15. After reading text, students should be encouraged to write questions about what they have read. They might pretend they are making up a test on the material. Later, the questions can be used for class discussion or read by the teacher only.

16. Previewing technical or difficult vocabulary and concepts for students before they read an assignment usually benefits all students but especially helps those who are struggling with comprehension. They can be given a glossary of words and concepts to use while reading. Such a list provides a preview of the content and also prevents them from becoming too confused as new words and ideas appear.

17. Many children with comprehension gaps need work in identifying main and supporting ideas in a passage. This can be done either through discussion, summarization after reading, underlining (using different colors for main ideas and supporting ideas), or diagramming.

18. When students lack sufficient prior knowledge in a subject, they may need tutorial support to acquire the substrate of basic facts. In a highly cumulative science course (such as chemistry), a tutor may need to return to material covered in the fall for a student to understand assignments in the spring.

19. Children who have difficulty with the conceptual content of a text should be using the techniques of mapping new concepts and of maintaining a conceptual atlas as described in chapter 4 (page 100).

20. Children whose reading comprehension difficulties are associated with weak language processing (chapter 4) may need specific forms of language therapy before they can make significant gains in reading. Teachers should also consider alternative ways of conveying knowledge, such as tape recordings, interactive software, and videos.

21. Collaborative activities often enhance the experience of reading. Teachers should create opportunities for students to meet in small groups, to discuss what they have read, to plan oral reports, or to carry out other projects relating to their reading. Teaming students with comprehension weaknesses with stronger readers can allow the delayed readers to show their strengths during the team effort (e.g., as illustrators, organizers, or emcees).

RUDY

Rudy is a thirteen-year-old boy who performs quite well in almost all areas in school. Spelling, however, is a serious problem for him. When he first started school, Rudy was a bit slow to learn how to read. Although he eventually acquired decoding skills and now is able to read at an appropriate rate and with good comprehension, his writing is seriously impeded by spelling problems. Most of Rudy's errors are phonetically correct but nevertheless inaccurate. He is likely to spell the word machine *as* musheen. *Using the spell check on his computer has been very helpful to Rudy, but he still makes numerous errors.*

INACCURATE SPELLING PATTERNS

Spelling is far from being the most indispensable of academic skills. In fact, many highly successful adults exhibit atrocious spelling. In an age of computers with spell checks readily available, one might argue that this skill is nearly superfluous. Nevertheless, accurate and rapid spelling greatly facilitates the writing process. Children who are good spellers take justifiable pride in what represents a very elegant fusion of language abilities, visual processing activities, memory functions, and rule applications. Additionally, accurate spelling in written products creates an impression of competency, motivation, and care.

Spelling: A Task Analysis

As with reading, a range of task components allow for proficiency as a child progressively masters the skill during the school years. Accurate patterns of spelling require the following competencies:

Phonological encoding—the ability to represent English language sounds with appropriate letter combinations. Not surprisingly, this capability correlates highly with overall phonological awareness.

Graphemic retrieval—the ability to recall the visual configurations of words. During spelling a child needs to be able to visualize at least the general appearance of the word to be spelled.

Segmentation—the ability to take apart words and put them back together again. Spellers need a strong sense of the component parts of the words they are attempting to spell.

Rule recall—the ability to appreciate and remember rules governing spelling. Students also form their own notions of rules and regularities, so that when they think about spelling they don't make use of letter combinations that are nonexistent in their native language.

Attention to detail—the tendency to focus on the precise internal characteristics of words. Good spelling requires some concentration, at least until it becomes nearly automatic.

Semantic networking and appreciation of morphology—an awareness of how words relate in their meanings, their roots, and their common derivations. Such awareness can help with decision making during difficult spelling. For example, in trying to decide on the ambiguously pronounced medial *u* in the word *industry*, it is most helpful to think about the word's morphological "cousin," namely, *industrial*. The latter must have a *u* in the middle.

Retrieval memory—rapid and precise access to stored spellings. Good spellers must retrieve convergently and often at the same time that they are recalling other materials (such as punctuation, letter formation, and facts).

Reading ability—strong word decoding skills. Children who read accurately are more likely to spell with accuracy.

A task analysis of spelling is represented in figure 6.5.

Forms of Inaccurate Spelling Patterns

Despite their dubious long-term significance, spelling problems continue to haunt children, their parents, and their teachers. Inaccurate orthography makes writing more labored and less gratifying for a student. Such difficult writing was part of the problem for Rudy in the case at the beginning of this section. Moreover, spelling is sometimes "the tip of an iceberg" from a developmental perspective. Difficulties with spelling may, in fact, reflect underlying language problems, memory weaknesses, or other forms of neurodevelopmental dysfunction.

The understanding of a child's delayed spelling skills can be enhanced greatly through meticulous analyses of his or her spelling errors. In fact, it is possible to define the forms of spelling delay on the basis of consistent patterns of errors the student tends to commit. For example, in Rudy's case, there are indications of phonetically correct but visually imprecise spellings. Table 6.1 summarizes common error patterns and provides examples of some of the observable phenomena associated with them.

Spelling

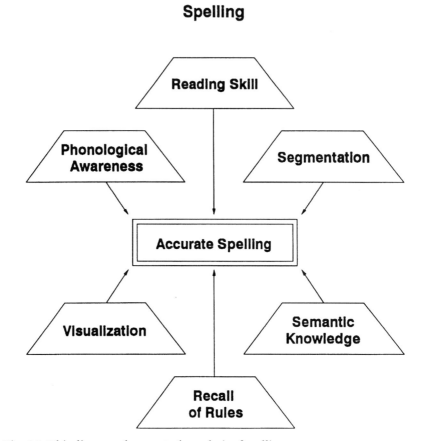

Fig. 6.5. This diagram shows a task analysis of spelling.

When trying to help a child deal with or overcome a spelling deficiency, adults can begin by characterizing the pattern of errors and the
ways in which these patterns reflect or are consistent with observable
phenomena in other areas of the child's life. For example, a particular
memory problem may affect both mathematical recall and spelling. A
student with diminished phonological awareness may encounter problems while decoding words as well as encoding words for spelling. Or,
attentional dysfunction may lead to careless, impulsive errors in spelling
and in mathematical computations. Children with inconsistent alertness
and mental effort may demonstrate highly erratic spelling, perhaps
spelling the same word three different ways on the same page. Such
recurring inaccurate patterns can even be used as evidence for the existence of a particular kind of observable phenomenon that is standing in

Table 6.1: Spelling Error Patterns and Their Associations with Other Observable Phenomena

ERROR PATTERN	ASSOCIATED OBSERVABLE PHENOMENA
Visually close, but phonetically poor (e.g., *boght* for *bought*)	May be seen in a child with a poor recall of language sounds (phonemes) and their representation by groups of letters (graphemes); also in those with segmentation difficulties
Phonetically close, but visually poor (e.g., *bawt* for *bought*)	Occurring in some children with weaknesses of visual recall from long-term memory; most common in early elementary grades, often seen in association with legibility problems; may persist in problems with irregular words
Accuracy with isolated words, but not in paragraphs	Found in children with poor simultaneous recall who have trouble spelling while recalling rules, vocabulary, ideas, letter formations at one time
Random/inconsistent errors	Frequently present in students with weak attention controls with inconsistent alertness and weak self-monitoring
Omissions within words (e.g., *bogt* for *bought*)	May occur in students who have trouble preserving data in linear chunks; they often omit groups of letters in the middle of words and/or confuse the letter sequences
Incomplete appreciation of spelling rules/regularities (e.g., *borgt* for *bought*)	Can be encountered in children with poor recall of regularity and rules or with weak recognition of patterns; they use letter combinations that don't exist in English and violate rules of spelling
Poor sense of word derivatives	Occurring in students with weak semantic abilities who fail to use word knowledge enabling them to spell a word when they can spell one related to it
Much better recognition than recall of spelling	Found in some students with memory gaps who may have trouble writing and spelling simultaneously but who can recognize correct spellings, as in a multiple-choice forma
Mixed spelling errors	Combinations of the above, likely to be found in some children with several neurodevelopmental dysfunctions

the way of school success. Finally, it is important to be aware of cultural factors that can influence spelling. For example, children who are exposed to strong dialects at home may have trouble recognizing the language sounds of standard English. These students may, in particular, omit or alter word endings when they spell.

Once a spelling error pattern has been described well, teachers and parents can formulate strategies to work on spelling accuracy at home and in school.

Managing Inaccurate Spelling Patterns at Home

Without overemphasizing the importance of spelling, parents may be able to assist a child to improve in this skill. In particular, they need to devise and use high motivational activities to make spelling palatable to a child who has had nothing but frustrating experiences with it.

1. The age-old technique of using flash cards lives on! Parents can drill children on both new and commonly misspelled words. As mentioned earlier, if done just before bedtime, rote learning consolidates best during sleep as long as there has been no intervening activity (watching television, etc.).

2. Children with phonological problems require help with grapheme encoding before they get too immersed in spelling real words. Games in which they are given a language sound (like *-ing* or *-out*) and asked to write out the ways that sound might be spelled can be helpful and fun. They can then try to think up real words that rhyme with that sound.

3. Children who often omit sounds within words must first become absolutely automatic in their appreciation and recall of the individual letter combinations and the sounds they regularly make. This, of course, will help them to remember these letter combinations during spelling. Parents should encourage these children to proofread, especially examining their spellings for "lost pieces of words." They can also benefit from exercises in which they are shown long words that have parts missing which they must supply.

4. Children with attention deficits and those who have trouble with simultaneous recall during writing must be encouraged to do their writing in stages rather than trying to spell, punctuate, and develop ideas all at once.

5. Some children who have spelling weaknesses may benefit from a word-family approach (page 172) in which they learn all the *-ought*

and all the -*ive* words as a "family" or visual category. This process can be especially helpful to children with visual memory problems. Categorizing the words actually reduces the need to revisualize.

6. Parents should investigate available spelling computer software which is likely to include high motivational activities to enhance spelling accuracy.

7. Playing word games like Scrabble and Spill and Spell at home may strengthen spelling accuracy.

8. Children can maintain a personal dictionary of words that they often use but commonly misspell. If they have access to a computer, they can enter these into the spell-check memory as well.

Managing Inaccurate Spelling Patterns in School

When a child has problems with spelling, the school needs to offer sensitive management. Teachers should put spelling in perspective for these children; for example, "We need to try to improve your spelling, but your problem with spelling is not worth feeling terrible or embarrassed about." A student who is having multiple academic problems (including spelling difficulties) should not allocate enormous amounts of time and effort to spelling.

1. When students with spelling problems also have serious reading decoding difficulties, the two problems should be addressed nearly simultaneously. Special educational consultation and/or intervention is clearly called for in such cases to select appropriate ways of enhancing the acquisition of sound-symbol associations.

2. Some children with memory-based spelling difficulties benefit from learning to spell using recognition memory rather than total recall. They can study alternative spellings and learn to choose the one that is correct. As they improve their proficiency at recognition, they are more likely to be accurate in recalling spellings during writing.

3. Students may need targeted help mastering specific letter combinations for spelling. Teachers can present common patterns (e.g., -*ion* and -*ness*) as units. Children then list words that contain these combinations as well as make up pronounceable nonsense words with the patterns. Teachers can also help students strengthen their skill by showing them different combinations of letters out of context and having them decide which ones exist and which ones do not exist in English.

4. Some of these students benefit from studying spelling rules and then looking at correctly and incorrectly spelled words to determine which rule applies and whether or not it is obeyed.

5. Teachers can use interesting spelling games in class. A child with a spelling problem can serve as scorekeeper in a spelling contest. Part of his or her responsibility will be to write the correct spelling on the score sheet along with the name of whoever spelled it correctly.

6. In some cases, spelling should be de-emphasized. When students have multiple academic problems, they can be assured that spelling accuracy will not contribute significantly to their grades. In addition, enormous amounts of resource, time, and emotion should not be spent on spelling with these students.

7. Students can maintain an evolving list of words that are hard to spell. Using such a list, students must spell a word correctly three times in order for that word to be taken off the list and replaced by a new unfamiliar word.

8. When spelling problems seriously impede writing, teachers can encourage students to make spelling a totally separate and later stage of writing. They should not try to spell and compose at the same time.

IMPEDED WRITTEN OUTPUT

Writing is one of the most complex activities in which a child is asked to engage. In part, this is because the act of writing involves the rapid and precise mobilization and synchronization of multiple brain functions, strategies, academic skills, and thought processes. It is not surprising, therefore, that so many children with learning difficulties find writing exceedingly taxing, unrewarding, and, perhaps, even humiliating.

Written Output: A Task Analysis

Proficient writers are able to recruit a multitude of functions and abilities to interact on paper. Among these are the following components:

Language production—facility at encoding thoughts into words, sentences, and discourse. Writing is a highly sophisticated form of literate and social language use.

Motor skill—the ability to coordinate muscles of the hand and forearm. The motor components of writing are intricate and therefore highly demanding, especially for novice writers.

Memory function—the capacity to recall a range of needs during writing. Very precise convergent, simultaneous, and ultimately automatic recall is essential for writing fluency. Active working memory also plays a vital role during writing (e.g., remembering what you wanted to state in a sentence while thinking about how to spell a particular word within that sentence).

Attention—having sufficient mental effort as well as control over the various regulatory functions needed for writing. During written output, there must be tight regulation of relative rates (e.g., the generation of ideas should not be proceeding faster than the recall of necessary vocabulary and spelling), keen attention to detail, and diligent self-monitoring. In fact, all aspects of attention control (chapter 2) contribute critically to the effectiveness of written output.

Problem solving—reflecting on and using strategies while writing. The act of writing often poses a challenge that needs to be met in a stepwise and flexibly strategic fashion.

Organization—the arranging of what is needed for efficient writing. Ideas, time, and materials need to be organized consciously in preparation for a writing activity.

REGGIE

Reggie is a twelve-year-old boy who simply hates to write. When he does so, his products are usually sparse and primitive. There is a marked discrepancy between the quality of his ideas in a class discussion and what he is able to produce on paper. In addition to being inconsistent, much of Reggie's writing is poorly legible. He writes very slowly, and the whole process is labored. Reggie also has difficulties with spelling and punctuation, although he is able to correct spelling and punctuation errors in paragraphs he is given to read. Reggie has a very awkward pencil grip. He holds the utensil near its point, perpendicular to the page, with great pressure. As the writing demands increase, Reggie is liking school less and less. He often tells his parents he has no homework, but later they find out that he has not been handing in his assignments.

Ideation—the generation of thoughts. This includes such issues as topic selection, topic development, research (using a variety of sources of information), creativity or insightfulness of ideas, use of prior knowledge, critical thinking, and the application of concepts.

Reading ability—the effectiveness of decoding and comprehension. Students who are good readers have a stronger likelihood of being effective writers.

Writing affinity and comfort—enjoyment of writing and a sense that written tasks are not a threat.

Perspective taking—understanding who the reader(s) will be and what that type of reader needs or expects from the writer. This includes a knowledge of how much background information needs to be provided, the kind of vocabulary that should be used, and the overall tone of the writing.

Adaptation to varied formats—an understanding of different kinds of writing and the rules, conventions, and limitations pertaining to them. Students need to be able to express themselves clearly in a letter writing style, a creative mode, or a critical essay.

Revision skills—the ability and willingness to refine ideas and mechanics. It has been said that writing is revising. Through ongoing revision, writing emerges as a craft.

Figure 6.6 presents a task analysis of writing.

Forms of Impeded Written Output

As we have seen, to be successful with the many components of written output, a child must mobilize and synchronize multiple skills and functions. Consequently, impeded written output may assume many different forms. Affected children often harbor one or more of the observable phenomena contained in this book. In the following pages we shall describe the most common forms of impeded written output.

Written language problems. Children who have weak language production (chapter 5) are apt to show deficiencies in their written expression. Their writing suggests gaps in word usage or semantics, proper sentence construction, and overall verbal sophistication. In some instances, the problem is that they commit conspicuous syntactic, morphological, or semantic errors. In other cases, what they write may be relatively free of language flaws, but the content is overly simplistic. These children write

Written Output

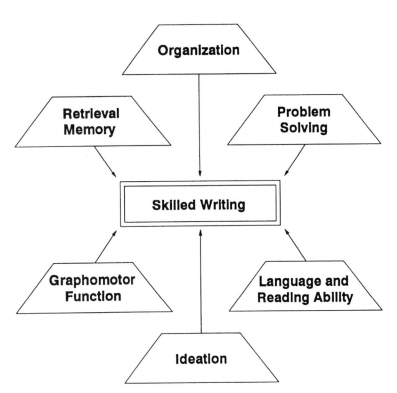

Fig. 6.6. This diagram presents a task analysis of writing.

brief sentences and overuse very common words, with a commensurate reduction in the complexity or development of ideas.

Graphomotor dysfunctions. Some children have motor problems which impair the precise coordination of the small muscles needed for fluent letter formation on paper. Their writing may suggest the presence of gaps or breakdowns in the connections between the brain and the fingers. These dysfunctions sometimes take the form of generalized fine motor deficiencies (page 134). A child so affected would have trouble drawing, difficulty tracing, problems using scissors, as well as impeded writing. There are many children, however, who show exclusively graphomotor dysfunction which means that they have fine motor problems that only affect their writing. In fact, such students may possess strong artistic or mechanical abilities, but their writing is slow, laborious, and sometimes illegible. Of the different types of graphomotor dysfunction that exist, we will describe three common forms.

Motor memory dysfunctions—Children with these conditions seem to have trouble integrating motor output with various forms of memory input. That is, they lack the procedural memory needed to know how to inscribe letters dependably on demand. In some cases, they are unable to recall the sequences of muscle movements (motor engrams) needed to form specific letters. Other children have difficulty with the rapid, consistent, and precise recall of letter shapes or configurations during writing. Eventually, these children are able to recall the shapes or the motor sequences, but then they cannot do so quickly enough to keep pace with the flow of their thoughts or consistently enough to write in a smooth and rhythmic manner.

The writing of children with motor memory dysfunctions is often slow, hesitant, and labored. It is characterized by inconsistent letter formations, frequent crossing out or erasures, and reduced legibility. Many of these children have spelling problems, since they find it even harder to picture the words than to visualize the letters. Their spelling errors generally are phonetically correct (e.g., *laft* for *laughed*). Very commonly these children much prefer printing (manuscript) to cursive writing. This is probably because, for manuscript, they need only remember twenty-six motor sequences and shapes while, for cursive, every word is a unique sequence of motor movements and a unique configuration, thus placing a much greater strain on memory.

Graphomotor production deficits—During writing, the writer must send messages to the very small muscles of the fingers telling them what to do when, as they form letters and words. Different muscles have different writing assignments at any given moment. In particular, the brain assigns some muscles to stabilize the writing utensil while it directs other muscles to move it to form the symbols. Some children have trouble transmitting these specific muscle assignments to their fingers. Consequently, they show poor graphomotor coordination. In some cases, too many muscles may be moving the pencil and too few stabilizing it, in which case the pencil grip is unstable and constantly changing. Such a child may keep dropping the writing utensil. In other cases, too many muscles may be stabilizing the pencil, and the student holds the pencil very close to the point, perpendicular to the page, and writes with extremely heavy pressure. Such writing was evident in Reggie, the child described at the beginning of this section. Some of these children ultimately develop a pronounced hook during writing. They stretch out the tendons on the back of the arm to such an extent that their fingers can no longer move very much, if at all, during writing. They write with the larger muscles of the wrist and forearm, which they discover they can control better than the small muscles of the fingers. Their writing, however, is often laborious and slow.

Children with graphomotor production deficits often write slowly. Their handwriting may or may not be difficult to decipher. It is interesting that these children often have a history of speech difficulty, especially articulation problems. It appears that many of them endure the same kind of trouble assigning mouth muscles to specific speech sounds as they do assigning hand muscles to specific letter formations.

Motor feedback problems—During writing it is imperative to be able to track the exact location of the pen or pencil point at all instants. By knowing where the utensil is, the brain is able to navigate its next destination within a word or even within a single letter. Small nerve endings in the muscles and joints of the fingers "report" their present locations on an ongoing basis during writing. For most people this happens automatically and unconsciously, but in some children this feedback system is deficient (a condition sometimes called *finger agnosia*). Affected students may compensate by keeping their eyes very close to the page in an attempt to visually monitor the pencil or pen point, since their fingers are failing to report back. Some students unconsciously start using their larger joints (such as those of the wrist) during writing because they do not get adequate feedback from the lesser joints in their fingers. This practice becomes manifest in an awkward and uncomfortable pencil grip. For example, a child may place the thumb over the other fingers, creating a fist-like grip and essentially preventing the fingers from moving the pencil. This role is assumed by larger joints in the wrist or further up the arm. In such cases writing may be painfully slow and exhausting. An affected child may come to despise writing and do as little as possible.

Exceeded Memory Capacity. As we have noted, effective writing requires the application of multiple memory functions. Long-term retrieval, active working memory, and short-term memory (chapter 3) must operate in concert and with tremendous speed during writing. These heavy memory demands may well exceed the current capacities of some students. As a result, their writing becomes sparse, highly inconsistent in its quality, and often disorganized. We will consider separately the common manifestations of the three kinds of exceeded memory capacity during writing.

Exceeded long-term retrieval capacity—During writing one must simultaneously and rapidly retrieve from long-term memory correct spellings, rules of grammar, punctuation and capitalization, vocabulary, prior knowledge, and letter formations (i.e., the motor memory described above). There are many students who cannot do so. They might be able to perform any one of these functions in isolation, but they have agonizing difficulty retrieving all of these critical resources at the same time. Thus, such a student might spell a word adequately in isolation but then misspell that same word in a paragraph. She or he might have no trouble correcting someone else's punctuation but commit glaring punctuation errors while writing a short story. Additionally, a child with this kind of memory overload may express remarkably perceptive and eloquently stated thoughts during a class discussion or a talk at the dinner table, but his or her ideas on paper are not nearly as sophisticated. This disparity occurs because the retrieval memory effort for that student during writing is so arduous that generating good ideas and writing at the same time becomes nearly impossible. In other words, trouble remembering undermines otherwise effective thought processes. In addition, such a child may write neatly when copying a sentence from the board but then display poor legibility when composing a paragraph. This is because long-term retrieval memory demands are minimal when transferring material from the board, whereas the multiplicity of demands when composing a paragraph tends to crowd out memory for letter formations, thereby causing illegibility. This is a likely explanation for some of Reggie's writing difficulties.

Exceeded active working memory capacity—During writing, students need to remember what they are currently doing while also remembering what they intend to express. Some children with insufficient active working memory have a problem with mentally maintaining both intentions and task components. While in the course of writing a report, they may lose sight of the original topic. While trying to recall a particular spelling, they may forget what idea they were going to express with that word.

Exceeded short-term memory capacity—Two writing activities are especially strenuous for short-term memory: copying and note taking. In both operations a child must hold a chunk of information in short-term memory long enough to be able to transcribe it on paper.

Children with copying difficulties are often very slow at getting material from the board to the paper. Moreover, the child can be seen looking up at the board or overhead much more frequently than classmates, who are able to retain a larger amount of the information in short-term memory while they are copying. The need of some children to keep looking up markedly decelerates copying and can also cause them to lose their places.

Students with note-taking weaknesses can have several reasons for their difficulty. Commonly, they are unable to hold a big enough chunk of verbal information in short-term memory while simultaneously listening to subsequent information, summarizing what they are hearing, and deciding what's important to note and what is not worthy of recording (i.e., saliency determination). Efficient note taking also is dependent upon the quality and rate of a child's comprehension of the speaker. Finally, there are some students who have trouble with note taking (and copying) because of graphomotor production deficits (page 186). Their slow motor output prevents them from keeping pace. Nevertheless, it is important to remember that problems with short-term memory are an important and frequently overlooked cause of poor note taking.

Unsophisticated ideation. Some students experience difficulty when they attempt to develop ideas in writing. They may have problems at one or more of the following levels:

- Topic selection—trouble deciding what to write about
- Research—difficulty knowing how to find factual material
- Brainstorming—trouble producing original thoughts, elaborating on ideas, thinking through possible responses
- Analytic/critical thinking—difficulty engaging in insightful thinking
- Use of prior knowledge—trouble applying facts and concepts learned previously

In thinking about a student whose writing reflects poor ideation, it is important to determine whether that student's other academic activities also are indicative of this pattern or whether the weak ideation is confined to his or her writing. If it is the latter, it is possible that the multiple demands required for writing are impeding the ability to generate ideas. This was true in Reggie's case.

Organizational problems. Writing demands organization. There are some students who feel overwhelmed when they try to write a report because they lack any kind of organizational schema for doing so. They don't know where and how to begin or what to do next. They seem unable to prepare a written product in a stepwise fashion. This and other forms of organizational deficiency were described in more detail in chapter 5.

Mixed problems. It is very common for children with impeded written output to have more than one source of their difficulty. Combined problems with graphomotor function and retrieval memory or weaknesses of organization, attention, and motor memory are examples of the many different patterns that can be found.

Figure 6.7 summarizes some common causes of impeded written output. These causes are often evident in samples of children's writing. Figure 6.8 shows some of the common patterns of difficulty as revealed in their writing.

Managing Impeded Written Output at Home

When a child is a poor or reluctant writer, it is insufficient to say simply that a student has *dysgraphia* (a term often used to label children with writing problems). To be most helpful to a child, one needs to know if the problem has its source in the motor area, in memory, in language, in ideation, in organization, or in some combination of these functions. Then it is possible to tailor a management program to the specific characteristics of that student. Carefully guided practice is always needed if a child is to make significant gains in the quality, quantity, and ease of written output. There is no way in which this can be accomplished ex-

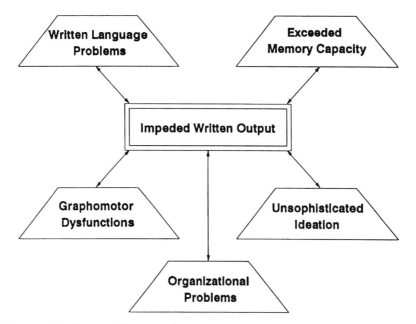

Fig. 6.7. This diagram illustrates five common sources of impeded written output.

clusively during classroom sessions. The following are some of the steps in management that can be performed at home.

1. Parents can encourage writing activities. Keeping a journal can be of great interest to a child at the same time that it provides daily writing practice. Other activities include writing a family newsletter, writing about trips and other family events, and writing letters (to friends, relatives, or pen pals). Some children like to write "far out" stories. They should be praised for doing so. They should also be urged to write about topics or areas in which they have a strong interest. Prior knowledge and a natural attraction to a subject can help to facilitate writing. Unfortunately, many children with writing difficulties wish to engage in as little writing as possible. Parents may need to provide additional incentives (such as prizes or special privileges) for this form of productivity!

2. If a child's pencil grip is clearly interfering with graphomotor fluency, a parent can work very gradually to modify this. The child should be taught a normal tripod grip (fig. 6.9) and be asked to write just a few sentences a night in a notebook using the new method. For all other writing activities in and out of school, the child can use the old accustomed grip. Slowly the number of sentences the student is asked to write using the new grip is increased. Eventually, in most cases, the child decides to write all the time with the newly learned grip. Sometimes the conversion can be facilitated by using an auxiliary plastic or rubber pencil gripper (sold at many stationery stores). It is important to emphasize that if a child has an awkward or unusual pencil grip but writes comfortably and easily, there is absolutely no need to alter it—if it's working, don't fix it!

3. Many children with graphomotor dysfunction have difficulty writing with ballpoint pens. They seem to function better with utensils that provide more friction with the paper (proprio-kinesthetic feedback). Parents should provide these children with a variety of pens or implements with a hollow shaft, such as a mechanical pencil, to try out until they find one that feels right. Taking time for trial-and-error experimentation is necessary.

4. When a child shows early evidence of graphomotor dysfunction, parents should have him or her begin the sometimes arduous effort at mastering keyboard skills. As early as age six or seven, a student can begin to feel comfortable at a computer. Initially, a "hunt-and-peck" approach to typing can be utilized, to be replaced by touch typing at a later age (when the child has developed some keyboarding efficiency).

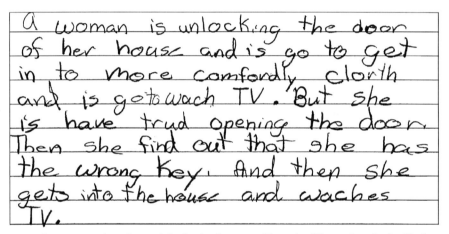

This space pen, shots, lasers. Writs with soting stars. I s aleticl and can fly. It has a digitl clock it can wright by it shelf.

Fig. 6.8. These five writing samples illustrate various forms of impeded written output. Sample A is that of a ten-year-old child who has difficulty with the multiple memory demands of writing. He becomes overwhelmed when he needs to write, and so writes as little as possible. His spelling is much better in isolation than in a paragraph.

A woman is unlocking the door of her house and is go to get in to more comfordly clorth and is go to wach TV. But she is have trud opening the door. Then she find out that she has the wrong key. And then she gets into the house and waches TV.

Sample B was written by a girl who is eleven and has significant chunk-size limitations. She has trouble spelling long words. She often omits endings, but she generally is accurate with the first several letters.

Wants There were a Man naMD Rrobert. He went out to get a Brthday prresint For His suns BcthDay. He got hiM a red anD yella Trnk Becouse He was wiy his 7 orray. He went Back to His Hous and uPinD The Door With His key anD Black gleas on His HunDs. He Put The Prasnt on His guns Bed, when

Sample C is taken from a story created by a twelve-year-old student with weak visualization. He makes many phonetically correct spelling errors, writes very slowly, and cannot perform cursive writing.

Sample D was produced by a sixteen-year-old adolescent with significant graphomotor production problems. This student has excellent language skills and is verbally fluent. (Text: The attitude a teacher takes toward her students governs their attitudes toward her class. I agree because from experience I know that when a teacher is derogatory, her students won't like to work for her. Derogatory treatment may lead to a bad experience and self-respect.)

Sample E is that of a twelve-year-old student with very good graphomotor function but significant problems with language production. This writer has a poor appreciation of syntax, making it hard for her to appreciate rules of punctuation and sentence structure.

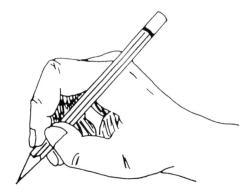

Fig. 6.9. A normal tripod pencil grip is illustrated here. The utensil is held about 1/2 inch from the point at a forty-five degree angle. Many children with graphomotor problems employ maladaptive grips, holding the pencil closer to the point, perpendicular to the page, or with a fist-like grip.

5. In many instances, word processing can be the salvation of a child with one or another form of writing difficulty. If possible, such children must be required to acquire facility with a computer. They can usually do so at school if a computer is unavailable at home. Ideally, they should be able to work with computers in both sites. Writing with a computer offers several advantages.

- The computer stresses recognition memory rather than retrieval. For many children recognition is less of a drain on memory. Spell checks, the symbols on keys, and computer icons all serve to reduce the recall burden during writing.
- Motor memory is less critical and complex. The computer recalls how to form the letters!
- Revision is easier, even fun.
- It is possible to create written products that actually look attractive. Many children have never been able to produce visually pleasing graphic material.
- With a reduced memory and motor burden, children may be able to allocate more effort to insightful thought, elaboration, creativity, and more organized expositions and narratives.
- Writing rate may be enhanced (particularly important for children with attentional dysfunction plus writing difficulty).

6. Children with impeded written output should not be allowed to give up entirely on writing. At the same time they are acquiring their keyboarding skills, they need to continue to practice graphomotor out-

put as well. It is also worth stressing that for many of these children learning to use the computer is about as hard as learning to write, but if done gradually and without undue pressure, it is definitely worth the effort.

7. Parents should be familiar with the principles of writing in specific stages. At home children should be encouraged to write reports and stories using these principles. The Report and Story Developers contained in Appendixes 4 and 5 can be used as guides both at home and in school. Parents can help model their use initially and then get students to verbalize their own plans.

8. Parents can be very helpful in assisting a child in getting started with a writing assignment. Children often feel overwhelmed with the enormity of the writing challenge. They can benefit from help interpreting the writing assignment, selecting a topic, finding reference materials, outlining or sequencing what they are about to write, and deciding what order to do things in for a long-range writing assignment. Again, the story and report planning worksheets can be used to facilitate this process.

9. As with other forms of home-based management, parents should avoid being too critical of a child's writing.

10. Parents can reward significant writing effort. For some children, simply handing in written assignments dependably (regardless of their quality) is a tremendous accomplishment. Parents should display and openly praise their child's writing progress.

11. Parents should not insist that a child use cursive writing. If manuscript writing is more comfortable and legible, the student should use it.

12. Children with weak attention control plus impeded written output may actually improve in the quality and quantity of their writing when they are given stimulant medication (page 264).

The Management of Impeded Written Output in School

Writing is hard to hide and, therefore, children who have difficulty with it often feel exceedingly vulnerable in school. They may be ashamed of the legibility or content of their writing. They notice their peers transcribing far faster and with greater efficiency than they seem capable of. If their writing appears terrible, then somehow the outside world may think they have a terrible mind. In addition, they may be accused of laziness and a poor attitude for problems that are largely out of their control. For these reasons, writing difficulties need to be managed with great sensitivity and caring. The following management suggestions may foster progress in writing while helping a student avoid public humiliation in school.

1. At least for a time, teachers may need to make accommodations for these students. These may include allowing more time for written responses on tests (perhaps permitting the student to answer the last few questions at lunch, after school, or at home), reducing the volume expected (i.e., accepting a shorter report), and prioritizing what should be completed. For example, a child might be told not to worry about spelling for a particular assignment. Often students who endure a memory overload during writing need to be allowed to forgo (i.e., not be evaluated on) one or more of the components of writing. In fact, different assignments can stress different aspects of writing.

2. In some cases it is justified to bypass writing entirely by allowing recorded or oral reports and multiple-choice or true-false testing formats or by permitting a student to submit a project instead of a written report. Such circumvention is called for when a student feels highly despondent about writing. A teacher needs to know a child's individual strengths and affinities and then identify some channel of output through which the student can convey ideas and feel a sense of accomplishment and mastery.

3. As noted, most students with writing problems gain from doing work in stages. This is especially valuable for those students with dysfunctions of memory, language, and/or ideation. In such cases, whatever aspect of writing is difficult for them can be a single stage on which they concentrate. In this way, nothing else will compete for mental effort with their weak area of function during writing. Teachers need to help children think of writing as a relatively long-term activity in which there are multiple stages of production. In no subject area should students have to do all of their writing under rapid "emergency" conditions; a good portion of written output should be in the form of long-term refined product development. The Story and Report Developers (see Appendixes) can be used to portray writing as a long-term activity.

4. It is important that long-term writing activities allow for good spacing between stages. For example, it is very hard for a student (as well as an adult) to proofread something very soon after writing it, while it is relatively interesting and even satisfying to proofread something

several days or a week later. Students should avoid doing everything at the last minute and can use their Report or Story Developer forms to document how they have staged their written output. Teachers need to evaluate and give positive support and encouragement to students at each stage.

5. Long-term writing assignments for children with impeded written output offer a good opportunity for collaboration between parents and teachers. Parents can monitor the completion of specific work stages.

6. Teachers should not insist that all students use cursive writing. Teachers should present cursive writing as an easy way to write for many people, but make it clear that it is not mandatory. A child with writing problems needs to try to learn it and then to decide how well it works. Children with motor memory limitations frequently prefer manuscript (printing) in contrast to students with fine motor production deficits and weak feedback (page 187) who often prefer cursive.

7. Teachers need to be conscious of how embarrassing messy or otherwise inadequate written work can be for these students. They should avoid having it corrected by their peers or putting it on display. In addition, they should never punish children with impeded written output by making them write sentences.

8. Whenever the equipment is available in school, these children should be exposed early on to using a computer. Teachers and parents need to coordinate their methods and software.

9. Children with note-taking and/or copying deficits require more time on these tasks. Teachers may provide them with duplicate materials even as they encourage them to continue practicing these activities in class. Teachers can ask students with weak note-taking skills to transcribe the most important points in abbreviated forms and then check their work. Children with copying deficits need help with the chunk size of the material they are trying to copy. They should whisper an entire sentence to themselves and then copy it. If they are copying nonverbal material (such as a design or diagram), they should try to visualize one small section at a time and then just copy that portion. They should gradually increase the size of the visual chunk they will try to hold in short-term memory during copying.

10. Children whose graphomotor dysfunction is severe enough may benefit from the services of an occupational therapist in school. Those whose writing is constrained by weak language production

(page 122) may require consultation with and possible treatment from a speech and language pathologist. Parents and school personnel should collaborate in determining the need for such services and deciding where and how they should be provided.

11. For children who need to make a conscious effort to write faster, teachers can assure them that it is all right to sacrifice some legibility in the interest of acquiring speed and ease of production.

12. Teachers should help students to understand the many benefits of writing—it is an important way of getting different parts of the brain to work together as well as an important way to think and to organize and communicate ideas.

13. All students, no matter how severe their writing difficulties, need to see their progress as reflected in a cumulative portfolio (ideally over years). Teachers should help them make and maintain such a record. There should be an emphasis on the pursuit of writing topics that genuinely interest the student. In this way, a student's writing accomplishments document his or her development as a focused thinker.

14. Teachers can encourage cooperative writing projects in the classroom. One student may be a researcher, another primarily a proofreader and reviser, another a brainstormer, and another an illustrator. Students should sometimes be grouped according to the parts of writing in which they are likely to excel. This will be good for their self-esteem. However, on occasion, children can be assigned to areas in which they are weak and need practice.

15. Children with impeded written output need practice with writing revision. Often this is best accomplished by providing them with text that they have not themselves written and having them make corrections of grammar, punctuation, and spelling. They can also use such text materials to improve the quality of written expression or to shorten or elaborate on the ideas presented. In doing so, students can pretend that they are editors of a magazine.

16. Metacognitive insight can be especially important for students with impeded written output. Teachers can help them understand what the writing process entails in terms of brain functions. They can learn, specifically, what kinds of memory, language ability, motor skills, and organization they will have to mobilize and integrate during a writing assignment.

DONNA

Donna is a nine-year-old girl who enjoys school very much and is very popular with her peers. She is good at reading and shows strengths in writing as well. Mathematics, on the other hand, is a serious problem. Donna has had great difficulty understanding arithmetic concepts. She was slow to develop counting skills as well as notions of place value. She appears utterly confused when her teacher explains simple multiplication to the class. Donna has tried to learn the procedures needed for problem solving in math class, but somehow such processes fail to make sense to her. Her parents and teacher have observed that Donna becomes exceedingly anxious when trying to solve arithmetic problems. Her anxiety itself is interfering with her performance in this subject area.

UNDERDEVELOPED MATHEMATICAL ABILITY

The learning of mathematics imposes its share of heavy cognitive burdens on the developing nervous system of a child. At the same time, the subject occupies a truly unique niche in a child's educational experience. Some of its intrinsic characteristics and the responses they elicit in students are summarized below.

- Mathematics is highly cumulative. The mastery of what has gone before is crucial for subsequent learning.
- Mathematics requires the integration of multiple developmental functions.
- Responses in mathematics usually need to be highly convergent, i.e., there is usually only one possible correct answer.
- The subject matter requires constant movement back and forth from very symbolic representations (numbers, operational signs, unknowns) to practical applications and implications.
- The learning of mathematics may be emotionally charged. Math anxiety and even phobia are common concomitants or complications of mathematics learning difficulty.
- It has been shown that many students believe that how you do in mathematics indicates how smart you are. Consequently,

performance in mathematics may have a significant impact on self-esteem. Ironically, some students may be afraid to excel in mathematics and thus be labeled a "nerd." Mathematical intelligence in certain settings is socially stigmatizing.

- Much of the content of mathematics may seem abstract and irrelevant to many students. In middle schools, for example, it is common to hear the lament, "Why do we have to learn this? I'm never gonna use it." Students may not have role models at home who make frequent use of mathematical processes.
- Mathematics is a subject that children tend to associate exclusively with school.
- Of all academic pursuits, none requires more accuracy and attention to fine detail. In this respect, it places great stress upon the attention controls (chapter 2).

Mathematics: A Task Analysis

Mathematical abilities demand that a series of functions be well developed in a child. The important components of skilled work in this subject area are described below.

Effective memory functions—the ability to recall what is needed to solve a problem. Mathematics entails the memorization and convergent recall of facts and procedures. Active working memory, pattern recognition memory, and short-term memory for visual and verbal material are all essential. As students advance in their studies, many functions need to become automatic so that their minds can concentrate on problem-solving strategies.

Accurate visual processing—the capacity to perceive, recall, and manipulate visually represented material. This ability is critical in geometry as well as for forming nonverbal concepts, such as fraction, ratio, or volume, and for grasping various aspects of measurement and estimation.

Conceptualization—the clear understanding of mathematical ideas, including number concepts, place value, and other such cognitive bases for mathematical operations.

Language ability—the use of language in a mathematical context. Verbal skills are critical in mathematics because they enable students to master difficult technical vocabulary, comprehend the content of mathematics textbooks, decipher word problems, and process the teacher's spoken explanations and instructions.

Problem-solving skills—the use of systematic approaches to finding answers. Such practices are essential for dealing with word problems, for formulating geometric proofs, and for undertaking a range of mathematical puzzles, while they are also vital in most other nonrote computational activities.

Mathematical comfort and affinity—a belief that mathematical learning is nonthreatening and at least potentially gratifying.
    A task analysis of mathematical learning is illustrated in figure 6.10.

Forms of Underdeveloped Mathematical Ability

Some students have a true affinity for mathematics. They are able to integrate deftly the multiple functions needed to learn and apply the subject matter, and they derive tremendous satisfaction from their skill. Regrettably, however, there are others for whom arithmetic learning is a chronic anathema. Some of them experience mathematical difficulty as part of a cluster of observable phenomena, while others have learning problems that are strictly limited to the domain of mathematics.
    Specific forms of mathematical learning difficulty can affect stu-

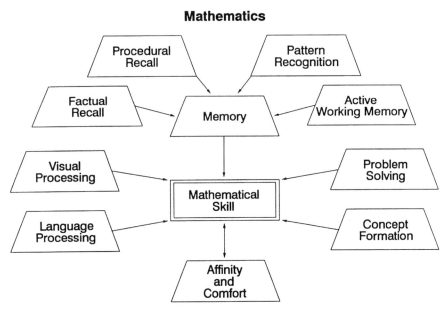

Fig. 6.10. This diagram shows a task analysis of mathematics.

dents. This is not surprising, since so many brain functions are needed for mathematical processes. The following are some of the common forms:

Memory-based deficits. Children with underdeveloped mathematical abilities may show one or more of the following phenomena related to memory.

Trouble registering facts in short-term memory—This phenomenon often appears when students are learning mathematical facts. This limitation can also slow up the copying of math problems from the board (page 188).

Trouble registering procedures and sequences in short-term memory—This causes students to have trouble with the initial mastery of multistep processes (such as division).

Insufficient active working memory—Students who chronically lose track in the middle of problems illustrate this phenomenon (e.g., a student carrying a number during long division who forgets what she or he intended to do after carrying the number).

Poor cumulative recall—These students may experience difficulty remembering in the spring what was learned in the fall. Their math grades may predictably decline during the last marking period each year.

Delayed automatization of facts and/or procedures—This weakness stands in the way of rapid and effortless recall during problem solving. Students may work so hard to recall facts that they have little energy to carry on reasoning at the same time. It is common for students to have problems only with the automatic recall of facts or only with the recall of procedures; some exhibit both weaknesses.

Weak pattern recognition—This deficiency makes it hard for students to discern a previously encountered form of problem and know (i.e., recognize) that they have seen it before, so that they can make use of previously acquired mathematical experience in tackling the new challenge.

Incomplete conceptualization. Children who fail to master fundamental concepts in mathematics usually depend completely on rote memory, using what has been called an extreme algorithmic approach. This pattern is seen in Donna, the girl described at the beginning of this section. Students like her may know how to do things, but do not understand why they are doing them. The result is a superficial grasp of mathematics which makes these students increasingly vulnerable to failure in the upper grades as the subject matter demands more understanding, while there is less opportunity to simply imitate procedures.

Weak language processing. There are students who struggle specifically with the semantics and syntax of mathematics and with word problems. They may prefer to learn by studying correctly solved problems rather than listening to a teacher explaining a process or concept.

Problematic problem solving. Children experiencing difficulty in mathematics may exhibit a random unsystematic approach in their work—using little if any planning, reviewing of possible strategies, or self-monitoring. They often lack an appreciation of the need for a stepwise approach to problem solving (page 150). Much of their mathematical work is, therefore, performed the hard way.

Slow data processing. For some students work in mathematics consumes far too much time. They cannot keep up with demonstrations and explanations and often fail to finish mathematics tests on time. Naturally, this makes them anxious and discouraged as they compare themselves to peers functioning at a far more rapid pace.

Deficient reasoning. There are children who become confused in the face of certain forms of reasoning in mathematics. Proportional thinking (needed to understand fractions and percentages) is especially critical and may be lacking in some students. Others struggle with analogical reasoning (e.g., x is to y as a is to . . . . .). Such confusion substantially interferes with problem solving in a mathematics class.

Poor symbolic understanding. Some students have chronic difficulty with the symbolism that pervades mathematics. Initially, they are likely to be baffled by operational signs. Ultimately, they are slow to comprehend algebraic representations (such as unknowns in equations).

Limited appreciation and application of rules. Children may reveal significant weaknesses in knowing how and when to make use of mathematical rules, for example, knowing what to do while solving a problem or having trouble comprehending and applying formal rules (such as those involved in balancing an equation).

Math anxiety and negative attributions. Many frustrated mathematical learners (or nonlearners) feel tense because of the highly convergent demands intrinsic to mathematics. Such anxiety is evident in Donna as well as in many others who are struggling to succeed in this subject. Some students feel intimidated, for no discernible reason, by mathematics teachers. Others believe that they are simply not smart enough to become competent in mathematics. This makes them feel that effort will do no good.

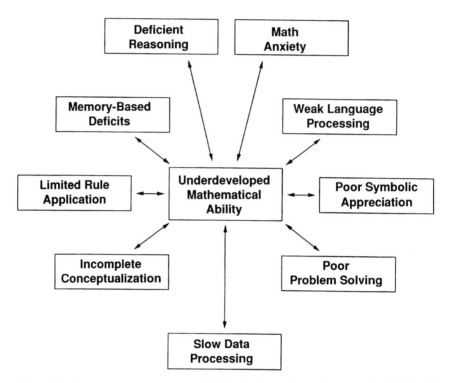

Fig. 6.11. Some common sources of difficulty in mathematics are depicted in this diagram.

Figure 6.11 identifies several reasons for students' difficulties in mathematics.

Managing Underdeveloped Mathematical Ability at Home

Parents can play a role in helping children approach mathematics assignments and studying for tests by stressing an organized approach. Even when a parent does not completely understand the arithmetic processes, she or he can try to learn with the child and can serve a useful role in facilitating self-testing and practice.

1. Because mathematics is such an emotionally charged area and children may be deeply embarrassed about the trouble they are experiencing, assistance must be offered sensitively. Parents should not hover over a child doing math. They should help him or her get started and be available to consult, to quiz the child (if requested to do so), and to assist in checking over work. The parent should not ever be critical or accusa-

tory while helping with mathematics. There should be an emphasis on praise, encouragement, and positive reinforcement for hard work.

2. Some parents feel very uncomfortable helping a child in this domain because they lack confidence in their own mathematical understanding. In such cases, they may need to arrange for a tutor to help their child. This individual may have experience as a math tutor or may even be a peer or a successful older student.

3. Parents should help children see the practical applications of what they are learning in school by trying to incorporate mathematical operations into activities children do for their own interest and as part of the family. Examples of the former could include keeping sports statistics, quantifying performance on video games, and calculating various mathematical dimensions for art or craft projects. Examples of the latter include giving a child responsibility for budgeting a family excursion or, during a car trip, having her maintain a log of miles covered, times and distances between stops, gasoline consumption per unit distance traveled, and the number of times per hour her brother had to be reprimanded.

4. Certain aspects of mathematics require rote memory. Parents can organize games that drill a child on mathematical facts until they become automatic. They may want to offer prizes for success and document progress on a wall chart.

5. If the family has a computer, parents should look for software that will enhance mathematical learning. High motivational mathematical games may bolster interest while helping a child improve skills.

6. As a parent comes to understand a child's specific reason(s) for mathematical difficulty, remedial steps can be individualized for that child. For example, a child with a language problem may need extra practice slowing down and interpreting word problems and technical vocabulary. A boy or girl with weak cumulative memory may benefit from review exercises covering material from several months ago. A child with poor concept formation needs opportunities to map the key concepts (page 100) and to talk about them or to try to teach them to a younger child.

7. Parents can collaborate with the teacher in modeling and reinforcing good problem-solving skills. The Problem-Solving Planner (see Appendix 1) can be used for this purpose. Children can practice using

the Planner to solve word problems. In doing so, they should be encouraged to verbalize the steps as they proceed.

8. Children should be encouraged to talk about what they have learned in mathematics. They should make believe they are teaching their parents about the concepts. Alternatively, if there are younger children in the family, they can try teaching them about mathematics.

Managing Underdeveloped Mathematical Ability in School

Schools can do much to prevent children from developing serious math phobias and becoming so far delayed that they feel justifiably overwhelmed amid the universe of numbers and manipulations. Teachers can make the subject as nonthreatening as possible for students who are struggling.

1. Children must not be permitted to fall too far behind in mathematics. Early intervention is more critical here than in any other skill area, since catching up can be so difficult and the anxiety caused by repeated failure so incapacitating.

2. Like parents, teachers can intervene at the level of a child's specific dysfunction and individualize instruction. Tasks should be designed so that a child's breakdown point becomes a solution or conclusion to a problem. In table 6.2 are examples of how to carry out this important form of intervention As children undertake one or more of the tasks described in table 6.2, they need to understand completely what that task is trying to accomplish. As part of this understanding, they must gain insight into the specific reasons why mathematics is hard for them. Thus, intervening at the point where a child's skills breakdown must be combined with clear demystification.

3. It is important to be flexible with these children and to allow them to use bypass strategies (page 261) so that their academic progress is not halted even though the dysfunction persists. For example, children with memory problems should be allowed to use calculators while taking math tests. They should, of course, continue to drill on facts at home. Students with slow processing as well as those with memory difficulty need to be given more time on tests (or allowed to take tests untimed).

4. Teachers should model good stepwise problem-solving skills for these children by articulating the specific steps in solving word problems. The children should then be able to restate these steps in their own words and identify the individual steps while actually solving problems.

Table 6.2: Tasks to Strengthen Mathematical Breakdown Points

BREAKDOWN POINT	DESCRIPTION OF TASKS
Understanding the language of a word problem	Activities that involve elaborating on and talking about computations and word problems; also, creating word problems for different processes
Recalling math facts and/or processes	Games that use timed drill on facts; also the use of educational software to achieve automatic recall
Attention to detail	Assignments rewarding a student for detecting careless errors in other people's work or their own
Systematic problem solving	Procedures in which a child is required to demonstrate and/or articulate a stepwise approach to solving a problem while working on that problem (e.g., while using the Problem-Solving Planner)
Mastering technical vocabulary	Lists of critical vocabulary words with definitions and examples that are compiled by the student as part of a personal mathematical dictionary
Understanding concepts	Paragraph descriptions or maps of the concepts with examples of their practical uses
Holding the parts or steps of a problem in memory while working on it	Approaches that stress writing down all steps and calculations and checking off each stage or step after completing it
Recognizing patterns in word problems or visual material	Tasks that involve studying a word problem, identifying the process needed, and then circling the key words that provided the clues; finding geometric parameters (radii) or shapes (trapezoids) within complex designs

Like parents, teachers can make use of the Problem-Solving Planner contained in Appendix 1 to help children develop these skills.

5. There needs to be considerable flexibility in the mathematics curriculum and in course selection. Not every student needs to be proficient at algebra. On the other hand, the problem-solving skills and symbolic representations of algebra and geometry can be of value to all students. Some students may need to acquire these skills through practical experiences (e.g., while repairing engines or programming a computer), while others will need to pursue the traditional algebra or geometry curriculum at a slower rate and with less threatening appraisal of performance than is applied to their peers.

6. It is important to consider the best ways of presenting information to specific students. Some are better at visualizing than they are at processing verbal instructions or assimilating long sequences of information. These students are likely to benefit from studying correctly solved problems (demonstration models) and diagrams rather than trying to follow prolonged verbal explanations. In the early grades, many students are helped through concrete manipulatives which provide proprio-kinesthetic input as well as visual confirmation of concepts and processes.

7. When children are very anxious about mathematics, it is inappropriate to call on them for rapid answers during class. They can be warned the day before that they will be asked to put a particular problem on the board.

8. Children should be discouraged from learning how to do things in mathematics without really understanding what they're doing. At every stage of skill acquisition, children should be asked to put into words what they have learned or to demonstrate through analogies, practical applications, and drawings or diagrams that they truly understand what they are doing. It is unfortunately possible for children to succeed at converting fractions into decimals without knowing what they are doing or why.

9. After a mathematics quiz or test, students should be required to go back over their incorrect answers to determine what went wrong. They should be given credit for good diagnoses.

10. A school should address any significant underlying neurodevelopmental dysfunctions that deter a child's mathematical learning. Help with language, treatment for an attention deficit, or strategies to

improve memory function may be needed before any progress in mathematics can be expected.

The Demystification of Delayed Skill Acquisition

Children with delayed skills need to be aware that there are possibilities for catching up. They should be encouraged to accept help and to realize that everybody sooner or later needs assistance with things they don't do well. They should be helped to see that many highly successful adults had serious problems with reading, math, or writing when they were students and that many grown-ups still can't spell very well.

The following suggestions are targeted at helping students develop a keener awareness of the reasons for their skill delays while feeling hopeful about the prospects for steady improvement.

1. These children need help to understand what aspect of a particular skill is lagging (e.g., automatic decoding for reading, punctuation and capitalization during writing, recall of procedures in mathematics). They should learn the vocabulary for their problem.

2. It is important to try to relate the skill delay to any observable phenomena (e.g., weak language production or poor problem solving) that are impeding a specific skill acquisition. Children need this vocabulary to be able to talk about and work on specific dysfunction(s). Sometimes students can gain insight by being helped to think about the part of a task that is causing problems for them. With guidance from an adult, they can come to understand and describe their problem with some precision. The On-Line Reading Review (Appendix 6) can be used for this purpose. The Mathematics Interview and the Writing Interview (see Appendixes 2 and 3) are also suitable for helping with the demystification process.

3. It is good to discuss how the child's strengths and interests can be used to try to speed up learning the skill. It is advisable to speak of problems learning a skill as taking too long to get there rather than being a fixed unalterable weakness.

4. If a child has more than one delayed skill, there should be some prioritization. If there are problems with spelling and math, the child should be told that the spelling problem isn't as important, and that a lot of effort needs to go toward learning more mathematics. When there are delays in both reading and mathematics, the student should be involved in discussions of how much time to devote to each.

5. Children should understand that having a delayed skill does not necessarily have to affect their careers when they grow up. In fact, many students with serious writing, reading, and math problems go to college and do well.

6. Every effort needs to be made to help these children feel less ashamed of their problems and more willing to discuss them openly with an adult.

Up until this point we have focused exclusively on school as a formal academic experience. Yet, there is more to school. The child's school day is replete with behavioral and social challenges. She or he must learn to adapt to a wide range of behavioral limits, controls, and expectations and, at the same time, maintain self-esteem and positive feelings. Such adaptation represents indispensable preparation for adult life. In the next chapter, we will look at a group of observable phenomena associated with poor adaptation to life at school.

CHAPTER SEVEN

Phenomena Related to
Poor Adaptation

A DAY at school can be gratifying or highly stressful; frequently, both conditions prevail. As children progress through school, they come to associate the experience not just with learning but also with performing and being judged. In the early grades students are apt to perceive their teachers as highly nurturant, in a sense, as substitute or auxiliary parents. But by secondary school they are conscious of their teachers as important figures who evaluate and make critical, objective determinations about them. In addition, social pressures intensify over the school years. Students come to sense increasingly that they are being evaluated by their classmates with whom they would like to be popular and with whom they are always competing. Harsh judgmental processes occur in settings where there is perpetual exposure, and the ever-present shadowy threat of embarrassment.

Many students adapt very well to school, having enough positive experiences to feel good about themselves and their school work. For others, however, school is threatening. They are likely to feel unsure of themselves and somehow inadequate compared to peers. Very often these are students who endure the neurodevelopmental dysfunctions that we have described throughout this book.

Students who have trouble adapting to school reveal an array of observable phenomena associated with their poor adjustment. In this chapter, we will examine five such phenomena and the forms they take: school-related sadness, bodily preoccupations, noncompliant behaviors, social inability, and loss of motivation.

DAVID

David is a ten-year-old boy who has chronic academic difficulty. He has shown some delays in virtually all skill areas. Over the years David has exhibited problems with attention, with memory, and with language function. There are signs that he is becoming increasingly discouraged at this point. He makes many self-deprecatory comments, such as "I'm a total and complete dummy in school." David's parents are concerned because he appears sad much of the time. His self-esteem is declining rapidly. Once he even suggested that he would rather kill himself than keep going to school. As a result of this comment, David began receiving help from a psychologist who has been trying to restore his self-esteem and diminish his high level of anxiety.

SCHOOL-RELATED SADNESS

Long-standing unhappiness in school can be part of a cyclical process. A child having trouble in one or more aspects of school life may become saddened and anxious. This phenomenon is certainly manifest in David's case. These feelings may make it hard to concentrate or to exert effort in school which, in turn, results in further failure and more negative evaluations leading to heightened levels of anxiety. Such cycles can be hard to break. Their optimal management depends, in part, on a good understanding of the sources and nature of a child's feelings of sadness.

Forms of Anxiety

Several different forms of anxiety are commonly encountered in school children. By sharing their observations, parents and teachers can determine the extent and nature of a student's anxious tendencies. The following are the most common patterns.

Targeted anxiety. In this form, a child's sadness and apprehension relate to a well-defined fear. A boy or girl may worry about embarrassment in physical education class, trouble with a peer, or difficulty relating to a specific teacher. Likewise a student may feel especially anxious about a particular content area in school; math anxiety is a common example. Targeted anxieties are not unusual. In fact, they represent universal experiences. However, they are problematic when they are long-standing, when they incapacitate or seriously compromise performance, when they become more generalized (see below), or when they evolve into phobias (e.g., school phobia, discussed below).

Test-taking anxiety. Some students experience exceedingly high levels of anxiety when they are tested. This may be because of poor test performance in the past or because of difficulty when working under timed conditions or when expected to use their minds in a highly convergent way.

Anticipatory anxiety. Children with this type of anxiety have an exaggerated fear of the future. They are very aware of how things may go wrong in their lives and tend to fear the worst. In their early school years they perpetually ask questions regarding the future ("When's lunch?" "When are we going out?" "When will we be coming in?"). Such students may evolve into chronic worriers, fearing the possibility of war, illness, loss of natural resources, and other potential threats to well being.

Generalized anxiety. Some students are pervasively anxious; their anxiety has no specific boundaries. In some instances this has been true since the child's earliest years. Sometimes other family members share this trait. Generalized anxiety may easily evolve into depression (see below).

School phobia. An overwhelming fear of school overtakes some children. It is common for them to refuse to go. The precise causes of school phobia are unknown, but it is likely that there are varying reasons for this behavior. In a few instances, the child eventually is able to pinpoint a source of anxiety that she or he is avoiding in school. In most cases, however, it is not that simple. The fear may represent a form of separation anxiety from parents or else an irrational concern that something bad may happen at home while the child is away. In most cases, however, the anxiety is diffuse, highly internalized, and undefinable. Milder forms of school phobia are encountered in children who are willing to attend school but who show bodily preoccupations, such as headaches and recurring abdominal pains, and make frequent visits to the health room or are absent excessively due to minor medical complaints.

Depression and bipolar illness (manic-depression). When a child feels very low much of the time, depression should be suspected. Children who are depressed feel extremely sad. They may show altered sleep patterns, lose interest in things they once enjoyed, allude to possible suicidal thoughts, and sometimes seem agitated. They are apt to make frequent negative comments about themselves. Those who have bipolar tendencies (sometimes called *cyclothymia* in its milder forms) may alternate between periods of despondency and phases during which they feel grandiose and too euphoric. In many cases, bipolar illness and depression run in families.

Obsessive-compulsive behavior. While obsessive-compulsive patterns are not necessarily associated with anxiety, they often are. Affected children reveal various ritualistic behaviors (such as excessive hand washing). In less dramatic cases, obsessive-compulsive tendencies are manifest in extreme perfectionism. A child may work extremely slowly in order to ensure positively that the work is flawless or that student may become anxious during the school day if his or her understanding of all new material is not absolutely perfect and complete. Obsessive-compulsive behaviors are sometimes part of the picture in children with Tourette Syndrome.

Managing School-Related Sadness at Home

Excessively anxious children need sensitive care and understanding from their parents. It is, of course, well beyond the scope of this book to present the many facets of anxiety and their specific treatments, but the following suggestions may prove helpful.

1. Parents need to make every effort to identify the sources of a child's anxiety. When the fears are specific, parents should eliminate, modify, and in whatever ways possible reassure the child about the perceived threat(s).

2. Aggravating factors that worsen the anxiety need to be reduced. For example, if a child's anxiety is intensified by sibling conflict, parents should educate the sibling(s) about the child's extreme anxiety and control verbal abuse and physical aggression when they exist.

3. Children with extreme anticipatory anxiety often benefit from keeping a diary in which they record each night their current worries. At regular intervals and with the help of an adult, they should review the concerns from the prior month. Such retrospective analyses can help the child to realize that most of the time these earlier concerns actually turned out well. This kind of desensitization may help alleviate patterns of anxiety.

4. Parents need to create a safe and confidential atmosphere in which children can discuss their anxieties. They should try to listen

and sympathize rather than to lecture and sermonize. Further, it is important to avoid being too cavalier or dismissive of the child's fears. Comments like "That's nothing," "Just ignore those kids," and "Don't worry about it" are not helpful and imply to the child that parents don't understand.

5. Parents should work closely with teachers to help children whose anxiety is entirely school-related. School-phobic students need to get to school—even for a short time. In many cases, however, professional help from a mental health professional is also necessary.

6. Children who are chronically anxious or who exhibit the signs of depression (discussed above) should receive professional diagnostic evaluation, preferably by a multidisciplinary team of professionals (page 245). If a child speaks of suicide (even casually), parents should arrange a prompt and complete evaluation by a child psychiatrist or psychologist. Likewise, children with obsessive-compulsive disorder require careful professional assessment and intervention.

7. Students who show excessive test-taking anxiety sometimes can be helped if parents give practice tests at home. Also, these students should be reassured that if they study hard, their parents will be pleased regardless of the test results. Such children often need reminding that a single test score in the long run of one's education is just plain trivial. Teachers can reinforce this idea.

8. When children are anxious, in part, because their parents are anxious, the child is unlikely to improve until the parents and perhaps the whole family learn to deal positively with their anxieties and problems.

9. Many children with mood problems appear to benefit from antianxiety medications. Some of these are listed in chapter 8.

Managing School-Related Sadness in School

Teachers need to be aware of anxious students and the educational care that they need. Often the manifestations of school-related sadness are most evident in the way a child appears and acts within a classroom.

1. Many anxious children improve dramatically when they feel school is a safe place. Teachers need to make classes as emotionally safe as possible. One way to do this is to avoid causing public embarrassment. Open criticism or ostracism in front of peers—for example, punishing a

child by having him or her sit out in the hallway to be viewed by all passersby—is never appropriate for these children.

2. Children who display anxiety in school may need direct help with their academic self-esteem. A teacher should look for roles or activities in which the student can display competency and feel needed. False praise should be carefully avoided. Children need to be praised for doing something well that most other children can't do. They often feel diminished when they are praised for doing something well that most others can do easily. Specific responsibilities, even errands, can give anxious students a greater sense of self-worth.

3. Students with test-taking anxiety may need some accommodation (see discussion of bypass strategies in chapter 8). In addition, teachers can talk with them about tests, explaining that life is full of tests, even outside of school. Therefore, it is important to learn not only how to be prepared for them but also how to avoid getting too nervous about them, that is, staying "cool." Teachers might also suggest that after completing a test or quiz the student rate his or her "test-taking coolness" according to some scale, such as, A=super cool; B=cool enough; C=partly cool; D=uptight; E=in a panic.

4. Teachers, like parents, should always be vigilant for students who show signs of depression (page 213) and should refer them to professionals.

5. When school-related anxiety is clearly targeted, teachers, specialists, and school administrators should try to intervene. Some common causes are fear of humiliation by one or more peers and fear of failure in one or more subjects or skills (such as physical education). When the source of anxiety is determined, it should be discussed directly and privately with the student. It is important to assess the level of anxiety. If it is great, some negotiating should take place to work through ways of diminishing the threat. It is inappropriate and even cruel to expect a child to solve his or her own problems or to face humiliation and just endure it. Remember, adults often take steps to avoid unpleasant or embarrassing situations. We should not expect children to endure experiences that no adult could tolerate!

6. Children who are anxious need to know that there is at least one person in school in whom they can confide their concerns. This person can be an advisor, a specialist, an administrator, or a teacher. As with parents, the school-based confidant should avoid moralistic preaching and be a good listener and a very willing advocate.

LETICIA

Leticia is a six-year-old girl who has missed a great deal of school this year. On many mornings she awakens with abdominal pain that is quite severe. Her mother keeps Leticia at home, and by afternoon the pain is frequently less severe. Leticia appears to be doing well in school despite her frequent absenteeism. Within the school setting, she is observed to be extremely shy, sometimes even withdrawn. She speaks softly and seems to want to be as inconspicuous as possible. Additionally, Leticia is a perfectionist. She works slowly and with great care when she is forming letters, drawing pictures, or completing other academic tasks. Because of her frequent abdominal pains, Leticia recently saw her pediatrician. She was found to have moderately severe constipation. Leticia admitted to the doctor that she did not like using the bathrooms in school.

BODILY PREOCCUPATIONS

For better or for worse, children take more than just their minds to school every day. Their bodies also have to meet the daily challenges. All students at all ages have somatic (i.e., bodily) concerns, but for some the concerns are extreme. Teachers and parents need to be especially sensitive to the somatic issues since often when these preoccupy a child, he or she may feel deeply ashamed and become highly secretive. Table 7.1 describes some of the common observable phenomena related to bodily preoccupations of school-age children and their specific effects.

Managing Bodily Preoccupations at Home and in School

The somatic preoccupations listed in the table can affect school performance and adjustment significantly. Since these varied conditions can have so many different sources and manifestations, we cannot offer specific suggestions for school and home management. Instead, the following generalizations pertain to most of the conditions delineated there.

1. Anxiety can promote these conditions and these conditions can promote anxiety! The suggestions offered in the previous section on the management of school-related sadness may need to be applied to help children with bodily preoccupations as well.

Table 7.1: Bodily Preoccupations—Some Examples

CONDITION	EFFECTS
Headaches	Intermittent pain on one or both sides of the head
Abdominal pain	Recurring discomfort often in a predictable time pattern (e.g., mornings, after meals)
Enuresis	Bedwetting or sometimes daytime wetting; child often very embarrassed, worried during school
Encopresis	Poor control over bowels; child is unaware of need to defecate, has "accidents"
Obesity	Child is overweight, often has poor self-image, may fear physical education classes
Menstrual discomfort	Student may experience serious cramping/ excessive bleeding
Acne vulgaris	Skin lesions may erode body image, cause great self-consciousness in school
Delayed or precocious puberty	Child may feel abnormally "developed" and fear public awareness and potential comments
Physical unattractiveness	Student may feel self-conscious and isolated, may have trouble making friends
Chronic illness (e.g., diabetes, asthma)	There may be a sense of bodily inadequacy and poor self-image
Appliance concerns	Child may feel "different" because of eyeglasses, hearing aid, braces, etc.
Eating disorders	Student may have unusual food intake as in anorexia nervosa; weight loss may be noted
Substance abuse	Excessive drug/alcohol use may take toll on attention and also create anxiety
Low threshold for feeling ill	Frequent absences; child often distracted by diffuse bodily discomforts

2. Parents and teachers should exercise care in the way they interpret a child's symptoms. It is often hard to know what caused a particular somatic condition. In fact we seldom find out with certainty. It is inappropriate, sometimes dangerous, to guess at or assume a cause. To say a child has abdominal pain because she is anxious might lead one to miss the fact that this anxious girl has colitis or an inability to digest milk products. Most chronic symptoms are worsened by anxiety and stress. That does not mean they were initially caused by psychological factors.

3. Somatic symptoms should be evaluated from both a medical and a psychological perspective. It should be emphasized that these are not mutually exclusive—a child's somatic status may be the culmination of both medical and emotional factors. This is most often the case. An affected child can benefit significantly from a treatment program that includes both medical intervention and some counseling or at least education about the problem.

4. Some children have predispositions to certain somatic conditions. Often they were born with these tendencies. Sometimes these tendencies represent bodily dysfunctions or normal variations rather than real abnormalities. Thus, a child may be born with the predisposition to have delayed puberty, obesity, or enuresis. Sometimes these tendencies run in families. Affected children may need reassurance about such patterns, so that they do not feel defective.

5. Children with bodily preoccupations may need special treatment. For example, students with bowel problems (constipation and encopresis) often have an enormous fear of school bathrooms because of their lack of privacy. This was true of Leticia described at the beginning of this section. Children like her avoid using the school bathrooms, become increasingly constipated, stretch out the muscles in their intestines and, in some cases, lose voluntary control over their bowels. Alternatively, they may develop severe abdominal pains (like Leticia). Permission to use a facility in the school that offers privacy and safety from peer comments could improve their situation. Another provision might be allowing children concerned over obesity or early or late sexual development to follow modified dressing requirements or procedures in physical education classes.

6. Teachers and parents need to be alert for students who are engaging in practices that endanger their health. Those with eating disorders and substance abuse need careful evaluation and counseling.

7. Students with somatic conditions may need help understanding the nature of their problem, learning how others have successfully dealt with it, and putting it in perspective. They should be encouraged to talk about their concern to a trusted adult.

8. Teachers and parents need to collaborate to assist children with excessive (and questionable) absenteeism. They should determine if there is a school phobia or a targeted anxiety underlying the absences. A physician may need to give the student strong reassurances that she or he is healthy.

NONCOMPLIANT BEHAVIORS

There are some students who seem to refuse to comply with the rules, the routines, and/or the work expectations imposed in school. In some cases, these students exhibit destructive and aggressive behaviors that harm or interfere with the rights of others. In others, they are strictly oppositional or defiant. That is, they may not be hurting anyone else, but they are refusing to meet expectations (e.g., failing to complete homework or being truant). Jonathan exhibits both of these patterns. Such children can be exceedingly frustrating to their teachers and parents as they become progressively "out of control." Table 7.2 summarizes some of the common forms of the observable phenomena associated with noncompliant behavior.

A child's noncompliance may resemble more than one of the forms listed. It is important and useful to identify the subtype(s) of noncompliance operating within an individual student. Often, in a sense, a child has a need to misbehave. To try to help regulate her or his behavior, adults must first understand that need.

A multitude of techniques have been described to help children with behavioral difficulties. These methods range from specific behavior modification techniques to programs of counseling to the use of certain medications. While it is not possible to be highly specific, some general guidelines can promote good collaborative management at home and in school.

Managing Noncompliant Behaviors at Home

A noncompliant child can create serious problems within a family. It is also true that serious problems in the family can foster noncompliance in a child! The successful management of difficult behavior depends very much on a realistic understanding of why the child exhibits a particular form of noncompliance.

JONATHAN

Jonathan is a fifteen-year-old boy who is frequently in trouble in school. He has been suspended twice during the last year. His infractions include smoking, the inappropriate use of profanity, and two episodes of stealing. Jonathan has also been truant on several occasions. He is a boy who has had a long history of academic frustration and failure. Currently, his reading skills are at grade level, but all of his other academic abilities are delayed. He is especially deficient in mathematics and in writing. Jonathan's parents feel they have lost all control over him. He stays out late and seems only to care about his friends. He loves skateboarding and music. He has a guitar which he likes to play, but he has refused to take lessons. Jonathan denies he is having any problems in school. He wants everyone to leave him alone. He seems to have no sense of the difficulty in life that rests ahead of him. He refuses to do any homework. He is likely to be retained in his current grade. In general, Jonathan reveals considerable resentment toward any form of authority.

---

1. Parents need to hold children accountable for their actions. An affected child should know that there will be consistent systems of reward and punishment based on his or her behavioral record. Both parents (when present) need to agree on these systems and implement them with complete consistency. This is critical for children with behavioral difficulties.

2. Sometimes using graphs or diagrams to document day-to-day behaviors can be helpful. Parents should emphasize scoring successful, or compliant, actions (e.g., points for completing homework, getting up in the morning without a struggle, having no outbursts for a whole day, etc.) and offer appropriate rewards when these tasks are accomplished consistently.

3. Parents need to avoid highly judgmental or moralistic terms, such as "bad" and "good," when discussing behavior with their children. Instead, descriptions like "in control" or "out of control" (e.g., of their impulsivity or insatiability) can provide more insight.

4. When parents (with help from an objective professional) understand the subtype of noncompliant behavior the child is showing, they

Table 7.2: Common Forms of Noncompliant Behavior

FORM	DESCRIPTION
Impulsive behaviors	Acting out without thinking, planning, or previewing the consequences, often associated with attentional dysfunction (chapter 2)
Insatiable behaviors	Difficulty getting satisfied, disruptive actions to provoke intensity, trouble with sharing and delaying gratification, extreme egocentricity, often associated with attentional dysfunction
Defensive patterns	Acting out or oppositional behavior to cover up feelings of inadequacy or to prevent criticism or ridicule, may take the form of aggression (a macho veneer) or of excessive "coolness"
Predatory actions	Premeditated destructive and/or aggressive behavior, often in a student who has serious personal/family/peer problems
Role-playing behaviors	Acting out behaviors as though following a role; repeating behaviors used for a long time; modeling negative behaviors to satisfy peer expectations
Poor coping manifestations	Aggressive outbursts in a child who can think of no better options for dealing with stress or conflict; this may be part of a broader picture of problematic problem solving and strategy use
Depressive acting out	Behavioral acting out in a student who also shows signs of depression
Temperamental difficulty	Actions that are part of a lifelong pattern of hard-to-manage behaviors (even evident in infancy)
Failure-avoidance tactics	Noncompliance in a student who is afraid to try because of a perceived strong likelihood of failure (see discussion of motivation, page 232)

should discuss this with him or her. Children can benefit from having the vocabulary to talk about behavioral issues. Thus, impulsive children need to be able to talk and think about their inability to preview and to control their impulses. Children with role-playing behaviors must understand their need for such patterns of behavior. Children with weak coping skills have to discuss and learn about ways people deal with stressful situations. Children with difficult temperaments need to recognize the effects their problem has and consider ways to work on changing their behavior. Some parents can conduct these kinds of discussions (in private) with a child, others may need the assistance of a counselor or therapist.

5. When serious domestic problems are stressing the child and eliciting or reinforcing the noncompliant behaviors, the family needs to get help resolving these difficulties.

6. Some children are defensive in their behaviors at home because they feel like a disappointment to their parents. They believe that because of their school difficulties they can never please a mother or father. They may react with anger, belligerence, or defiance. Alternatively, they may display aggression toward a higher achieving sibling. Most children sense that their parents do love them, but many (especially those with neurodevelopmental dysfunctions) truly wonder if their parents respect them, whether a mother or father might, for example, boast to friends or relatives about them. Parents need to find ways to show authentic admiration (in addition to love) on a regular basis.

7. Some children's noncompliant behaviors are treated with medication. For example, impulsivity and insatiability in certain individuals can be curbed by drug therapy. Although it sometimes can help (see chapter 8), a medicine is never the whole answer.

8. Even the most competent parent requires outside help when a child seems behaviorally out of control. A professional who can serve as an objective source of practical behavioral management advice is what is needed. This individual should also work closely with the school.

Managing Noncompliant Behaviors in School
Difficult behavior in school can represent an enormous challenge for teachers who have the responsibility to impart knowledge and skill to large numbers of students. At the same time, school has the potential to be a major source of humiliation and it can be the actual cause

of noncompliant behavior in such children, especially when school personnel have an incomplete understanding of their plight. Although it is very hard to provide optimal treatment for those who are non-compliant, by using understanding and flexibility, a teacher can see positive results and, at the very least, can avoid creating further damage to a child whose self-esteem is likely to be fragile.

1. The measures suggested to reduce anxiety in school (page 215) pertain as well to children with noncompliant behaviors.

2. Accountability for actions is as critical in school as it is at home. A child should have a clear idea of the inevitably of certain punishments or constraints that will follow noncompliant behaviors.

3. Teachers should continue to express praise and friendship for noncompliant children, so that they do not feel they are disliked.

4. Teachers are in an excellent position to help define the subtypes of a child's noncompliant behaviors. They can share their insights with the child, with the parents, and with any professionals who may be involved.

5. Once a subtype of noncompliant behavior has been identified, management should be based upon it. For example, if students are believed to act a certain way because they are embarrassed about their poor performance in math class, it is critical to protect them from further shame in that setting.

6. Whenever possible, "the punishment should fit the crime." A child who does not complete homework might be given additional work to complete during lunch or some other "leisure" interval.

7. All students can benefit from insight into why kids act as they do in school. Teachers should initiate discussions of defensive behaviors and peer modeling, in particular. By using case studies which the class can try to analyze, a teacher may provoke dialogue which can be particularly revealing to students with noncompliant behaviors.

SOCIAL INABILITY

Although it may seem hard to believe, children are born with certain innate social competencies, just as they are born with potential strengths or weaknesses in their language or motor functions. These innate capacities enable children to form good relationships, to maintain friendships, and to act in a way that appeals to peers. Siblings growing up within the same family and sharing many of the same experiences can

---

LUANN

Luann is an eight-year-old girl who does very well academically. However, her parents and teachers are concerned about her failure to make friends. Luann spends much of her time at school all alone. The other girls seem to avoid her. When she is with her peers, Luann has a tendency to be too aggressive with them. She is unable to share. She must be the first one in line. She boasts a great deal and is often inappropriate in her behavior on the playground. For example, when the other children are trying to play a sport, Luann will often interrupt them and try to do funny things or make strange sounds to entertain the others. No one finds this amusing, except Luann. She seems unable to detect the disapproval or even anger of other children. Luann often wonders why she has no friends. Her teachers this year and last year have commented on her apparent lack of effective "social skills."

---

differ dramatically in their social skills and in their abilities to form friendships and to gain acceptance by peers.

Within any school the children can be classified sociometrically. That is, they can be grouped according to their level of peer acceptance. The following list provides an example of this kind of classification:

- Popular children—those who are very well liked by most or all of the student body
- Amiable children—those who are pretty well liked but not very well known by most of the student body
- Neglected children—those who are ignored or go unnoticed by their peers for no apparent reason or because some of these students want to be neglected
- Controversial children—those who are popular with some students and rejected by other students
- Rejected children—those who are widely disliked, excluded, and possibly ostracized by a substantial part of the student body

In our discussion we will focus on the most vulnerable of these groups, students who are rejected and reveal a lack of social skill. Children with such social inability are likely to experience profound unhappiness in school. Their more popular peers may be verbally or physically abusive to them. These students may encounter overt and covert rejection throughout the school day. Some of them constantly endure the refrain, "Sorry, this seat is saved." Social setbacks occur most commonly outside of the classroom in such sites as the bus stop, within the school bus, in the lunch room, in the bathroom, in the corridors, and in the locker room. At these social "hot spots" children with poor social skills frequently suffer damaged feelings and, in the worst cases, even physical harm from bullying. Unfortunately, in many settings the more socially accepted students prey upon those with deficient social skills.

The symptoms of social inability can vary. In general, affected children are conspicuously unpopular. Many of them have trouble forming and maintaining friendships. They may spend a great deal of time alone or else with people of any age group except their own. For some reason, many of them can relate to younger children, older youngsters, or adults far better than they are able to interact with their own age peers. These children with weak social ability crave meaningful relationships but lack the skills needed to form and nurture them.

There has been considerable research into the very specific capacities that children (and adults too) need to become socially successful. Two of the references in the Suggested Readings (see Asher et al.) review this area of research. Students with weak social abilities have been found to differ from each other in their precise social skill deficits. Table 7.3 summarizes some of the common deficits that may occur in various patterns among children with social inability.

It should be clear from this table that all children and adults have experienced some or many of these social difficulties. But some individuals struggle with these inabilities daily. This is certainly the case with Luann whose social inabilities are described at the beginning of this section. Children like her acquire a poor reputation with their classmates which can stigmatize them for years. The result is often a deep erosion of self-esteem and sometimes pervasive anxiety about school.

Children with social inability can be divided into two groups, those who are aggressive and disruptive and those who are shy and withdrawn. The aggressive and disruptive children behave in a way that their peers find offensive. Often they have little or no idea of how their actions are creating social difficulties for them. The shy and withdrawn group show extreme passivity and sometimes anxiety in the presence of peers. They show little social initiative and spend much of their time in isolation.

Sometimes weak social ability occurs in association with other dysfunctions. For example, some children with weak language production (chapter 5) have difficulty with the use of language in social contexts, generally referred to as *verbal pragmatics*. These students are unable to regulate their choice of words, their tone of voice, and other verbal skills to fit in socially.

About one third of children with weak attention controls (chapter 2) show social inability. Often in these cases, impulsivity seems to thwart the prediction of social responses. Additionally, their weak self-monitoring makes it hard for them to realize when they are offending or losing the respect of a peer. The insatiability that affects many students with attentional dysfunction may interfere with skills at negotiating conflict and learning to share.

There are children with social inability and attentional dysfunction who fit a picture of autism. Such youngsters may have serious problems relating to others and communicating. They may seem to be in their own world much of the time and they may exhibit ritualistic mannerisms (such as periodic flapping of their arms). Milder forms of this pattern are known as Asperger Syndrome (sometimes also called high-functioning autism).

Other children have weak social abilities that are seriously complicated by additional factors beyond their control, such as poor gross motor skills (with consequent humiliation during athletic pursuits) and unusual physical appearance, such as obesity, unattractiveness, or short stature. There are also children with weak social abilities who show no evidence of neurodevelopmental or other problems beyond the social realm and who are competent students.

Some of the most popular students in a school may find that they can enhance their social and political status by leading the offense against peers with weak social abilities. Other students, seeking to gain admiration and acceptance by popular classmates, become willing collaborators, to the detriment of the rejected child. Schools need to intervene in such situations (see below).

It is important to stress that not every student wants to be popular. Nor should students conform to rigid social expectations from their peers. We need to admire those children (and adults) who are willing and able to be different. Individuality should be differentiated from weak social ability in that it does not entail a lack of social skill. Children with real social inability, on the other hand, simply lack the necessary skills.

Social inability may be a lifelong affliction. When these problems persist into adult life, they can interfere with job performance, marital stability, and even child rearing. Therefore, it is essential that teachers and parents try to help affected children to understand their dysfunction and to work on remedying it.

Table 7.3: Some Common Skill Deficits of Children with Social Inability

SKILL DEFICIT	DESCRIPTION	EXAMPLE
Weak greeting skills	Trouble initiating smoothly a social contact with a peer	Child interrupts two others while they are talking or playing
Poor social predicting	Trouble previewing peer reactions before acting/talking	Child on playground, for no reason, imitates a bird without anticipating negative impact on reputation
Inappropriate presentation	Trouble presenting self in a manner pleasing to peers	Child dresses in a manner others perceive as odd or inappropriate
Problematic conflict resolution	Trouble settling social disputes without aggression	Child starts a fight when peer takes his or her seat on bus
Reduced affective matching	Trouble matching moods with others	Child talks about an upcoming test while peers are joking
Social self-monitoring failure	Trouble knowing when in trouble socially	Child alienates friend, doesn't sense it
Low reciprocity	Trouble sharing and trouble supporting/ reinforcing others	Child keeps boasting about ability, never praises peer
Misguided timing/staging	Trouble knowing what to do when in a relationship	Child talks to strangers as if they are old friends

Poor verbalization of feelings	Trouble using language to communicate true feelings	Child sounds angry, hostile but is not
Inaccurate inference of feelings	Trouble perceiving others' feelings through their use of language	Child doesn't realize a friend is sad or in a bad mood
Failure of code switching	Trouble matching language style to current audience	Child sounds like an adult while with friends
Lingo dysfluency	Trouble using the parlance of peers credibly	Child uses word cool/in wrong contexts
Poorly regulated humor	Trouble using the right kind of humor at the right time, in the right place, and with the right people	Child keeps telling jokes and acting silly while teammates are trying to win soccer game
Inappropriate topic choice/maintenance	Trouble knowing what to talk about when and for how long	Child keeps talking about snakes, although no one looks interested
Weak requesting skill	Trouble knowing how to ask for something inoffensively	Child says "Give me that . . . ." in a gruff manner
Poor social memory	Trouble learning from previous social experience	Child repeats noises that offended peers in the past
Unregulated assertiveness	Trouble exercising optimal levels of control over group vs. personal will	Child tries to dominate others during a game; or child acts out just to please peer
Social discomfort	Trouble feeling relaxed while relating to peers	Child acts nervous, shy, inhibited at a party

Managing Social Inability at Home

Parents are often in a good position to detect interpersonal difficulties in their children as they observe them interacting during play and other informal activities. The following recommendations suggest ways to offer help:

1. If a child has weak social abilities, a parent should accompany that child and a friend to a specific activity (lunch, the mall, a sporting event) and then observe closely how the child relates to the peer. That night, as the child is lying in bed, the parent can review the event from a social standpoint: "Do you remember at lunch today how you grabbed Jim's French fry? Did you notice how angry he got?" Or: "You know, you talked a lot about how great you are at video games, but I was a little surprised that you never said anything to make Tom feel good." Or: "That was excellent the way you shared your ice cream sundae with Joan; she really liked that." Such regularly scheduled specific feedback and social coaching can be of tremendous benefit to a child who lacks sensitivity to these issues.

2. Parents need to think about the specific weak social skills of their children before abruptly placing them in group situations (e.g., a sports program) where they are likely to experience failure and embarrassment. It is better to proceed slowly and help the child form one or two good relationships before exposing him or her to the complexities and stresses of large competitive groups.

3. When a child does become enrolled in a group activity (e.g. scouting, summer camp, or dance), parents can alert the adult leader to the social problem. That adult should monitor the child's interactions closely to prevent him or her from being rejected.

4. Parents need to be highly supportive of children's individuality. If children with weak social abilities prefer solitary activities and somehow feel safer during such pursuits, a mother or father should avoid discouraging them. In fact, it is wise to praise children for being so good at "entertaining" themselves. Many of these children crave and need relief from the social tension they endure in school. Such relief can and should take place either alone, with older or younger people, or with pets. Children should not be made to feel guilty about such solitude.

5. A mother or father can play a valuable role in helping a child develop the products and strategies to become socially accepted. Some

examples of this might be picking out clothing, discussing issues of personal appearance (i.e., how to look "cool"), reviewing ways of resolving social conflict without fighting, and developing socially integrating abilities. An example of the latter might be learning to play the drums which could allow a child to become part of a musical group. Parents should be sensitive to issues of projected image when helping a child choose activities (e.g., perhaps a boy who keeps getting rejected by peers should not play the piccolo). Although responding to such stereotyped biases can be repugnant to parents, regrettably, they play a significant role in everyday peer interactions.

6. In many communities, there are now excellent social skill groups for children. They are led by a professional. Participating children learn about social abilities and share social experience. Parents may find out about these groups by inquiring at school or asking their pediatrician or family doctor. Such groups have been found to be very effective in helping children to understand their weak social abilities and to start working on them.

7. When social skill groups are unavailable, a child may benefit from individual counseling about social skills. It is important that the therapist in such cases be a professional who has a background in social development and social skill training.

8. Children whose weak social abilities are associated with other neurodevelopmental dysfunctions may gain socially when these other difficulties begin to improve. Thus, progress in language skill or attention control may enable these children to relate more effectively to their peers.

Managing Social Inability in School

Since many of the excruciating social stresses occur during the school day, teachers and school administrators have a major role to play in the management of social inability. Schools need to be especially sensitive to the inhumane suffering of children who are repeatedly rejected and humiliated by peers.

1. If a child is being victimized by peers, it may be necessary for a teacher or administrator to address the issue with the entire class. The child experiencing rejection should be present but not specifically identified. There should be discussion of the cruelty of rejection and bullying and of the cowardice of the perpetrators. It should be made clear that

true heroism rests in helping unpopular kids; anyone can hurt them! It should also be made clear that verbal or physical bullying is unacceptable, and disciplinary action may need to be taken to punish those who commit these acts.

2. All children can benefit from learning about social skills and social inability. Ultimately, all schools should teach this subject matter at several different grade levels either by inserting units on this topic within a health or other course or by integrating it with the subject matter of such content areas as English or social studies. For example, in reading a story children can analyze the social skills of the characters.

3. Teachers should try to elevate the social status of rejected children by offering them public praise, giving them leadership roles, and finding ways in which they can gain the respect of their peers.

4. Teachers need to avoid exposing these children to situations in which their peers will ridicule them. For example, a child with serious verbal pragmatic weaknesses should not be asked to make up a story and tell it to the class.

5. When schools have social skill training groups, teachers should encourage these students to participate.

6. It can be very helpful if a classroom teacher lets a student know that he or she is aware of the student's problems socially. The child should know that it is possible to talk with the teacher when the social stress is becoming unbearable.

MOTIVATIONAL LOSS

Motivation is innate in humans. When a child appears unmotivated for school, then something has interfered with this inborn or inherent drive. A loss of motivation is probably the most common complication of academic frustration. Children may lose motivation when they feel that academic effort is futile, that somehow success is unattainable, or that it would require extraordinary effort. One can detect this pattern in Craig's case. Ironically, such a lack of motivation almost ensures further failure and frustration. The following beliefs and predicaments are common, observable phenomena in these children:

- A belief that success is somehow "out of their hands," that forces beyond their control are determining results in school. Such students may feel that they are simply unlucky when it comes to school or too dumb to learn well. These negative attributions, or

---

CRAIG

School has been chronically frustrating for Craig. Now, at age nine, Craig appears to have given up. His poor reading and spelling are especially troubling to Craig. When he needs to read a story, an inordinate time is required. In fact, it takes him so long to read that he forgets what he is reading! As a result, Craig is reading less and less. He has told his father that he will never be able to read. On numerous occasions he has been embarrassed in class by having to read aloud in front of his peers. Craig is a very sensitive boy. Recently, Craig's teachers have noted that he seems to be working less than ever, that he doesn't really try to succeed at much of anything. He shows some clowning behavior in class. He recently told his mother that he was never going to be smart in school and that he didn't care anyway.

---

external loci of control, lead students to think that school attainment is beyond their control, so why try?

- A tendency to associate with peers who are likewise unmotivated toward school work. These friends can justify and/or reinforce a lack of motivation. Together they may find alternative (and sometimes troublesome) paths to satisfaction, such as abusing chemical substances, committing violent acts, and forming gangs.
- A chronic neglect of schoolwork and studying. As a result, they lose ground daily and feel increasingly overwhelmed and hopeless in school. Often they lose the capacity to work and fail to develop the habits and the momentum needed to accomplish school tasks efficiently and with consistency.
- A tendency toward denial and denigration. Students who have lost motivation may outwardly deny that there is any problem. They refuse to think about or show concern over the future, living instead in a world where plans for next weekend are as far ahead as one looks. They may also tend to denigrate or deny the importance of things they have trouble doing (e.g., "Who needs Spanish, anyway? I'm never gonna use it."). In Craig's case, there was evidence that he was trying not to care or show concern over his problems. Like Craig, beneath the surface, many of these children are pessimistic about their school performance.

- A pattern of poor relationships with teachers. Many children with lost motivation frustrate and even antagonize their teachers. The students frequently state, "I can only work well if I like my teacher." They may actually feel frightened and intimidated by their teachers who may symbolize their inability to achieve at the level of their classmates.
- A decline of self-esteem. Although they may appear not to care about school, unmotivated students feel profoundly inadequate and sad about themselves. They are traumatized by being a disappointment to their families and to themselves. This situation may become further complicated by extreme anxiety or actual depression (page 213).
- A life of conflict at home. Students with low levels of motivation often elicit anger from their parents which, in turn, triggers further alienation. The child is likely to feel hostile toward a mother or father who is extremely critical of the lack of motivation. In the worst cases, the child may try to punish the parents by committing acts in the community that will bring disgrace to the family.

Not all academic motivational loss is due to learning problems or overt academic frustration. Some children lose academic motivation because they are depressed or preoccupied with personal problems. Others may be nearly obsessively diverted into other interests from which they derive enormous gratification. These outside interests (or perhaps distractions) might include interpersonal and/or sexual relationships, athletic pursuits, or an irresistibly compelling avocational activity (e.g., computer games, horses, a part-time job, or cars). School work may be unable to compete with these more accessible forms of instant gratification.

Many cultural and environmental factors can influence motivation. Students may find it hard to devote themselves to academic endeavors if these are not valued and modeled at home. If a child never encounters a parent reading, writing, or discussing issues in the news, that child may never perceive the relevance of education. It is especially hard for such a student to work diligently when those she or he lives among (including older siblings, friends, and neighbors) seem to function without any academic orientation whatsoever. Then, too, the opposite scenario may also create this effect. A child who is part of an achievement-oriented, intellectually and academically vigorous family may endure so much implicit or explicit pressure to succeed in school that this causes him or her to lose motivation. This child may feel an inability ever to successfully fulfill the expectations of the family. The problem sometimes worsens when the child is competing with one or more high-achieving siblings.

Whatever the cause(s) of a motivational loss, the consequences can jeopardize the ultimate happiness and life adjustment of a developing child. Any effort aimed at helping a student succeed must include a plan for restoring lost motivation.

Managing Motivational Loss at Home

Parents need to be certain that they are not contributing to a child's motivational loss. There is much that can be done at home to bolster a child's incentives and will to strive.

1. As with many conditions, the optimal treatment of motivational loss is prevention. As children are growing up, it is important for them to sense strongly that their parents respect and value their abilities, intellectual and otherwise.

2. Parents must be sensitive to balancing criticism with praise. A child who comes to feel that it is impossible to please parents is likely to lose motivation.

3. Parents need to ensure that their children are not experiencing a condition called *chronic success deprivation*. They should provide opportunities for them to feel personal gratification and some sense of mastery. Successes of whatever kind contribute to children's beliefs in themselves. Table 7.4 summarizes various kinds of beliefs about personal success that are important for children's development. Children who have good feelings in none of these areas are desperately at risk. Adults need to confirm regularly for children these feelings of success by providing positive and honest feedback.

4. In a family where siblings are very successful at a particular activity, parents may want to find one or more separate and distinct pursuits for the child who is at risk for losing motivation. When siblings are especially adept at sports, the unmotivated child might be encouraged to learn to play a musical instrument (or to pursue some other activity that interests him or her). The activities and unique abilities of all the children should be explicitly valued.

5. Parents and children need to share in their understanding of motivational loss and discuss it in an objective nondefensive, nonaccusatory manner. When this is not possible, the family may benefit from professional counseling.

Table 7.4: Sources of Success Beliefs during Childhood

SOURCE	DESCRIPTION	EXAMPLE
Intellectual	A belief that one's mind works well	Good feelings about an ability to do math or to read and talk about complex issues
Motoric	A belief that one's body is effective	Good feelings about swimming skill, riding horses, or building models
Social	A belief that one is liked by others and can relate to them well	Good feelings about the care and respect received from friends
Creative	A belief that one is capable of originality	Good feelings about the cartoons one draws, stories one writes, gadgets one invents
Problem-solving	A belief that one is effective at figuring things out	Good feelings about being able to fix motors
Altruistic	A belief that one is helpful to others	Good feelings about visiting and helping elderly people one knows

6. Parents should limit activities that interfere with children using their minds for intellectual purposes, for example, hours spent playing video games, watching television, or talking on the telephone. Limitations need to be put into effect early in the life of a child because when they are imposed suddenly during adolescence, children are likely to be resentful and angry.

7. It is important for children to see their parents interested in continuing to learn. Ideally, there should be times set aside during which all family members are engaging in intellectual activity. At such times, they can help each other learn and perform intellectual work. During car

trips and at the dinner table, there can be discussions of topics that are being studied in school. This may help to bridge the intellectual gaps between home and school, thereby increasing the personal relevance of school for a child.

8. Sometimes children need to be given additional incentives to be motivated. Parents should reinforce effort and productivity rather than specific results on a report card. A child might be materially rewarded for not missing any assignments during the coming semester or for studying for each test for at least an hour. This is preferable to rewarding straight B's on a report card because the latter is too dependent on chance, and often children can attain good grades without developing effective study or work habits.

9. Sometimes parents find it helpful to enter into a contract with a child in order to increase motivation and compliance. An example of such a contract is shown in figure 7.1.

Managing Motivational Loss in School

Because schools are in a powerful position to influence motivation either positively or negatively, it is essential that teachers understand and try to sympathize with the reasons for a student's motivational loss.

1. Sometimes teachers assert: "He'll start succeeding as soon as he gets motivated." While this may be true, it is even more likely that: "He'll get motivated as soon as he starts succeeding"! Consequently, teachers need to program successful experiences for these students in whatever manner they can.

2. As we noted earlier, children with motivational loss are apt to be highly sensitive about their relationships with teachers. Therefore, teachers should try to communicate directly with these students to establish a positive relationship. A teacher may need to make it explicit that she or he does not dislike, disrespect, or "have it in for" a child. The teacher should show that she or he understands and feels compassion for the student's plight. Children with lost motivation should not be humiliated or criticized harshly in front of their classmates. Condescending or accusatory comments, such as "You could do better if you really wanted to," are out of place.

3. A teacher may need to discover methods for increasing a child's belief in his or her own success within the classroom. A good artist may be encouraged to create pictures or diagrams to help teach the rest of the class. A student may be given responsibility for taking attendance,

STUDENT CONTRACT

_____(student), agrees to the following goals and/or accomplishments and will try as hard as he/she can to do these things:

#	ACCOMPLISHMENTS OR GOALS
1.	
2.	
3.	
4.	

If_____ succeeds in meeting these goals and/or accomplishments, she/he will receive the following beneifts:

#	BENEFITS
1.	
2.	
3.	
4.	

This contract will start on_____ and continue until _____.

Agreed to and Signed By: **_Date Signed_**_____

_____   _____
(Student)   _(Parent or Parents)_

_____
(Teacher or Others if Needed)

Fig. 7.1. Often children with motivational problems can benefit from the use of a behavioral contract which is signed by them, their parents, and possibly their teachers. This relatively simple example can be used to encourage homework completion, the accomplishment of chores at home, or other behavioral goals. More detailed contracts exist that can be administered with the help of a mental health professional.

erasing the blackboards, planning a field trip, or keeping a record of birthdays. Even simple responsibilities such as these can enhance self-esteem and help to restore motivation.

4. Teachers should be aware of those students who are feeling justifiably overwhelmed in one or more subject areas because of their learning problems. They may need to reduce, prioritize, or stage demands for students, as described in management sections and in chapter 8 of this book. By making success more attainable in vulnerable areas, a teacher may be able to enhance motivation.

5. Teachers should be especially attuned to those students who have shown a recent and dramatic decline in motivation. Such children may actually be depressed or heavily burdened with personal problems. In some cases, substance abuse may manifest itself in a sudden loss of motivation. Teachers can alert appropriate people in school or in the community to explore what is happening and then to direct the child and family to the relevant therapy.

The Demystification of Poor Adaptation

Children with problems adapting to school need to understand why they act and feel the way they do. Knowing "how I got this way" can help a student find a more comfortable way of life in school. The following points can strengthen the demystification of such a student.

1. These children need to realize that many other children behave or feel the way they do in school. So many of these youngsters believe they are the only ones in the school with such a problem; they need to realize that they are far from unique.

2. After a thorough evaluation has been completed, adults need to sit down with these children to review why they act and feel the way they do. For example, it is important for a child with neurodevelopmental dysfunctions that are causing some learning problems to see how these relate to his or her trouble adapting to school. In a sense, the adults are helping to tell the stories of these children. It can be most therapeutic if the children join in to talk about why they think they behave or feel the way they do in school.

3. It is always relevant to discuss the role that other children are playing in a child's maladaptation. The need to impress peers, fear of public humiliation, and the desire for role models are all issues that are familiar even to very young children.

4. Noncompliant children should understand that a person can do bad things without being a bad person, that a kid might even have good reasons for acting bad! On the other hand, once the reasons are well understood, better solutions need to be found. Adults should review carefully and sympathetically with the child the presumed reasons for the noncompliant behaviors (page 220).

5. There are children with some form of maladapted behavior who may not respond very well or very promptly to demystification. They simply may not be ready to hear it and they may deny their difficulties. In such cases, demystification must become part of ongoing therapeutic counseling from a mental health professional.

Adaptive Strengths

While many children with school problems show evidence of maladaptation as described in this chapter, there are others whose adaptive capacities are truly admirable. Despite having significant learning problems, some children display a remarkable, even heroic, ability to strive and thrive in school. These students are commonly said to display *resiliency*.

Many factors combine to create resilient children. These include the following:

- Highly supportive and understanding parents
- Highly supportive and understanding schools
- A home life that is not beset with extreme family stresses
- A family that values and pursues education
- A child with effective coping skills
- A child with usable compensatory strengths
- A child with an "easy temperament," allowing some insulation from stress

Children who show good adaptation deserve recognition for their valor under pressure! They should be praised for maintaining their self-esteem and effort despite the adversity of school problems. It is likely that their excellent coping skills will serve them well throughout life.

The first seven chapters of this book have amply demonstrated the extraordinary complexity and the vast network of interacting factors that can undermine the educational life of a growing and developing child. We have stressed repeatedly the importance of understanding the unique ways in which the observable phenomena we have described interact over time with each other, with strengths, with temperaments, and with life circumstances. We have emphasized the importance of understanding the individuality of these struggling students if we are to be meaningfully allied with them in their struggles. In the next chapter, we will provide an overview of a systematic approach to humane educational care.

CHAPTER EIGHT

The Provision of Educational Care: Assessment and Management

S CHOOL problems are likely to in-
flict the greatest harm when they
are misunderstood. It is essential, therefore, that affected children, their
parents, and their teachers acquire a valid awareness of the strengths
and weaknesses of a student who is, in whatever way, unable to fulfill
expectations in school. It is equally important that all who are involved
share similar understandings and interpretations of the child's difficulties.

In this chapter we will examine the process of assessment for children with school problems and then describe an overall approach to
their management at school and at home. Up until this point we have
delineated many specific recommendations for parents and teachers. We
will now see how these suggested interventions fit within a broader
framework of assessment and management.

ASSESSMENT: THE FAIR AND THOROUGH INTERPRETATION OF A CHILD

A child with school problems has a need and a right to be understood.
Misinterpretation of such a student can cause far more damage than the
learning difficulty itself. A proper assessment entails objectivity, the seeking of evidence from multiple sources, and a recognition of the multiplicity of factors that together obstruct the child's success in school. In the
following sections, we will examine the various components and levels of
assessment needed for accurate interpretation.

Assessment should always begin with informed observation. The
adults in a child's life should watch that child performing, behaving, inter-

acting, and learning. The observers will begin to discern patterns that recur. Many such patterns are likely to correspond to the observable phenomena we have described in this book. A familiarity with these phenomena can help to guide and interpret that which is seen. Classroom teachers, in particular, are in a unique position to make such observations, especially when they are knowledgeable about the observable phenomena and the forms they take at the age level and within the content and skill areas they teach. No other single source of information regarding a school-age child's development is apt to be as valid as the observations of a knowledgeable teacher. Parents can augment such observations with their perceptions of the child's function at home.

It is important to make the distinction between observation and diagnosis. We are not suggesting here that teachers and parents become clinicians or diagnosticians. Instead, we hope that they will be informed and able to recognize the common phenomena and the forms they are taking in an individual student. When further evaluation is needed after such recognition occurs, they will be able to ask more specific questions and be of greater assistance to the clinicians involved.

Levels of Assessment

Not every child with a school problem needs to undergo an extensive evaluation. There are distinct levels of assessment that can be offered (fig. 8.1). When the problems are not overwhelming and the parents and school feel they have a good understanding of the student's needs, a formal assessment may not be called for. The teacher and the parent may feel able to develop their own management strategies to deal with the child's problems at home and in school.

One level of assessment occurs when a specialist from within the school or in the community offers consultation which might include some testing, further direct observations, and a review or discussion of the concerns of the teacher and parents. Such additional assessment might be performed by a psychologist, a learning disabilities specialist, an occupational therapist, a speech-and-language pathologist, a developmental pediatrician, or some other professional with expertise in school problems.

Another level of assessment makes use of a multidisciplinary team. This kind of assessment is likely to be needed when a student's difficulty is long-standing, difficult to manage, causing other problems, and/or hard to interpret. Multidisciplinary assessments may be undertaken within a school or in a community clinical setting. The exact composition of the team is likely to vary, depending upon local needs and available resources.

Levels of Assessment

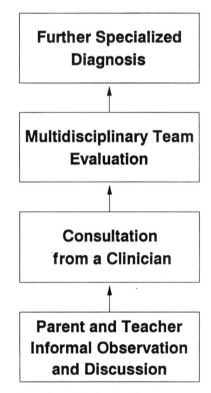

Fig. 8.1. The diagram above shows the levels of assessment which a child might undergo. The complexity of her or his difficulty is likely to determine the most appropriate level.

Additional assessments might include highly specialized evaluations, such as an ophthalmologic examination, in-depth language testing, a genetics consultation, or a psychiatric evaluation.

Principles of Assessment: A Phenomenological Approach

The principal aim of assessment is to formulate an exact profile of the child—his or her strengths, weaknesses, affinities, and life circumstances. Such a description can then lead to an individualized prescription. Some principles that should guide the assessment process are listed below.

• Assessment should consist of the search for recurring themes, patterns of strength, weakness, and affinity that are noted by multiple observers and/or examiners in different contexts (e.g., at home, in school, during testing). Any conclusion or interpretation based on a single observation by an individual observer or a single test must be considered inconclusive and susceptible to numerous possible interpretations. Observations require corroboration. Individuals who are assessing children should be familiar with the observable phenomena and the forms these take at specific age or grade levels and in specific content areas. For example, someone evaluating an eight-year-old with poor school performance, should be familiar with the forms that weak language processing or problems with short-term memory take in second graders. Areas covered in chapters 2 to 7 of this book can translate into a core of critical assessment questions which are summarized in table 8.1.

- The result of assessment should be a description of a child rather than a label (such as L.D. or A.D.H.D.) or a score. If either of these is needed for pragmatic purposes (e.g., to obtain services or reimbursement for services), it can be provided, but the label or score should never be the final product of assessment. It should represent only an incidental part of a multifaceted description that includes strengths, weaknesses, patterns of behavior, and content affinities.

- There is a difference between an evaluation to determine whether a child qualifies for services and an evaluation to uncover the sources of his or her poor functioning. The former generally involves giving tests to determine if a child has a particular problem, while the latter involves searching for an understanding of the phenomena in order to develop a program to manage the difficulties at home and in school.

- It is important to stress that many of the observable phenomena we have discussed in *Educational Care* are not easily detectable on standardized tests. This further emphasizes the need for other sources of information, including direct observations by parents and teachers.

- All professionals are susceptible to strong disciplinary biases related to their clinical training or to a form of therapy they feel most comfortable administering. They may have a tendency toward certain diagnoses. Having an assessment by a multidisciplinary team may protect children from such biases (as long as the team itself isn't in a diagnostic rut or too heavily under the influence of one discipline).

- Even though schools often are capable of performing good evaluations, children, parents, and teachers may benefit when a multidisciplinary evaluation is performed independently outside of school.

Table 8.1: Relevant Assessment Questions

AREA	RELEVANT QUESTIONS
Attention	What is the status of child's attention controls? Are there specific forms of weak control of mental energy, processing, or production? How are these affecting learning, behavior, and social interactions? Does this child show attentional assets?
Memory	What are his or her memory strengths and weaknesses? Are there observable phenomena relating to problems with short-term memory, low capacity of active working memory, consolidation in long-term memory, or access from long-term memory?
Understanding	Are there notably strong or weak forms of understanding? Are there observable phenomena relating to weak language processing, incomplete concept formation, deficient visualization, slow data processing, trouble with chunk sizes, or poor regulation of top-down and bottom-up processing?
Output	What strong and weak modes of output does this child exhibit? Are their observable phenomena related to weak language production, disappointing motor performance, poorly organized output, or problematic problem solving and strategy use?
Academic Skills	What is the current status of this child's skills? What sub-skills are deficient (see page 250)? Can the observable phenomena in chapters 2-7 help account for delayed skills? If so, in what way(s)?
Adaptation	How effectively has this child adapted to school? Are there indications of school-related sadness, non-compliant behaviors, bodily preoccupations, social inability, or motivational loss? In what ways does this child display resiliency?

- Assessments should be free of political or economic conflicts of interest. For example, the fact that a school has no funds for language therapy should not prevent that school from discovering that weak language processing is impairing a child's reading comprehension. Likewise, a child with attention problems should not be misinterpreted or deprived of help because the school board feels too many children are being identified with these difficulties.
- Most children with school problems have more than one source for their poor performance. Therefore, it is inappropriate to overuse the word "or" to ask, "Is this some kind of a learning disorder *or* is it emotional?" Often it is both. A better question might be: "What are the contributions of behavioral factors and of neurodevelopmental factors in this child's school difficulties?"
- Assessments should focus as much on strengths as they do on weaknesses.
- A good assessment is a form of treatment. Following an assessment, children and their parents should feel uplifted, energized, and more optimistic about the future.

While the actual content of an evaluation is likely to vary depending upon local resources and practices, it is possible to divide most high-level evaluations into five basic components and their subcomponents which are described in table 8.2.

We will now examine more closely the individual assessment components.

Educational Assessment

This type of evaluation is performed by an educational diagnostician who may be a psychologist or a special educator with experience and qualifications in evaluation. Generally, this person does individual testing of specific academic skills to detect delays and strengths; the results are usually expressed in grade levels or percentile ranks.

Educational diagnosticians can provide valuable insights to guide management when their work is process-oriented, that is, when they focus on how the child accomplishes a task or where the breakdown in performing it occurs. For example, during the mathematics portion of a psycho-educational assessment, the diagnostician may ask: What happens when this student tries to solve a word problem? Does he have trouble understanding the language? Is he unsystematic in his problem-solving skills? Does he have difficulty recalling facts or procedures? Is it hard for him to recognize what to do when in a problem? Are there gaps

Table 8.2: Common Evaluation Components

EVALUATION COMPONENT	GENERAL DESCRIPTION OF SUBCOMPONENTS
Educational	• Psycho-educational testing—observations of academic performance on standardized testing with documentation of "breakdown points" • Direct classroom observations and error analyses by teachers • Interpretations of historical data from parents and possible interview with the student
Behavioral and Affective	• Direct interviewing of the child to assess affect, seek other psychological conditions, determine child's feelings about school problem(s) • Use of parent, teacher, and (when possible) student questionnaires to elicit patterns of behavior and behavioral concerns
Cognitive and Developmental	• Direct intelligence, neuropsychological, and/or neurodevelopmental testing to detect strengths and weaknesses in relevant neurodevelopmental domains • Use of questionnaires to document past and present neurodevelopmental function, affinities, and styles
Environmental	• Interview with parents to elicit relevant factors in the current and past home environment of the child • Consideration of cultural, peer-related, and community-based issues related to the student's performance
Medical	• Review of child's medical history to uncover current or previous factors affecting school performance • Complete physical examination to rule out any definable medical disorder associated with the child's learning difficulty • Complete neurological examination to detect any possible central nervous system disorder

of attention? Does he understand the concepts? Similarly, while observing the writing process in a child with writing problems, the diagnostician might wonder: Is this a graphomotor breakdown? Or, are there problems with the language or mnemonic aspects of writing? Is she having trouble generating or organizing ideas? The answers to these questions can serve as strong evidence for the existence of one or more specific neurodevelopmental dysfunctions impeding performance. When integrated with the results of cognitive and developmental testing, analyses of student work samples, and the impressions of teachers, parents, and the student, some revealing recurring themes are likely to emerge.

The process-oriented approach also encourages dynamic assessment. This highly flexible technique for testing allows the clinician to modify tasks in order to determine if such changes lead to improvement. For example, the tester might dictate a sentence more slowly to see if the child's spelling improves.

A thorough educational assessment needs to include a description of specific dimensions of performance within each academic skill area. These dimensions will obviously vary according to grade level. Table 8.3 provides some typical subskills that merit consideration as part of educational testing.

Educational diagnosticians, like other clinicians, should spend time speaking with the child alone. The student at any age can offer valuable insights into the nature of his or her academic struggles. Standardized interview formats are sometimes helpful. Two examples (for writing and for mathematics) are found in the Appendixes of this book. Educational diagnosticians may also learn a great deal about a child's particular learning problems by working directly with that child in a specific subject area or, alternatively, observing that student during class sessions.

Behavioral and Affective Assessment

Because it is beyond the purpose of this book to review the many ways of assessing a child's affective (mood) patterns and behaviors, we will identify instead four techniques that are commonly used: (1) parent, teacher, and student questionnaires (generally inventories of different problem behaviors and signs of anxiety); (2) direct interviews with the child conducted by a clinician; (3) projective (personality) tests on which the child reacts to a design, a provocative phrase or a revealing picture; and (4) observation of the child in the classroom and/or at play.

Behavioral and affective evaluations serve to identify psychological factors that may be causing or aggravating a child's school problems. In many cases, the behaviors or mood problems are largely attributable to

Table 8.3: Important Educational Skills, Subskills, and General Observations for Assessment

SKILL AREA	DIMENSIONS
Reading	• Decoding accuracy and speed • Comprehension • Recall • Summarization skill • Overall speed and automaticity
Spelling	• Accuracy • Error types • Spelling in context (i.e., during writing activities)
Writing	• Pencil grip • Graphomotor fluency, rhythm, ease of output • Legibility (manuscript and cursive) • Mechanics (actual use of punctuation, capitalization; recognition of errors) • Language usage (compared to oral language) • Ideation (topic selection and development) • Organization
Mathematics	• Factual recall and degree of automaticity • Procedural recall and degree of automaticity • Understanding of concepts • Word problem-solving skill • Visualization/geometric ability
General Observations	• Patterns of attention during academic work • Use of strategies to facilitate work • Level of performance anxiety • Understanding of learning (metacognition) • Enthusiasm, degree of interest • Creativity • Specific content affinities

the student's frustration and anguish in school. Most of the time it is fruitless to speculate about cause and effect, that is, to try to decide whether the behavior problem is the cause or the result of the learning problem. It is safe to assume that anxiety or maladaptive behavior is both a cause and a result of school difficulties.

Cognitive and Developmental Testing

Psychologists often administer intelligence tests as well as other neuropsychological tests that examine specific cognitive abilities. Increasingly, pediatricians perform neurodevelopmental examinations (such as the PEEX and the PEERAMID) on their patients. When the results of all these tests are considered together, they are likely to reveal helpful information about many of the observable phenomena described in this book. The following principles should guide professionals in their assessments of children's cognition and development:

- They should not overrely on intelligence tests. Many students with neurodevelopmental dysfunctions achieve inconsistent results on these tests. This is especially true of children with attention deficits. Moreover, intelligence tests do not come close to assessing all the developmental functions needed to succeed in school. Many important parameters of attention, memory, language, strategy use, and motor function (among others) are not well evaluated on intelligence tests. For example, a child who has language difficulties at school may still perform adequately on the verbal subtests of WISC III, a widely used intelligence test for children.
- Choosing a specific test or test battery may not be nearly as important for a successful evaluation as carefully observing relevant skills or functions during any examination. For example, patterns of attention control can be evaluated during educational tests, neurodevelopmental examinations, or interviews with the student. It may not even be necessary to use a direct test designed specifically to evaluate attention.
- Clinicians should avoid tests with strong cultural or gender biases.
- Interpretations of a child's difficulty should not be based on a single test result or on one encounter with the child. Evaluators need to search for recurring themes and multiple interlocking pieces of evidence in order to derive valid explanations of a child's learning difficulties. For example, there are many children with attention deficits who appear to concentrate adequately when they are tested one-to-one, but who function very differently in a class-

room setting. In such circumstances, daily observations at home and in school have greater weight than the limited clinical view of the child during an evaluation.

- Test items need to be selected to shed light on a student's specific academic difficulty. Thus, the cognitive assessment of a second grader with reading problems must include tests of phonological awareness. A sixth-grade child with writing problems requires an assessment of his or her motor, language, and memory functions.
- Dynamic assessment techniques mentioned under psycho-educational assessment can also be applied to the evaluation of cognition and development. Diagnosticians should alter tasks on tests (e.g., provide more time or present verbal stimuli visually) and attempt to teach children how to perform some of them in an effort to understand more thoroughly the breakdowns in a child's learning.
- Clinicians should engage in a dialogue with the child during some or all of the testing. As part of dynamic assessment it is helpful to uncover a child's own insights. If she or he fails an item, the examiner might ask: "What was hard about that?" Likewise, when a child does very well on a task, one can say: "That was great. Can you tell me how you did it?" Such information can provide valuable clues and often reveals the observable phenomena described in this book.
- As clinicians perform assessments of cognition and development, they should be looking for a child's strengths as well as dysfunctions.

Environmental Assessment

The assessment of issues relating to a child's environment is usually undertaken by such professionals as social workers, psychologists, and guidance counselors. They explore aspects of the child's home and community life that are affecting performance at school. They often use interviews to obtain their information, sometimes supplementing this with data from standardized questionnaires. Table 8.4 lists some of the issues covered in this part of an assessment.

The environmental assessment should serve to identify specific stresses and shortcomings in a child's environment that may be contributing to a child's school problems. Likewise, actual or potential assets in the child's milieu should be identified. When a child comes to school from a chaotic, stress-laden, or deprived environment, these factors certainly have the potential to impair school performance, but it is important never to automatically blame everything on a child's environment. Often school difficulties result from the complex interplay between environmental stresses and a child's neurodevelopmental dysfunctions. In

Table 8.4: Issues Relating to a Child's Environment

AREA	ISSUE
Home Life	• Marital stability and quality • Level of financial stress • Extent of sibling rivalry • Extended family and other supports • Organizational patterns at home • Presence of substance abuse • Overall living conditions
Parent-Child Relationship	• Availability of parents to child • Parents' understanding of child's problems • Parents' awareness of child's strengths • Quality of communication between child and parents • Parents' methods of rewards and punishment • Parents' feelings about child's education • Parents' willingness to collaborate with school
Community	• Services, supports available to child • Neighborhood stresses • Socioeconomic factors • Cultural values and pressures • Adult role models • Violence, other dangers
Peer Group	• Child's social ability • Peer pressures • Role models among peers

fact, children from difficult environmental situations are more likely to have neurodevelopmental dysfunctions.

Medical Assessment

Many health factors have a bearing on school performance. Therefore, a careful medical assessment should be part of the assessment of any student with school problems. A medical assessment has several components which are summarized in table 8.5.

Table 8.5: Components of a Medical Assessment

COMPONENT	KEY ISSUES AND PROCEDURES
Health History	• Detection of any early health risk factors that may have predisposed child to neurodevelopmental dysfunction (e.g., prematurity, recurring ear infections) • Review of current health to identify present illnesses (e.g., asthma) or symptoms (e.g., headaches) that may affect school function
Physical Examination	• Assessment of overall physical health • Detection of any condition that might be associated with learning problems (e.g., a thyroid deficiency or a chromosomal problem, such as Fragile X) • Assessment of growth and physical maturation • Evaluation of any specific bodily complaints
Neurological Examination	• Detection of underlying central nervous system condition (e.g., tumor) • Uncovering of localized neurological findings (e.g. uneven reflexes) suggestive of a problem in an area of the brain
Sensory Examination	• Assessment of visual acuity • Assessment of auditory acuity
Neurodevelopmental Examination (see also, Cognitive and Developmental, table 8.2)	• Elicitation of minor neurological findings suggesting dysfunction • Use of developmentally appropriate tasks to screen attention, language, memory, visual processing, sequencing, motor functions, and approach to tasks
Additional Assessments (if called for, based on the above forms of medical assessment)	• Laboratory tests as needed to diagnose conditions such as anemia, hypothyroidism, lead intoxication • EEG and/or brain scans to detect seizure disorder or abnormal brain structure

Multidisciplinary Teams

As we have noted, proper and thorough assessment demands a well-balanced and unbiased multidisciplinary team approach. Parents, teachers, and the child need to be an integral part of the team, offering their observations and impressions. In communities where no such teams exist, it is important for parents to advocate for their development within clinics, hospitals, or the offices of private clinicians. Schools often offer team assessments but may not offer the depth and breadth of evaluation available outside of the school. Often schools themselves find it helpful to request another opinion from a team when a child is puzzling.

The Role of Parents and Teachers

Parents and teachers must be an active part of the assessment process. Their perspectives and observations need to be considered a vital contribution to the evaluation. Parents and teachers can also assist clinicians by identifying the phenomena in this book that appear to pertain to a child with school problems. Finally, parents and teachers should be wise consumers of evaluations. If an assessment does not "fit" with what they are seeing and hearing on a day-by-day basis, they should be skeptical about that assessment. On the other hand, parents and teachers can't always have the diagnosis or description that they'd like to have. Clinicians are obligated to portray objective impressions of a child, even if the findings somehow displease a parent or school personnel.

The Assessment "Product"

The final product of a good assessment should be an excellent written description of a child's strengths, dysfunctions, psychological health, and any other relevant factors. The report should contain a list of highly specific suggestions for the school and the parents to carry out. It should also include an explicit commitment to long-term follow-up of the child's progress by one or more members of the assessment team.

It is of course a basic premise of this book that excellent management follows from an excellent understanding of the child. In earlier sections of the book we presented specific management suggestions relating to specific phenomena. In the remaining sections of this chapter, we will provide a broader view of such management strategies.

MANAGEMENT: THE HUMANE AND INFORMED TREATMENT OF A CHILD

Good management of their learning problems should enable children to feel increasingly engaged and effective in school. They should perceive tangible evidence of their progress at the same time that they are developing positive feelings about future possibilities for themselves as students and as adults. Good management depends on parents and teachers sharing in its implementation. We will describe seven basic components of this shared management: (1) demystification; (2) the use of bypass strategies; (3) direct remediation of dysfunctions; (4) direct remediation of skills; (5) medical therapies; (6) preservation of pride, protection from humiliation, and strengthening of strengths; and (7) provision of advocacy and longitudinal monitoring.

Demystification

We cannot emphasize enough the importance of children understanding themselves. When they are unable to perceive the causal relationship between their specific weaknesses and the problems they are experiencing when they attend school, they tend to fantasize about themselves. Unfortunately, their fantasies are most often far worse than the realities. They may believe they are retarded, crazy, or just born to lose. Such attributions promote fatalistic feelings and a strong belief that effort does no good in school. In addition, when children feel pervasively defective, they are likely to suffer a serious loss of motivation.

Demystification is a process which provides children with more accurate personal insight. Through open discussions with adults who are working with them, they put borders around their deficits and come to recognize that like everyone else they have strengths and weaknesses. Very importantly they learn the vocabulary of their problems. It is exceedingly hard to work on something when one doesn't know the name for it! If a student is confused in class, it is far healthier for him or her to think, "There goes my visual processing problem again" than it is to feel, "Boy, am I a dummy."

Demystification can take place at any age when a child is experiencing frustration in school. Different forms of demystification can occur in various settings and under specific circumstances. If an assessment has been done, a child needs to learn about the findings and their implications. Both at home and in school, children should have opportunities to learn about and discuss their problems. Demystification can take place with small groups of children or in a one-to-one format with a clinician, counselor, or teacher. Parents too can undertake demystification, although sometimes the information may feel more objective if it does not come from a family member.

One-to-one demystification should consist of five steps.

- Introduction. Children should learn the importance of under-standing themselves. They should be reassured that everyone, even students who get all A's, have parts of their minds that need to be worked on. The overall tone should be very positive, optimistic, nonaccusatory, non-"preachy," and supportive.
- Discussion of strengths. The child needs to be told about his or her areas of competency. Specific concrete examples should always be cited ("I saw that drawing you did; you are really great at that kind of art work"). Whenever possible, strengths should be expressed in comparison with peers ("Very few kids your age can draw like this; you have a great talent"). False praise must be avoided. Children see it immediately. They may feel that the adults they know have low expectations for them, and this perception can become a self-fulfilling prophecy.
- Discussion of weaknesses. Children should be told about their ar-eas of dysfunction. These should be explained in plain language. Often it is helpful to use analogies. For example, one can use the Concentration Cockpit (chapter 2) to explain weak attention con-trols to young children. In this case the control of attention is lik-ened to the controls in an airplane's cockpit. Whenever discussing weaknesses, it is important to start with a specific number (e.g., "Susan, there are three kinds of weaknesses that your mind has and that we need to be working on. First, there is a problem with . . ."). After describing the weaknesses to these children, they should be asked if they feel these are right. They might also be asked to talk about some times they have trouble in these areas. Finally, children should be asked if they can remember the areas of weakness and repeat them in their own words. Numbering and enumerating the problems can help children feel less over-whelmed, less pervasively deficient.
- Induction of optimism. Children should be helped to see that they can improve, that their weaknesses can be worked on, and that their strengths can keep on getting stronger. Students need to rec-ognize that neither they nor anyone else is to blame for the prob-lems they are experiencing. They should realize that their kinds of minds aren't quite right for what they are being asked to do at this time in their lives. Each child should be helped to see real possibili-ties in the future for his or her kind of mind. This phase of demystification is aimed at bolstering motivation and feelings of personal efficacy.

- Alliance formation. The person leading the demystification should assure the child that he or she wants to be helpful in the future. The child should be reassured that everyone needs help in life, that no one can be completely independent. Children need to feel that the adults helping them are really on their side and are not overly judgmental. They also should believe that these adults have genuine respect or admiration for them and for what they can become.

As we have mentioned, demystification can also take place in group settings. A small group of students or even an entire classroom can have organized discussions of their strengths and weaknesses. Sometimes it is good to use case studies for this purpose. They can be found in the author's books for children—*All Kinds of Minds* (for elementary school students) and *Keeping A Head in School* (for secondary school students)—listed in the Suggested Readings. In these sessions it is important to stress the fact that different children have different kinds of minds, different strengths and weaknesses, different interests and specialties. Such variation should be legitimized in the eyes of students, so they need not feel ashamed of the way they are. Of course, this reduction of guilt and shame is especially soothing to students with learning difficulties.

Finally, it is important to stress that demystification needs to be a continuing process. Affected children may not be able to process, retain, and fully internalize the information the first time. There need to be recurring opportunities for them to discuss these issues in a relaxed, nonthreatening way with adults who are important to them.

Dealing with Resistance and Denial

Much of the material in this book is based on the premise that the parents, the school, and the child all agree that there is a problem that needs to be worked on. Unfortunately, such consensus does not always exist in reality. Let us consider some common scenarios.

- The school denies there is a learning disorder. In such a case the parents need to obtain an evaluation from an outside source, preferably from a multidisciplinary team. Once objective assessments are completed, if the parents feel the school is neither understanding nor meeting the student's needs, they can call a meeting with school representatives. If it is possible, a member of the outside assessment team should be present for the written report to be discussed. If the school continues to disagree about the assessment and management of the problem, parents may need to consider obtaining an advocate or initiating due process.

- The parents deny there is a problem. Schools can become exasperated because parents will not admit or recognize that a child is having difficulty. Sometimes this is because the parents have low expectations or in some instances they may have similar difficulties. At other times the parents may be embarrassed by the problem or lack trust in the school. Teachers and administrators need to make every effort to communicate effectively with these families through a parent conference. Sometimes the child's pediatrician, a clergy person, or a caring relative can be asked to participate and to help present the school's point of view.

- The child denies there's a problem and/or refuses help. Unfortunately, this scenario is very common. It is especially likely to occur between the ages of eleven and fifteen when students are heavily preoccupied with being like everyone else, with being "perfectly normal." Often these denying but hurting children simply make believe their troubles are not really happening. They are embarrassed about getting help and they carefully avoid any talk about school at home. This form of resistance can be the hardest to deal with. The following suggestions may be helpful:

1. These students require strong demystification to dispel their misunderstandings. Part of the process needs to include convincing them that it is possible to have a learning disorder and still be a normal person. Group sessions may be especially helpful in removing any stigma from their situation.

2. Many children feel embarrassed when their parents assist them with work or learning. The parents of such students may need advice about ways to preserve the self-esteem of their children while helping them with school work.

3. Children need to "take ownership" of their school careers. They must be helped to realize that the future is in their own hands and that the longer they deny the problems, the harder these will be to solve. Professional counseling may be necessary to facilitate this degree of involvement on the part of the child.

4. Parents may develop contractual arrangements with some children to get them to accept help and to show increased productivity in

school. This procedure was mentioned in chapter 7 and illustrated in figure 7.1.

Bypass Strategies

Throughout this book we have presented bypass strategies to deal with specific phenomena. Bypass strategies are techniques that are employed in regular classroom settings to circumvent or work around a student's dysfunctions. Bypass strategies thus enable a child to continue to acquire skill, knowledge, and a sense of competency despite the presence of a problem with processing, remembering, or producing in school. These techniques must be a part of the management of every child with significant learning problems. Their implementation costs no money but demands understanding, tolerance, and flexibility on the part of the school administration and teachers.

Table 8.6 delineates ten forms of bypass strategy that are often used.

Bypass strategies can make a student feel safer and more confident in the classroom when teachers are adept at devising and applying such tactics. On the other hand, some teachers and school administrators oppose their use. Table 8.7 lists some objections to the use of bypass strategies and some arguments to make in response.

Children should understand the bypass strategies that are being used. They should look forward to a time when fewer of such tactics will be needed. These strategies should not be perceived as a way of making school easier. In fact, it can be appropriate to "charge" a child something for a bypass concession. For example, a child might be asked to read an extra book in exchange for writing shorter reports.

Parents are often in a good position to suggest bypass strategies that the school might use with a child. The recommendation of "humane" accommodations represents an important part of child advocacy for those with learning problems.

Direct Remediation of the Forms of Observable Phenomena

It is, of course, possible and desirable to intervene directly to strengthen a weak function or skill. We have suggested approaches to such intervention throughout this book. Remediation may take place outside of the regular classroom, although, increasingly efforts are being directed toward interventions (beyond bypass strategies) within regular classrooms (so-called inclusionary models of service). A special educator may visit a classroom to help a child, or the regular teacher may be educated to help that student directly.

Professionals may work to strengthen specific functions (such as

Table 8.6: Bypass Strategies

STRATEGY	DESCRIPTION	EXAMPLES
Rate adjustment	More time to process, to complete a task, to demonstrate knowledge	Taking untimed SAT's, being told a question before class to have more time to prepare an answer
Volume adjustment	Smaller amount of material to process or produce	Writing a shorter report, solving fewer math problems
Complexity reduction	Fewer details or complicated ideas to create or interpret	Reading a simpler text, finding a manageable topic to write about
Staging	Tasks completed in logical steps or increments instead of all at once	Writing a report in stages (page 292); prereading, reading, and rereading a difficult chapter
Prioritization	Certain task components are stressed or de-emphasized during a complex activity or task	Telling a child to concentrate on ideas and grammar in a report and not to worry about spelling
Shifting of processing format	Information gets presented in a way that child can process more effectively	Providing a correctly solved math problem (demonstration model) to a child with language problems or explaining verbally about geometry to a child with poor visualization
Shifting of production format	Student is allowed to demonstrate competency using a medium that works well	Allowing a student with a graphomotor problem to present an oral report or to do an art project
Modification of evaluation system	Performance is assessed differently for the student	Using a different grading system, providing daily or weekly feedback on progress
Curriculum modifications	Requirements and/or timing of requirements are changed	Postponing or not requiring a foreign language, delaying algebra
Use of supports or aids	Specific tools are used to facilitate learning or output	Using a calculator in math class, writing reports on a word processor, using card on desk to remind a student to concentrate

Table 8.7: Possible Objections to Bypass Strategies

OBJECTION	RESPONSE
"There isn't enough time to do special things for her; I have thirty other students to worry about."	It is hard, but with planning it can and has been done for other students.
"It isn't fair to the others if I treat him differently"	All students should be helped to understand that people have different kinds of minds and different ways of learning.
"This child doesn't want to appear different in class."	Bypass strategies can be used discreetly, and the child needs demystification.
"Such allowances will compromise the academic standards of our school."	Creating more successful children will foster higher standards of performance for all.
"How will she ever learn to be independent?"	No one ever needs to be independent; successful people should be collaborators not soloists!
"This course is required for graduation."	There should be more than one way to show competence and educational success.

memory or language ability). For example, a child with weak language production may receive language therapy from a speech and language pathologist. Or, an occupational therapist may provide treatment for a graphomotor dysfunction. Psychologists and special educators have used a form of intervention called cognitive-behavioral therapy to help students with attention deficits and various other cognitive dysfunctions. In this form of treatment children are taught about their weaknesses and then given specific exercises or tasks to work on them. Sometimes children can learn effective memory strategies (such as rehearsing, self-testing, making diagrams). It is not clear whether these techniques actually strengthen a function like memory, but they are likely to lessen the impact of reduced remembering.

Unfortunately, very little is known about how effectively these interventions work. We really do not know if it is possible to build up more memory or to "fix" a motor deficit. It is likely that certain children benefit more than others, but it is not easy to predict who will make gains. It is probably justified to seek to help all children strengthen their weak functions. At the very least, such efforts will help them understand the nature of their weaknesses.

Direct Remediation of Academic Skills

Remediation is often used to enhance weak academic skills. Tutorial support for reading difficulties, mathematics delays, or writing problems is commonly sought. Tutors or educational therapists are likely to be most effective when they are knowledgeable about children's profiles of strength and weakness. Often strengths can be mobilized to compensate for weak areas. Also, a method of teaching can be selected based on the child's unique preferred learning style.

An important aspect of skill remediation involves intervention at students' breakdown point(s). The following steps are involved:

1. There should be a determination of where breakdowns occur when a child tries to perform a particular kind of task. For example, in word problem solving a student may have trouble with the language of the problem. This determination is made during cognitive and psycho-educational assessments (pages 251 and 247).

2. The child should be helped to understand these breakdown points. This can and should be part of the demystification process.

3. Tasks should be designed so that the breakdown point becomes the end point. If children have trouble recognizing phrases in a word problem that call for a particular mathematical process, then they might be given tasks in which all they have to do is inspect word problems, identify the process called for, and circle the words that indicate this process. In fact, proceeding with the solution to the problem could obscure the critical step or message the therapist needs to impart.

4. Students should be taught to slow down and take much more time when they reach one of their typical breakdown points during a task.

Appropriate computer software can also be helpful. There are programs for improving reading skills, spelling, and mathematical abilities.

Parents and teachers are likely to need help in selecting the most effective software.

In many cases it is possible for a parent or other relative or adult friend to serve as a tutor. Such assistance can be best undertaken when there is very good communication with the child's teacher(s). Sometimes it is possible to obtain educational help from an older student (in high school or college). This arrangement may have the advantage of providing a role model as well as a tutor. In addition, there are programs for peer tutoring which may have advantages under certain circumstances, especially when children have certain skills or interests they can teach their peer tutors!

Medical Interventions

Certain kinds of medical interventions may be important in the care of children with school problems. When there are neurological problems (such as a seizure disorder or migraine), these children need to treated and monitored by a physician. This is also true for children with somatic preoccupations (such as enuresis, abdominal pain, or growth delays).

The use of medication to treat learning and/or behavioral difficulties has become widespread. Most frequent is the use of stimulant medications in the treatment of attentional dysfunction. Methylphenidate (Ritalin), dextroamphetamine (Dexedrine), and pemoline (Cylert) are most commonly prescribed. These drugs often enhance a child's ability to mobilize mental effort, concentrate effectively, and become significantly less impulsive. There is abundant evidence that these drugs are highly effective in many children with attention deficits. However, very little else has been established scientifically. There are still unanswered questions regarding the optimal dosages, the frequency with which the medicines should be taken, their long-term side effects, the ability to predict in advance who will benefit from them, and the mechanisms through which they actually work.

Other classes of medication are used when children with attention deficits are not benefiting sufficiently from stimulant therapy. Drugs are also used to treat tics (involuntary muscle movements as seen in Tourette Syndrome), anxiety, depression and bipolar illness, obsessive-compulsive disorder, and other conditions that may accompany learning difficulties. Table 8.8 summarizes some of the commonly used medications and their effects.

Although much excellent research on the use of these medications continues, surprisingly little is actually known about them. Their precise dosages, their long-range side effects, and use in various combinations require further investigation. For this reason we strongly recommend a conservative approach to their use.

Parents, teachers, and clinicians should consider the following guidelines whenever medication is part of a child's management.

1. Drugs are not a panacea and should never be viewed as the whole answer. They can comprise only one aspect of a management program that might also include ongoing demystification and other counseling, remedial help with schools, and bypass strategies.

2. The drug therapy should not be considered a permanent treatment. The physician, the parent, and the child should keep working on ways of possibly tapering off the medication. There should always be a plan in mind for ultimately discontinuing this form of treatment. In many cases, it is good to have regularly scheduled "drug holidays" during the school year. These are intervals during which the children take no medicine and try to gain control over their own attention, learning, and/or behavior.

3. Physicians should try to use the smallest possible effective doses of these drugs. Since their long-range effects are not entirely known, it is wisest to be conservative with dosages. It is also prudent to use as few different medications as possible, since drug interactions can cause significant problems.

4. Physicians should regularly monitor children who take medication to evaluate their current progress and to discuss the benefits and side effects of the treatment. During follow-up visits, they need to perform complete physical examinations to seek possible adverse effects and to monitor growth and development of the children. The physical examination is also a good time to elicit any bodily preoccupations of the child (page 217).

5. There needs to be good communication between the clinician and the school regarding the drug's effects. Teachers can often be helpful in completing questionnaires about the child's attention and behavior in school. This kind of input can help clinicians decide if the medication is working and whether the dose needs adjustment.

6. Children need to understand just what the medicine does and does not do. They should realize that they will need to keep working on their problems. The pill can't do it all!

7. Physicians who administer and monitor these medications should be experienced in doing so. Those who manage very few chil-

Table 8.8: Medications Commonly Used to Improve Behavior, Mood, and Learning

CATEGORY	MEDICATIONS	THERAPEUTIC ($\Uparrow$) EFFECTS AND SIDE ($\Downarrow$) EFFECTS*
Psychostimulants	Methylphenidate HCl (Ritalin) Dextroamphetamine Sulfate (Dexedrine) Pemoline (Cylert)	$\Uparrow$ May reduce impulsivity, increase attentional strength, diminish motor activity, enhance certain memory functions $\Downarrow$ May cause tics, loss of appetite, growth delays, sleep problems, personality change; Pemoline may disrupt liver function
Tricyclic Antidepressants	Desipramine HCl (Norpramin, Pertofrane) Clomipramine HCl (Anafranil) Amitriptyline HCl (Elavil, Endep)	$\Uparrow$ May reduce anxiety, depressive symptoms, aggression, obsessive-compulsive signs, and overactivity $\Downarrow$ May cause sedation, changes in heart rhythm, gastrointestinal disturbance
Aminoketones	Bupropion HCl (Wellbutrin)	$\Uparrow$ May reduce hyperactivity, anxiety, and aggressive tendencies $\Downarrow$ May cause insomnia, headaches, gastrointestinal distress, seizures
Lithium Preparations	Lithium Carbonate (Eskalith, Lithotabs)	$\Uparrow$ May be effective in bipolar illness (manic-depression); may also help in depression when other drugs fail $\Downarrow$ May cause gastrointestinal upset, tremor, weight gain, urinary symptoms, or poor motor coordination
Serotonin Re-uptake Inhibitors	Fluoxetine HCl (Prozac) Sertraline HCl (Zoloft) Paroxetine HCl (Paxil)	$\Uparrow$ May reduce anxiety, impulsivity, overactivity, obsessive-compulsive tendencies $\Downarrow$ May worsen attention deficits, cause nervousness, result in oversedation

Table 8.8: *(continued)*

CATEGORY	MEDICATIONS	THERAPEUTIC (⇑) EFFECTS AND SIDE (⇓) EFFECTS*
Antipsychotic Agents	Haloperidol (Haldol)	⇑ May help attention in low doses, reduce tics in Tourette Syndrome, lessen aggressive symptoms ⇓ May be overly sedative, interfere with cognition and learning, cause movement disorder (tardive dyskinesia)
Alpha-Adrenergic Agonists	Clonidine HCl (Catapres) Guanfacine HCl (Tenex)	⇑ May increase frustration tolerance, reduce impulsivity, improve task-oriented behaviors in children with motoric overactivity, lessen tics in Tourette Syndrome, improve sleep ⇓ May overly sedate, cause fall in blood pressure, induce depression or other mood disorder

* All of these medications have additional, possible effects, both detrimental and beneficial. Different children are apt to respond or react differently to the same drug. There are some differences in effects between the drugs within a single category. Some of these medications have not been fully tested in children.

dren with learning and behavior problems should refer these patients to more experienced clinicians or work in close consultation with a physician who has expertise in psychopharmacology.

Physicians can also help parents by reviewing possible "alternative" health therapies. These are treatments that frequently appear in the press promising cures for learning and behavioral difficulties. Diets, nutritional supplements, exercise programs, training activities, and special devices might be very tempting to parents who are feeling frustrated and rather desperate. Proponents of these treatments almost always provide anecdotal testimonies to their effectiveness. Yet there is likely to exist little if any scientific evidence that they work. Unfortunately, there is often a strong "placebo effect" whereby almost any therapy works for a while. However, such treatments can delay the implementation of more appropriate management at the same time that they confuse the parents and the child. To avoid this situation parents should look to their child's physician for guidance and strong consumer advocacy.

Preservation of Pride, Protection from Humiliation, and Strengthening of Strengths

Through all of our efforts to help these children we must aim steadily toward the strengthening of self-esteem and the maintenance of personal pride. These vulnerable students must be insulated from public humiliation in school and at home. In so many cases the embarrassment is more hazardous than the learning disorder. Teachers can provide great benefits by protecting these youngsters from humiliation before their peers. Examples of such exposure might include having others correct the papers of a child with illegible writing, the posting of poor grades, repeatedly criticizing a student in public, having a child sit out in the hall for misbehaving in class, calling on a child with attention deficits who has not been concentrating, or forcing a child with an expressive language problem to elaborate on an idea in class. Children can be criticized and they can endure punishment, but like adults, they have a right to privacy. In medicine a very important part of the Hippocratic Oath is "primum non nocere"—"first of all, do no harm." This admonition certainly applies to children with learning disorders; their humiliation constitutes serious harm. Therefore, protection from humiliation must be an important component of educational care. Four common sources of humiliation are described below.

- Consistently low grades. When grades must be assigned, students with neurodevelopmental dysfunctions are particularly in need of report cards with grades and teacher comments that do not make them feel discouraged and powerless. They must be given the benefit of the doubt when there is any question about a grade to assign. Teachers' comments should avoid the one-sided blaming of children for their disappointing performance. These students should be acknowledged for making progress and working hard even if the results remain poor. Teachers need to be aware of the potential motivating effects of giving a student a very good grade.
- Consistent negative, accusatory feedback. Students become discouraged when they are perpetually confronted with comments that strongly imply that they are somehow morally guilty for their learning difficulties. Teachers' comments can be especially humiliating. Evaluations by two different teachers of Susan, the girl with

attentional dysfunction who was described briefly in chapter 2 (page 16), illustrate two different approaches.

Teacher A (moralistic and accusatory):

Susan is performing very poorly, yet I know she can do the work when she makes up her mind to succeed. There are days when she decides to put forth effort and accomplish things in class. On other days, she fails to hand in work, she is unwilling to study, and she seems more interested in her friends and what is going on outside the classroom than she is in learning anything. I am sure Susan has potential, but she will not reach it until she changes her attitude and chooses to become motivated.

Teacher B (observant and supportive):

Susan is puzzling to me. Some days she comes to class and is very alert and productive. On other days, she is distractible and appears tired or "burnt out." On her tired days she is fidgety and restless and accomplishes very little. She has shown that she has a great deal of ability, but somehow it is very hard for Susan to make use of this ability consistently. She needs to try hard to become more consistent. I know how much Susan would like to succeed. She and I will have to find ways to work on this problem.

When children are constantly exposed to comments like those of Teacher A they are apt to become discouraged and lose motivation. Even more importantly, children often accept without question the evaluations of their teachers. Consequently, if students keep on hearing that they are responsible for their problems, they are apt to feel guilt and to blame themselves for all of their academic woes. Such self-blame thwarts true insight and may lead to a serious loss of motivation.

- Tracking. Many children with learning problems come to feel stigmatized when they are victims of a tracking process in school. These students may frequently be placed in classes for slower learners while many of their peers pursue normal or accelerated programs. Whenever practical, tracking should be avoided. Within regular classrooms, teachers should be able to be flexible in their expectations of individual children. Students should be able to proceed with the subject matter at varying rates. Those with learning problems should be able to use their strengths to make unique contributions to class activities. They should have opportunities to interact with higher achieving students and learn from them. The more rapid learners can also benefit from their interactions with students who possess different ways of learning and different strengths from their own. High-achieving children can also gain from opportunities to help their peers.

• Grade retention. Retaining a student in a grade can represent the most severe setback to a child's pride, especially after first grade. Moreover, grade retention has not been shown to help children succeed in school. Those who have been retained in a grade are more likely to leave school without graduating. They are also highly susceptible to a variety of behavioral and other mental health complications. Parents, teachers, and school administrators need to seek alternatives to grade retention. These options include extra help at home or during the school day, summer school, and after school remedial programs.

It is critically important to ensure that children with learning problems attain gratification from the things they enjoy and are good at. In fact, the strengthening of their strengths becomes an indispensable part of their management. It may be that some children, who appear to have learning disorders, instead (or in addition) have highly specialized brains, minds that could flourish in the adult world when they are permitted to practice these specialties. As we have stressed throughout this book, it is essential to discover, nurture, and employ whenever possible a child's natural assets and affinities. Parents and teachers need to facilitate the processes through which children can acquire expertise and ever-increasing levels of skill in these areas, even if they do not represent the areas adults might have selected for these children! It is also important for students to have tangible evidence of their progress in strengthening their strengths. Cumulative portfolios of their art work, recordings of their musical renderings, and photographs of their athletic triumphs should be compiled over time.

Facilitating Collaboration through Communication

Throughout this chapter we have stressed the need to base management on good assessment. Evaluation findings enable parents and teachers to work out collaborative arrangements for the optimal educational care of the child. To do so there must be excellent communication between parents, teachers, and other involved adults who need to be reporting to each other on a regular basis.

While planning a child's management, it is especially critical that all concerned arrive at an agreement on what needs to be done and how it will be implemented. One method of doing this is through the use of the Collaboration Worksheet (Appendix 7) which is a form that can be completed by parents, teachers, and clinicians to facilitate the planning process.

The Long-Term Commitment

So often parents and children need help that will remain available over the years. It is impossible to predict with certainty what a child will be like in five years. New issues and problems come forth unpredictably over time. There is a clear need for continuing outside help to offer advice, to serve as a sounding board, and to provide vigorous informed advocacy. Sometimes this commitment can be provided by personnel within the school. Often it must come from someone within the community, such as a physician, an educational therapist, or a mental health professional who can offer regular follow-up visits to assess progress and plan next moves. Managing these complex problems can be confusing and lonely for a parent. Mothers and fathers shouldn't have to confront the challenges in isolation. Nor should their children!

CHAPTER NINE

Implications and Applications

W E HAVE much to learn from children who have been unsuccessful in school. They teach us about the need to appreciate, preserve, and respect varied abilities among people. They teach us that there are many different kinds of minds and that a mind's specialization may well commence early in life. They force us to acknowledge the disparity between an adult world where specialized talents are celebrated and a child world where a universality and uniformity of expectation for performance prevails. These children sensitize us to their own fragility, to the lurking dangers to us and to them when early life failure is an inevitable consequence. In this chapter, we will explore some of these broader implications and the changes in attitude and practice that will be needed if our society is to meet the challenge of pluralism among the minds of children.

THE MISINTERPRETED CHILD

The observable phenomena articulated in *Educational Care* cause widespread suffering and embarrassment everyday in every school. With great frequency they result in repeated failure and exasperation. But their immediate short-range effects may be minimal compared to the durable impacts of their misinterpretation. When students are falsely accused of laziness, when problems are attributed glibly to poor attitudes, when children come to believe that they were "born to fail," the result is a population of functionally crippled individuals, young persons who may then seek alternative, perhaps even antisocial and potentially self-destructive, pathways toward gratification. A loss of aspiration, deflated self-esteem, a profound sacrifice of individuality, alienation, and criminal behavior are among the many potentially devastating complications of growing up misinterpreted.

While human minds share a multitude of common goals, it is also the case that different minds are destined to serve different purposes. If we believe in such uniqueness of purpose, then it is critically important that the educational care of children include sensitive observation of them as individuals. We must be able to detect and nurture those special purposes as they emerge. They may not be the purposes we might have selected for these youngsters, but they are authentic and they cry out for recognition. To use a mind for purposes for which it was not "wired" is to misuse it. To help a mind fulfill its authentic promise is to celebrate it.

AN ATTITUDINAL SHIFT AND ITS IMPLICATIONS

Obviously, we are calling for a major modification of public attitude. As societies become willing and able to acknowledge and respond to the diversity of minds during childhood, a series of compelling implications for policy and for practice present themselves.

The redefinition of what we mean by "normal." We have to affirm that being different is not synonymous with being abnormal or psychopathological. We must preserve and even broaden the scope of what constitutes normal variation (as opposed to deviation). We must combat the temptation to label glibly any child who shows divergent patterns of thinking and attending. While it is important to acknowledge that a child has a particular kind of neurodevelopmental dysfunction, it is hazardous to employ a label with such frequency and intensity that it becomes an integral part of the child's personal identity. Sadly, there are too many children who have come to think of themselves as "a dyslexic" or as "an ADHD kid." They would be better off having deeper insight into their own array of strengths and weaknesses rather then reducing themselves to a compressed label. We need to seek out, encourage, and support unusual or even eccentric children.

The broadening of educational requirements. Our knowledge of neurodevelopmental variation must lead us to the firm conclusion that we cannot impose the identical requirements for learning on all children. If we insist on doing so, we will cause endless intimidation and precipitate ever more failure among our children. We will incur great costs for the rehabilitation of young citizens whom our communities have declared incompetent and who have responded with self-destructive and antisocial actions. To avoid this calamity, we must resist uniform tests of competency, rigid graduation requirements, and unyielding educational standards. Instead there need to be multiple acceptable ways of qualifying to be a successful child. We do not require adults to meet standards in all areas of cognitive function. We should not demand that children do so. Some may wish to be generalists, to display their competencies in broad areas. All children need to be exposed to the widest range of forms of knowledge and types of skills, but those with less versatile minds should only have to demonstrate true mastery in one or more areas of specialization, if they and their parents choose for them to do so.

The creation of multiple pathways toward success in childhood. Every child without exception should be provided with opportunities to succeed. Since, as we have seen, different children are likely to succeed in different ways, schools, parents, and communities need to encourage a range of choices through which children may be challenged. There should be a continuing emphasis on schools which themselves are specialized (e.g., in the arts or in science) and on a greater variety of choices within schools. Every child should benefit from an Individualized Educational Plan (IEP) that emphasizes her or his developmental strengths and their utilization to foster success. In high school, students should be evaluated (graded) in such a way that the greatest weight is given to their chosen area(s) of specialization or affinity. In other words, we need to assert that the strengthening of strengths is one of the most important of educational missions.

The encouragement of true expertise. Schools may tend to place their emphasis on breadth of knowledge rather than depth. Yet, every child, regardless of his or her neurodevelopmental profile can benefit from being knowledgeable in a specific area. A student should be helped to find a unique topic or field of interest and encouraged in its study over the years. Knowledge helps to build skill. Unique expertise can also bolster academic motivation and self-esteem, two invaluable facilitators of school performance. Students should begin the quest for expertise early in elementary school. Parents and teachers should help them renew or redefine this periodically throughout their educational careers.

The erasing of stigmas. We need to work to remove the stigma from various educational programs and types of jobs. Being a truck driver may be as rewarding as being an attorney. Children who find trucks romantically attractive and whose learning styles enable them to problem solve magnificently under the hood of a vehicle must not be perceived or categorized as less able when compared to their peers who excel linguistically. The vocational education to which they have a right and for the which they have a need before adulthood should emphasize excellence just as much as more traditional academic programs do. Someday, these students may own a vast fleet of trucks. Someday, they may operate a national chain of truck repair facilities. Someday, they may be designing new models of trucks. In other words, the content of a child's affinities should not limit her or his ambitions in life.

Attuning schools to neurodevelopmental diversity. For childhood neurodevelopmental diversity to be recognized and well-managed, teachers, specialists, and school administrators need to be educated in the content and implications of this subject area. Schools need to define the critical neurodevelopmental issues that can become problems at specific ages or grade levels. They need to be sensitive, for example, to the important language acquisitions and expectations for children in first grade, fourth grade, eighth grade, etc. They then can be alert for the neurodevelopmental dysfunctions likely to present themselves in children at these times in their lives. Schools can develop developmentally appropriate observation/assessment procedures and ideas for the management of individual children.*

Attuning parents. Central to the philosophy of *Educational Care* is the belief that schools can help children with far greater efficacy when parents become informed collaborators with teachers and other school personnel. Thus, a knowledge of childhood neurodevelopmental variation can enable parents to help teachers at the same time that this information can facilitate the job of parenting as well. There need to be educational programs for parents as well as schools, so that they may learn the relevant concepts and keep abreast of new knowledge in this important field. Such programs can be offered by parent support groups, including various national organizations (see Appendix 8). They can consist of

---

*The author of this book and his colleagues have actually implemented a national project called "Schools Attuned." Schools throughout North America are provided with curriculum materials, a syllabus, educational videotapes, and observation instruments that enable teachers to be more responsive to diversity of learning among their students. Data from the participating schools demonstrate that this effort has resulted in marked improvement in student performance as well as teacher's knowledge and skill. The preparation of regular classroom teachers in this way is of critical importance for the application of inclusionary service models for children with learning disorders. To place such children in regular classrooms with teachers who lack the preparation to understand and manage them effectively is unfair to the students and to the teachers themselves.

discussion groups, lectures, videotapes, case-study presentations, collaborative problem-solving sessions, and other formats. In this way the misinterpretation of children by parents can be minimized and perhaps even prevented entirely.

Attuning children. Students themselves need to acquire an understanding of the neurodevelopmental variations that are most relevant at their grade levels. Such teaching should be an ongoing process in schools. While it is especially critical for those children who are having problems in school, learning about learning can help all students! The process can also permit children to become more tolerant of the individual differences between them. Such an attitudinal change can empower students to develop as authentic individuals rather than always feeling compelled to conform to the imposed uniform standards and values of their peers.

Attuning clinicians. At present, there is wide variation among clinicians with respect to their knowledge, their use of terminology, their diagnostic preferences, and their favored management routines. Pediatricians, psychologists, psychiatrists, educational diagnosticians and others who offer assessment and management provide very different and often contradictory approaches to the care of children with learning problems. A child receiving an evaluation is subjected to very strong biases depending on a clinician's professional background and training, current interests, and therapeutic beliefs. There is little common ground between disciplines; often the same phenomena are described with different words. There is a continuing need for interdisciplinary professional education in the domain of neurodevelopmental variation in order to create a shared frame of reference, while facilitating communication across disciplines and between clinicians, parents, children, and schools.

The discovery of new modes of success for children. We need to uncover new ways in which children can exhibit their competency. Traditional multiple-choice tests, written reports, and grading systems may unfairly favor certain groups while discriminating against others. Fortunately, there is considerable interest in cooperative learning and working, activities in which children team up with peers who have different strengths and weaknesses from their own in order to accomplish specific activities. This model much more clearly replicates the demands currently operating in most adult careers where much important work is accomplished by teams rather than individuals in isolation. In addition, encouraging children to accumulate portfolios so that their evaluations are based on their cumulative products and accomplishments rather than final examinations may be more apt to tap important strengths (for example, creativity as opposed to rote memory).

The firm commitment to the identification of dysfunctions at any age. Neurodevelopmental dysfunctions can create problems at any age. We are never really "out of the woods." As a child's brain develops, some functions may start to lag at any point. As the demands of the curriculum undergo change over time, as new or more complex expectations emerge, dysfunctions can appear. Schools need to have systems in place for the timely detection and proper identification of these problems at any point during a child's education. It is common to screen very young children for educational readiness. In reality, issues of readiness extend well beyond kindergarten. For example, the readiness of twelve year olds for adolescence or of seventeen year olds for young adulthood should be a matter of prime concern for communities. Sometimes communities believe that by investing the bulk of their resources in early (preschool) detection and education, they will prevent most problems from emerging later. While this early identification and intervention is of great importance, it is a serious mistake to assume that all critical neurodevelopmental dysfunctions can be detected and treated early. If we neglect the later-onset dysfunctions, we will misinterpret and mismanage many children. Communities must invest in prevention throughout the years of childhood.

A long-term investment in the function of children. The leaders of our society need to become knowledgeable and committed to the fostering of optimal function among our children. They need to recognize the enormous toll of misinterpreted and mismanaged early life failure. Resources must be allocated to provide for the excellent educational care of these children. This includes comprehensive diagnostic and monitoring services as well as effective individualized teaching. There should be ample support for programs to educate professionals, parents, and children about neurodevelopmental variation. There is also a need for continuing research into the understanding and management of impaired learning during childhood.

The pain and suffering of large numbers of children with learning problems may not be as visible as the mortality rate from various life-threatening illnesses. Yet, the devastation is there. When communities fail to invest in educational care, they are likely to incur far more draining of their resources as they pay for the later-life damage caused by their neglect.

EDUCATIONAL CARING

Children are at once delicate and resilient. They are simultaneously very much alike and remarkably different from one another. We cannot construct a child's mind. We may not even be capable of reconstructing it—at least not very much. We can, however, try to understand a mind, seek to nurture it, learn to love it, and strive not to harm it. This is a highly complex, artful, and vitally important process, one that entails far more than conveying large quantities of fact and skill. To provide true educational care is to demonstrate authentic respect for a child's unique mind while caring about it and caring for it.

APPENDIX ONE

The Problem-Solving Planner

T HE FORM contained on the next several pages is intended to help students become more systematic and strategic in their approach to problem solving. The form can be modified to be more suitable for specific age groups or academic content areas. Children can use this planner to solve a wide range of problems. It is good to start with everyday practical issues, such as settling a dispute with a friend or deciding whom to invite to a birthday party and areas of strong interest or ability. For example, a child might practice by solving problems relating to sports, fixing a broken bicycle, or using a computer.

As they progress in their problem-solving skills, students can apply them in more academic contexts, such as solving word problems, writing a report, or tackling issues in the news.

Children should have an opportunity to explain their problem-solving plans to others. Using the Problem-Solving Planner, they can articulate their stepwise approach and their strategies. As they become more consciously aware of the problem-solving process, students can generalize this organized approach to a wide range of academic and nonacademic challenges.

The Problem-Solving Planner

Name _____   Date _____

Collaborators _____

1. Is there a problem I need to solve?

   Yes_____   No_____   Possibly_____

2. What exactly is the problem?

   Statement of the problem _____

   _____

   _____

   _____

   _____

3. What information do I need to solve this problem? Where do I find this information?

Information Needed	Place(s) to Find it
1.	
2.	
3.	
4.	
5.	
6.	

4. Can I solve this problem?

- Yes, Easily_____ Yes, with a Lot of Work_____ No_____ Maybe_____

- By Myself_____ With Help_____ From Whom?_____

5. How long will it take?_____ How much time do I have?_____

6. What is familiar in this problem (what I've seen, heard, or been through before)?

   Familiar Patterns _____

   _____

   _____

   _____

7. What should be the order of my stepwise approach for solving the problem?

   (1) _____

   (2) _____

   (3) _____

   (4) _____

   (5) _____

   (6) _____

8. What strategies can I use to solve this problem?

   Strategies_____

   _____

   _____

   _____

   _____

9. Do I have back-up strategies in case the first one doesn't work? If so, what are they?

Back-Up Strategies _____

_____

10. Roughly, how will this be or look when it is finished or the problem is solved?

Preview or Estimate _____

_____

11. [To be answered in the middle of the problem-solving activity] Are things going according to plan? Am I satisfied with how I'm doing?

Yes_____   No_____   Partly_____

Comments _____

_____

12. [To be answered when the problem has been solved] How did this turn out?

- Very Successful_____   Pretty Successful_____   Unsuccessful_____

- Is Really Finished_____   Could Use Some More Work_____

- Was Harder_____   Was Easier_____   Was As Hard As I Expected_____

- Took Longer_____   Took Less Time_____   Took What I Thought_____

13. Can I use the solution and/or these problem-solving strategies in the future? If so, how?

Future Uses _____

_____

_____

_____

APPENDIX TWO

The Mathematics Interview

OUR UNDERSTANDING of a child's learning problems in mathematics can be expanded simply by discussing the difficulty with the student. The Mathematics Interview provides a format for obtaining the student's perspective. Statements often made by students about mathematics are divided into areas of function, such as comprehension and memory. Their wording is intended to help students recognize that many children have trouble succeeding in this subject.

The child being interviewed indicates the extent to which such statements are true for him or her. These responses should help to pinpoint specific areas that are causing problems. At all points during the interview, children should be encouraged to elaborate on their answers and to give examples when they can. Such added information can be entered in the Comments section of the interview form. The last section of the interview contains some open-ended questions designed to elicit the child's feelings and attitudes about the subject.

The Mathematics Interview is intended for use with students in fifth grade and up. However, teachers may find they can adapt parts of it for younger children. This interview is not meant to be scored. It is to provide a qualitative overview which can contribute to a narrative description of a child's patterns of learning, while at the same time providing insight into that student's own understanding of the learning problem and his or her willingness to talk about it.

The Mathematics Interview

PART ONE

Key to Part One
0 = Always True for Me; 1 = Mostly True for Me; 2 = Sometimes True for Me; 3 = Not True for Me

Statements				
COMPREHENSION	0	1	2	3
1. Some students say they get pretty mixed up the first time a teacher explains something in math class.				
2. There are kids who can do plain math problems pretty well, but they have lots of trouble figuring out word problems.				
3. Some kids have a tough time understanding vocabulary words that come up in math classes.				
4. There are students who find it very hard to explain something they've learned pretty well in math.				
5. It is possible for someone to learn math more easily by studying a correctly solved problem than by learning about that kind of problem in class.				
6. Some people when they do math have a lot of trouble picturing shapes, dimensions, and sizes of things in their minds.				
7. There are students who can do a lot of things the right way in math, but they don't really understand what they're doing.				
8. It is possible to try to memorize things in math instead of understanding them.				
9. Some students think they understand something during class and then later on realize they didn't really get it.				
10. For many students thinking is harder in mathematics than it is in other subjects.				

MEMORY	0	1	2	3
11. It can take too long to remember math facts (like multiplication) on a test or on homework.				
12. Some kids have trouble remembering how to do things in mathematics.				
13. It can be much faster and easier to do hard math problems using a calculator.				
14. There are students who forget what they're doing in the middle of a math problem.				
15. Some kids can do much less math in their heads than other kids.				
16. A lot of students find that when they look at a math problem, it just doesn't look familiar to them. Every problem seems very different from all the others.				
17. Doing things in the right order is one of the hardest parts of mathematics.				
18. Some people have to stop and think about everything in math; none of it seems to be fast and automatic for them.				
19. In math it can be very hard for some people to remember exact shapes when they hear the names.				
20. Some kids complain they understand how to do things in class and then they forget how on an assignment or a test.				
ATTENTION	1	2	3	4
21. It is possible to make too many careless mistakes in math because of rushing through stuff.				
22. It can be very hard to keep concentrating during math class.				
23. Some kids say they keep getting very tired when they do math.				
24. A student might complain that there are too many little details to think about in math.				
25. There are students who sometimes have trouble in math because they don't really stop and think and plan enough before they do a problem.				

	0	1	2	3
26. It can be very hard to get started on math problems				
27. There are students who have problems estimating; they have no idea about what the answer will be before they start a problem.				
28. Some students have minds that don't like subjects like math because there's only one correct answer all the time.				
29. For some people it is extremely boring to check over math work.				
30. Some kids are very inconsistent in math; they do really well sometimes and very poorly other times.				
PROBLEM SOLVING/ORGANIZATION	**0**	**1**	**2**	**3**
31. There are students who have trouble figuring out what to do first when they try to solve a math problem.				
32. When some kids get stuck doing a math problem one way, they just can't think of new things to try to solve the problem.				
33. It can be hard to figure out what's important and what isn't in a word problem.				
34. It can be very hard knowing what and how to study for a math test.				
35. Some students never bother to test themselves when they're studying math.				
ATTRIBUTIONS	**0**	**1**	**2**	**3**
36. Math makes certain people very uptight.				
37. Some kids mess up on tests because they get too nervous.				
38. Doing math makes some people feel dumb.				
39. There are students who believe they are so far behind in math that they can never catch up.				
40. It is possible to be very unlucky in math.				

Comments and direct quotations:

PART TWO

1. What part of math have you enjoyed most?

2. Have you found some ways to make math a little easier for yourself? What are they?

3. What do you do when you're having trouble with a math assignment? Is there anything else you could do?

4. Some people think you can tell how smart a kid is by how he or she is doing in math. What do you think about that?

5. What kind of mind do you think a kid has who has trouble in math?

6. What kind of mind does someone need in order to do well in math?

APPENDIX THREE

The Writing Interview

THE WRITING INTERVIEW uses a format similar to that of the Mathematics Interview. Children are presented with statements about writing that have been made by other students. They, then, indicate how true each item is for them. The statements are organized into areas of function that are important for writing. These areas include language, graphomotor function, ideation, memory, and organization. A child may indicate significant difficulties in one or more of these areas. Such responses can then be examined along with samples of the child's writing, observations made by teachers and parents, as well as any relevant testing. In this way a broad description of the child's writing problems can be developed. Such a description can be vital in formulating a plan for management at home and in school.

The Writing Interview, like the Mathematics Interview, is not intended to be scored. It is designed for use with children who are in fifth grade and beyond. The wording of the items can be adjusted for use by younger children or by those with weak language processing. Children should always be prompted to elaborate on their answers and to give examples of times that they have experienced a particular problem. The last section of the Writing Interview allows students to give open-ended responses to questions relating to their feelings and attitudes toward writing.

The Writing Interview

PART ONE

Key to Part One
0 = Always True for Me; 1 = Mostly True for Me; 2 = Sometimes True for Me;
3 = Not True for Me

Statements				
GRAPHOMOTOR FUNCTION	0	1	2	3
1. Kids sometimes complain that their hand gets very tired when they have to write a lot.				
2. Some students have an unusual way of holding a pencil or pen.				
3. There are kids who think they write too slowly on tests and homework.				
4. Some people can print much better than they can use cursive.				
5. Lots of students say forming letters is not as easy for them as it is for other kids.				
EXPRESSIVE LANGUAGE	0	1	2	3
6. There are students who find it hard to get their ideas into words when they speak in school.				
7. Some kids make too many grammar mistakes when they write.				
8. While they write, some students have to think too long about how to say their ideas on paper.				
9. When some people write, they have trouble using good vocabulary; they use a lot of easy words.				
10. Some kids have trouble describing things well in a class discussion.				
IDEATION	0	1	2	3
11. Some students find it very hard to think up topics or decide what they want to write.				
12. There are kids who would hate to have to write a story.				

13. It can be very difficult to know what to write or include in a report.				
14. A lot of kids say it's not easy for them to come up with their own original ideas about things in school.				
15. Some people say it's really hard to write about their opinions or what they think about things.				
MEMORY	**0**	**1**	**2**	**3**
16. It is confusing to remember so many things at once (like spelling, punctuation, vocabulary, etc.) while writing.				
17. Some kids have much neater handwriting when they copy from the board than when they write a paragraph.				
18. When writing a report or story it's not always easy for some kids to remember what they wanted to write.				
19. Some kids have said that they have much better ideas when they speak than when they write.				
20. Problems with spelling make writing especially hard for some people.				
ORGANIZATION	**0**	**1**	**2**	**3**
21. It can be really hard to get started with a writing assignment.				
22. When they write, some students have trouble getting their thoughts down in the right order.				
23. Some students don't think much in advance about what they are going to write; they just start writing.				
24. There are students who have trouble getting together the books, paper, and other tools they need to write things.				
25. It is hard to know how long it will take to write a report or a story.				

Comments:

PART TWO

1. Is there any kind of writing that you enjoy in school?

2. What's the hardest part about writing for you? What's the easiest?

3. Is there anything you've learned to do that makes writing easier for you?

4. Do you ever feel embarrassed when other kids look at things that you've written?

5. If you were having trouble writing a report, what could you do?

6. Have you used a computer for writing? Has this made writing easier for you? Are there problems for you in using a computer?

7. You need muscle coordination for writing, for playing sports, and for doing art or fixing things. Which of these things do your muscles work well for and which are problems for your muscles?

8. What does a kid have to be good at to write well?

APPENDIX FOUR

The Report Developer

THE REPORT DEVELOPER can be used to help students develop an organized approach to expository writing. It is meant to convey the idea that most writing needs to thought out in advance and prepared in stages. The Report Developer also enables students to monitor and evaluate their writing experience.

Children can be assigned to write a report and to fill out the Report Developer while doing so. Different parts of the Report Developer can be completed at different stages of report writing. The form can be reviewed at these times with a teacher and a parent.

When students first encounter the Report Developer, an adult should model its use. A teacher or parent can make up a hypothetical title and go through the steps of completing the form in front of the student. During their initial attempts to use it, students may require assistance.

Teachers may wish to evaluate students on how well they completed the Report Developer. This form of evaluation communicates to students that how you go about writing a report is just as important as how well the report comes out when it's finished.

The Report Developer

Student's Name _____ Today's Date _____

Class _____ Type of Writing _____ Due Date _____

Assignment or Topic _____ Probable Length _____

Audience(s): Teacher   Classmates   Parent(s)   Other_____

A. Staging and Scheduling—The Timeline

Stage	Time Needed	Date and Time	Done
Brainstorm			
Read/Look Up Things			
Outline			
First Draft			
Revise Ideas/Sentences			
Second Draft			
Revise Sp., Punct., etc.			
Final Version			

B. Deciding on the Major Topic of Report

_____

_____

C. Thinking about How It Will Be (Circle Words)

How Much Fun	How Hard	How Valuable	How Well I'll Do
A Lot of Fun	Easy	Very Good to Do	Excellent
A Little Fun	Pretty Hard	Pretty Good	Good
Not Much Fun	Hard	Not so Good	Fair
Boring	Very Hard	Waste of Time	Poor

D. Listing Major Kinds of Information to Be Included

1. _____

2. _____

3. _____

4. _____

5. _____

E. Finding Additional Information

Information Needed	Place(s) to Find it
1.	
2.	
3.	
4.	
5.	
6.	

F. Organizing Paragraphs/Sections in Best Order/Subheadings

1. _____

2. _____

3. _____

4. _____

5. _____

6. _____

7. _____

G. Previewing the Ending or Conclusions

_____

_____

_____

_____

H. Deciding on a Title _____

I. Judging How It Turned Out (To Be Filled Out after Handing In)

Excellent_____   Good_____   Fair_____   Poor_____

How Hard Different Parts Were (1 = Very Hard; 2 = Hard; 3 = Not Hard)

Part of Writing	How Hard	Part of Writing	How Hard
Writing Fast Enough	1 2 3	Understanding Topic	1 2 3
Writing/Typing Neatly	1 2 3	Brainstorming	1 2 3
Using Good Grammar	1 2 3	Finding Information	1 2 3
Using Punctuation	1 2 3	Organizing Ideas/Facts	1 2 3
Spelling	1 2 3	Stating Ideas Well	1 2 3
Proofreading/Revising	1 2 3	Writing Enough	1 2 3
Concentrating Well	1 2 3	Using Rep. Developer	1 2 3

J. Other Notes and Comments

_____

_____

_____

_____

_____

APPENDIX FIVE

The Story Developer

THE STORY DEVELOPER can be used in a way similar to the Report Developer. Students can plan, document progress, and evaluate the experience using the form.

There are many different ways to use the Story Developer. Before the child starts the activity, a teacher can provide some of the information asked for on the form. For example, students might write a story that fits a particular title or they could be given the last line of a story and asked to write the rest of it.

Teachers should model the use of the Story Developer for students. Eventually, they are likely to be able to use it independently.

As with the Report Developer, students submit the form for evaluation at various stages of their story writing.

The Story Developer

Student's Name _____	Today's Date _____
Class _____ Type of Writing _____	Due Date _____
Assignment or Topic _____ Probable Length _____ (pgs/wds)	
Audience(s): Teacher Classmates Parent(s) Other _____	

A. Staging and Scheduling—The Timeline

Stage	Time Needed	Date and Time	Done
Brainstorm			
Outline			
First Draft			
Revise Ideas/Sentences			
Second Draft			
Revise Sp., Punct., etc.			
Final Version			

B. Picking and Describing the Major Characters in the Story

Character	Brief Description
1.	
2.	
3.	
4.	
5.	

C. Providing the Background

Setting_____ Place_____ Time_____

D. Listing Major Events and/or Conflicts to Be Included

1._____

2._____

3._____

4._____

5._____

6._____

E. Organizing Events in the Best Order

1._____

2._____

3._____

4._____

5._____

6._____

F. Previewing How the Story Ends

_____

_____

Last Line of Story_____

_____

G. Adding Other Interesting or Entertaining Details

1._____

2._____

3._____

4._____

5._____

6._____

H. Picking a Title _____

I.　Thinking about How Writing This Story Will Be (Circle Words)

How Much Fun	How Hard	How Good to Do	How Well I'll Do
A Lot of Fun	Easy	Very Good to Do	Excellent
A Little Fun	Pretty Hard	Pretty Good	Good
Not Much Fun	Hard	Not so Good	Fair
Boring	Very Hard	A Waste of Time	Poor

J.　Deciding How It Turned Out (To Be Filled Out after Finishing)

Excellent_____　Good_____　Fair_____　Poor_____

How Hard It Was (1 = Very Hard; 2 = Hard; 3 = Not Hard)

Part of Writing	How Hard	Part of Writing	How Hard
Writing Fast Enough	1 2 3	Choosing Title	1 2 3
Writing/Typing Neatly	1 2 3	Thinking Up Story	1 2 3
Using Punctuation	1 2 3	Getting Story in Right Order	1 2 3
Using Good Grammar	1 2 3	Writing Enough	1 2 3
Spelling	1 2 3	Concentrating on Work	1 2 3
Using Story Developer	1 2 3	Proofreading/Revising	1 2 3

APPENDIX SIX

The On-Line Reading Review

T HE ON-LINE READING REVIEW is intended to help adults understand students' reading difficulties. It can also be used to assist older students in gaining insight into the problems they are having while reading.

The student first reads or is read to and helped to understand the introductory page. Then, she or he reads a passage or chapter. At one or more designated points, the student pauses and rates the reading experience on the form.

Common kinds of reading problems, which appear on the right side of the form, are described in the following list:

- Attention. Some students have trouble concentrating hard enough when they read. Their minds wander. They may lose their place and miss important details. Sometimes they feel tired and/or bored while they read.
- Mood. There are students who get nervous when they read. Others become uptight. These feelings may be caused by their difficulty with reading.
- Memory. Children have to do a lot of remembering while they read. They need to recall facts they learned a long time ago as well as to remember what they are reading while reading it. Sometimes memory problems make it hard to read well.
- Chunk Size. Some students have trouble when they have to read large amounts. They have trouble with "chunk" size. They can read much better if they don't have so much to read.
- Language. Understanding words and sentences is a big part of reading. Some students get mixed up about the language when they read.

- Concepts. Concepts are the ideas that children need to understand during reading. They can become confused if they don't really grasp these.
- Background. Sometimes students have difficulty reading because they don't know enough about the subject to figure out meanings.
- Decoding. To read well students have to be able to figure out each word quickly and easily. Some of them have trouble understanding because they have to work too hard to decode a lot of the words.

The On-Line Reading Review

Name _____ Grade _____ Today's date _____

Teacher _____ Class _____

Book or Article Read _____ All of it _____ Part of it _____

Chapter/Section Read _____ Number of Pages _____

Directions: Many students have a hard time with reading. This form is designed to help students, their teachers, and their parents understand these reading problems better. Please look over the form and then read your assignment. Before you start, divide your reading into four sections or time periods. Put an X in the right box if any of the things on the list have been a problem during the part you just read. This may help you think about why reading is hard for you.

PROBLEM	1	2	3	4	KIND OF PROBLEM
Mind wandered					Attention
Felt tired					Attention
Missed important details					Attention
Lost my place					Attention
Lost track of ideas					Attention/Memory
Wanted to move around/get up					Attention
Felt bored					Mood/Attention
Felt nervous/uptight					Mood/Attention
Couldn't decide what's important					Attention/Background
Hard to remember what I read					Memory/Language
Forgot facts needed to understand					Memory
Would have trouble summarizing					Reading/Memory/Language
Too many new facts					Chunk Size/Background
Too many new ideas					Chunk Size/Background
Vocabulary too hard					Language
Sentences too complicated					Language
Paragraphs too complicated					Language/Background
Ideas hard to figure out					Concepts/Language
Didn't know enough to understand					Concepts/Background
Couldn't picture things					Visual Processing
Trouble with diagrams/charts/maps					Visual Processing
Had trouble reading some words					Word Decoding
Read too slowly					Word Decoding/Language

APPENDIX SEVEN

The Collaboration Worksheet

THE COLLABORATION WORKSHEET is intended to help teachers, parents, and clinicians work together to understand and plan for a child's educational care. There are several different ways in which the form can be used.

Teachers, parents, and other involved adults can complete the Collaboration Worksheet independently and then compare notes at a conference. Alternatively, they can compile their findings together on one form during or after a discussion of the child. This form can also be used by teachers as a training activity. They can read *Educational Care* and then practice completing the form on students whom they know or on hypothetical case studies.

Many different sources of information might be sought in filling out the Collaboration Worksheet. Direct observations by parents, teachers, and clinicians can be documented. The results of testing, interviews with the child, and various specialty consultations may provide further input.

The Collaboration Worksheet is not meant to be a diagnostic instrument. Instead, it should help all of those involved to organize their findings and ensure that parents and teachers are viewing and managing a child in a consistent manner.

The Collaboration Worksheet

Child's Name_____ Grade_____ Date _____

Person(s) Completing Worksheet _____

Parent_____ Teacher_____ Clinician_____ Other (Specify) _____

Observed Phenomena

AREAS	OBSERVED PHENOMENA	SEVERITY*				SPECIFIC FORMS OF PHENOMENA
		1	2	3	4	
Attention	Weak Mental Energy Control					
	Weak Processing Control					
	Weak Production Control					
Remembering	Problems with Short-Term Memory					
	Insufficient Active Working Memory					
	Incomplete Consolidation in Long-Term Memory					
	Reduced Access to Long-Term Memory					
Understanding	Weak Language Processing					
	Incomplete Concept Formation					
	Weak Visual Processing					
	Slow Data Processing					
	Small Chunk-Size Capacity					
	Excessive Top-Down or Bottom-Up Processing					

*Key to severity rating: 1 = Not a problem; 2 = A slight problem;
3 = A moderate problem; 4 = A severe problem

AREAS	OBSERVED PHENOMENA	SEVERITY*				SPECIFIC FORMS OF PHENOMENA
		1	2	3	4	
Output	Weak Language Production					
	Disappointing Motor Performance					
	Persistent Organizational Failure					
	Problematic Problem Solving					
Skill Acquistion	Slow Reading Development					
	Inaccurate Spelling Patterns					
	Impeded Written Output					
	Underdeveloped Mathematical Skills					
Adaptation	School-Related Sadness					
	Bodily Preoccupations					
	Noncompliant Behaviors					
	Impaired Interactions					
	Lost Motivation					

*Key to severity rating: 1 = Not a problem; 2 = A slight problem;
3 = A moderate problem; 4 = A severe problem

Strengths and Affinities:

_____

_____

_____

Elaboration and Additional Comments on the Observed Phenomena:

_____

_____

_____

_____

Academic Subskills

SKILL AREA	SUBSKILL	STATUS* 1	2	3	4	COMMENTS
Reading	Decoding Accuracy					
	Decoding Speed					
	Recall of Facts					
	Comprehension					
	Summarization					
	Speed/Automatization					
Spelling	Accuracy in Isolation					
	Accuracy in Context					
Writing	Pencil Grip					
	Fluency/Ease of Output					
	Legibility					
	Mechanics during Writing					
	Mechanics in Isolation					
	Written Language					
	Ideation					
	Organization for Writing					
	Organization of Writing					
Mathematics	Factual Recall					
	Speed of Factual Recall					
	Procedural Recall					
	Procedural Speed					
	Word Problems					
	Mathematical Language					
	Visualization					
	Symbolic Representation					
	Understanding of Concepts					

*Status Ratings: 1 = Above grade level; 2 = At grade level; 3 = Less than one year below grade level; 4 = More than one year below grade level.

Comments on academic content areas (e.g., history, science, foreign language):

_____

_____

Comments on academic interests:

_____

_____

Assessment and Management

Summary of Recent Test Results (If Applicable)

Additional Consultation and/or Assessment

1. _____

2. _____

3. _____

4. _____

5. _____

Management Proposal

Demystification Plans:

_____

_____

_____

Major Priorities for Management:

_____

_____

_____

_____

_____

_____

Suggested Bypass Strategies in School:

_____
_____
_____
_____
_____

Suggested Forms of Direct Remediation in School:

_____
_____
_____
_____
_____
_____

Suggested Program for Management at Home:

_____
_____
_____
_____
_____
_____
_____

Use of Strengths and Affinities:

_____
_____
_____

Provisions for Humilation Protection:

_____

_____

Additional Services and Treatments:

_____

_____

_____

_____

Monitoring and Follow-up Plans:

_____

_____

_____

_____

Helpful Resources for Parents, Children, and Teachers

T HERE ARE many excellent local and national organizations that are devoted to helping schools and families deal with the kinds of problems elucidated in *Educational Care*. The following list includes some of the major national organizations. It is advisable to investigate additional organizations that might exist locally.

Children with Attention Deficit
Disorders (CHADD)
499 Northwest 70th Avenue,
    Suite 308
Plantation, Fla. 33317

Learning Disabilities Association of
America (LDA)
4156 Library Road
Pittsburgh, Penn. 15234

National Center for Learning
Disabilities (NCLD)
99 Park Avenue
New York, N.Y. 10016

Orton Dyslexia Society
Chester Building, Suite 382
8600 LaSalle Road
Baltimore, Md. 21286

Tourette Syndrome Association
Park 50 Tech. Center
Milford, Ohio 45150

Those wishing information about additional organizations and about schools and other resources for children with learning problems are referred to the *Directory of Facilities and Services for the Learning Disabled* which is published and revised regularly by Academic Therapy Publications, 20 Commercial Boulevard, Novato, Calif. 94949.

SUGGESTED READINGS

T HE FOLLOWING books and articles provide further information about various learning disorders. They may be especially helpful in adding to the management suggestions offered in *Educational Care*. A brief description follows each of these references.

Aaron, P., and Baker, C. *Reading Disabilities in College and High School: Diagnosis and Management*. Parkton, Md.: York Press, 1991. This book can be especially useful for teachers trying to assist older students with delays in reading skill. It provides good insights into the problems themselves and presents useful ideas for management.

Asher, S.R., and Gottman, J.M., eds. *The Development of Children's Friendships*. Cambridge: Cambridge University Press, 1981. This volume contains a collection of papers on various aspects of social skill development during childhood. There are excellent discussions of how children succeed or fail in gaining acceptance by peers.

Asher, S.R., and Coie, J.D., eds. *Peer Rejection in Childhood*. Cambridge: Cambridge University Press, 1990. This collection of essays focuses on research into children who are rejected by their peers. There are useful reviews of specific social skills and their roles as well as papers on social skill training methods.

Berninger, V.W., and Hooper, S.R., eds. Preventing and remediating writing disabilities: Interdisciplinary frameworks for assessment, consultation, and intervention. Mini-series in *School Psychology Review* 22(1993):590. This is a collection of articles dealing with various aspects of writing difficulty. There are useful discussions of assessment techniques as well as good reviews of management practices.

Bley, N.S., and Thornton, C. A. *Teaching Mathematics to the Learning Disabled*. 2d ed. Austin, Tex.: PRO-ED, 1989. The authors provide recommendations for teachers at various grade levels who are working with children who have problems acquiring mathematical skills.

Brooks, R. *The Self-Esteem Teacher*. Circle Pines, Minn.: American Guidance Service, 1991. This guide offers a systematic approach to helping children maintain their self-esteem in school. Although the book is directed toward teachers, much of the advice is also suitable for parents.

Carlisle, J. *Reasoning and Reading*. Level 1 and Level 2. Cambridge, Mass.: Educators Publishing Service, 1993 and 1983. These two workbooks provide a range of exercises for the improvement of reading comprehension. There is an emphasis on the development of sophisticated thinking skills at the same time that students are enhancing their reading abilities.

Chall, J.S. *Stages of Reading Development*. New York: McGraw Hill, 1983. Dr. Chall has written a very readable account of how children normally acquire reading skills as they progress through their school years. Her book helps the reader to understand why certain children can experience reading difficulty at particular periods in their education.

Chapman, R.S., ed. *Processes in Language Acquisition and Disorders*. St. Louis: Mosby Year Book, 1992. This collection of papers provides an excellent and very sophisticated overview of current issues related to normal language development and to the problems of children with weak language processing and production. It contains thorough reviews of the literature on these topics.

Christenson, S.L., and Conoley, J.C., eds. *Home-School Collaboration*. Silver Spring, Md.: National Association of School Psychologists, 1992. The essays in this book cover many areas of potential collaboration between home and school. Parents and teachers can find good suggestions for dealing with such issues as discipline problems, homework supervision, divorce, and communication between parents and schools.

Clark, L. *SOS! Help for Parents*. Bowling Green, Ky.: Parents Press, 1985. This highly readable book is filled with excellent suggestions for parents about how to manage behavior problems at home. Practical methods of punishment, reward, and time out are described.

Cohen, G. *The Psychology of Cognition*. 2d ed. Orlando: Academic Press, 1983. This textbook provides excellent discussions of concept formation and problem solving as well as other aspects of reasoning and remembering. While the book focuses on normal human cognitive processes, it has significant implications for understanding children with learning problems.

Devine, T. *Teaching Study Skills: A Guide for Teachers*. 2d ed. Boston: Allyn and Bacon, 1987. This volume contains an approach to the teaching of study skills. Its ideas can be integrated into curriculum across grades and subject areas.

Fowler, M. *CH.A.D.D. Educators Manual.* Plantation, Fla.: CH.A.D.D., 1992. This manual offers practical suggestions for working with children with attentional dysfunction in school and is most helpful when discussing the management of their behavioral problems.

Gerber, A. *Language Related Learning Disabilities.* Baltimore: Paul Brookes Publishing Co., 1993. This book is a well-written, comprehensive resource for parents, clinicians, and teachers who wish to learn more about the language aspects of learning as well as weaknesses of language processing and production. It also contains many helpful suggestions for management in school and for language therapy.

Levine, M.D. *Developmental Variation and Learning Disorders.* Cambridge, Mass.: Educators Publishing Service, 1987. This referenced book deals in detail with specific forms of learning disorders. It describes the manifestations of the disorders and provides information about their assessment and management. The book is written primarily for teachers and clinicians.

Levine, M.D. *Keeping A Head in School.* Cambridge, Mass.: Educators Publishing Service, 1990. This book is designed to help older children (ages eleven up) to understand the nature of their learning disorders and strengths. It reviews issues relating to attentional dysfunction, various kinds of learning disorders as well as difficulties with motor function, self esteem, and social skill. Students are given suggestions for working on their problems and using their strengths. Cassette tapes of the book are available.

Levine, M.D. *All Kinds of Minds.* Cambridge, Mass.: Educators Publishing Service, 1993. This book is written to help younger students (under eleven) understand different kinds of learning disorders. It is a fictitious account of a group of children with specific kinds of difficulties in school. The book describes how they come to understand and deal with their problems. Cassette tapes of the book are available. There is also a manual (*Guidelines for the Use of All Kinds of Minds*) to help adults make use of the book with children.

Lyon, G. R., Gray, D.B., Kavanagh, J.F., and Krasnegor, N.A., eds. *Better Understanding Learning Disabilities.* Baltimore: Paul Brookes Publishing Co., 1993. This collection of papers provides an excellent overview of research in learning disabilities, and it provides various theoretical models to explain them. The book also covers issues relating to future research and educational policy.

Lyon, G. R., ed. *Frames of Reference for the Assessment of Learning Disabilities.* Baltimore: Paul Brookes Publishing Co., 1994. This volume of rather technical papers provides an excellent overview of the kinds of assessment tools and approaches that are available for the evaluation of children with learning disorders. A wide range of academic areas and cognitive functions are covered.

Meltzer, L. J., and Solomon, B. *Educational Prescriptions for the Classroom*. Cambridge, Mass.: Educators Publishing Service, 1988. This is a well-organized manual designed to help teachers accommodate to the needs of students with specific forms of neurodevelopmental dysfunction. The book offers many specific suggestions that are easily implemented.

Meltzer, L.J., ed. *Strategy Assessment and Instruction for Students with Learning Disabilities*. Austin, Tex.: PRO-ED, 1993. This volume contains a number of excellent essays on assessing the strategies used by students and on helping them to apply effective strategies in specific academic skill areas. There are particularly good discussions of strategies children may use to improve language and memory function.

Moss, R.A., and Dunlap, H.H. *Why Johnny Can't Concentrate*. New York: Bantam Books, 1990. This well-written volume provides a very readable overview of attentional dysfunction which will help both parents and teachers. It includes many practical suggestions aimed at the needs of specific age groups. It also offers good insights into medical therapies.

Pennington, B.F. *Diagnosing Learning Disorders*. New York: Guilford Press, 1991. The author of this book, a neuropsychologist, provides a useful discussion of various conceptual models of learning disability and then elucidates a variety of methods of assessment. The book has particularly helpful discussions of interactions between various forms of autism and learning disorders.

Reed, M. Educational assessment of learning difficulties: A developmental, descriptive, and process-oriented perspective. In *Developmental-Behavioral Pediatrics*. Ed. M. D. Levine, W. Carey, and A. Crocker, 2d ed. Philadelphia: W.B. Saunders, 1992. This chapter provides a clear synopsis of the objectives and general content of a thorough educational assessment for a child with learning difficulties.

Rief, S. F. *How to Reach and Teach ADD/ADHD Children*. West Nyack, N.Y.: The Center for Applied Research in Education, 1993. This book should be particularly helpful to teachers in their daily management of children with attention deficits. It also offers some good suggestions for dealing with learning disorders in children who have attention problems.

Rudel, R. *Assessment of Developmental Learning Disorders*. New York: Basic Books, 1988. The neuropsychological perspective on learning disorders is described very well in this volume. The book is especially effective in elucidating the assessment techniques used by neuropsychologists in the evaluation of these children.

Sedita, J. *Landmark Study Skills Guide*. Prides Crossing, Mass.: Landmark Foundation, 1989. This manual offers abundant suggestions to improve study skills. The book presents specific methods for reading, taking notes, and organizing time and space. It is especially geared to the needs of children with learning disorders. There is a Spanish version as well.

Steere, A., Peck, C.Z., and Kahn, L. *Solving Language Difficulties*. Cambridge, Mass.: Educators Publishing Service, 1984. This workbook is comprised of a large number of exercises designed to help children with language disabilities. There is a stress on the improvement of morphology. The book is aimed at fourth to sixth-graders, but some of it can be adapted for use in younger and older students.

Stoner, G., Shinn, M.R., and Walker, H.M. *Interventions for Achievement and Behavior Problems*. Silver Spring, Md.: National Association of School Psychologists, 1991. Although written specifically for school psychologists, this volume of essays is filled with excellent ideas for dealing with a wide range of learning and behavioral problems within the school setting.

Sugden, D.A., and Keogh, J.F. *Problems in Motor Skill Development*. Columbia: University of South Carolina Press, 1990. This book describes different forms of motor difficulty. The introduction and several of the chapters are especially relevant to the understanding of children with motor problems affecting writing.

Tierney, R.J., Readence, J.E., and Dishner, E.K. *Reading Strategies and Practices—A Compendium*. Boston: Allyn and Bacon, 1985. This book contains excellent descriptions of many curricula and techniques that are used to teach reading at various levels. There are numerous methods described, many of which could easily be adapted for use by parents and teachers working with students who have delayed reading skills.

Traub, N. *Recipe for Reading*. 3d ed. Cambridge, Mass.: Educators Publishing Service, 1990. This book presents a series of excellent activities designed to enhance phonological awareness and reading decoding skills. The exercises can also play a role in helping children improve spelling and writing abilities.

Turecki, S. *The Emotional Problems of Normal Children*. New York: Bantam Books, 1994. Dr. Turecki, a psychiatrist, provides much practical advice on the understanding and management of common behavioral problems in childhood. His wisdom reflects his abundant clinical experience, and his philosophy is refreshing, as he stresses that even "normal" children have problems.

Vail, P.L. *Smart Kids with School Problems*. New York: E. P. Dutton, 1987. In this general book about learning styles and learning disorders, the author provides excellent insights into the multiple factors that relate to academic success and failure. The book is equally relevant for parents and teachers.

Vail, P.L. *Common Ground: Whole Language and Phonics Working Together*. Rosemont, N. J.: Modern Learning Press, 1991. Making use of an eclectic approach, this short volume offers a remarkable number of practical suggestions for teaching decoding skills to children in first to fourth grade.

Wolfgang, C. H., and Glickman, C.D. *Solving Discipline Problems*. Boston: Allyn and Bacon, 1986. This book contains a useful survey of various methods that have been devised and evaluated for the management of children with behavior problems in the classroom. The authors assess the pros and cons of each approach.

INDEX

ABOUT THE AUTHOR

Dr. Mel Levine is a professor of pediatrics at the University of North Carolina School of Medicine. He is the director of the Clinical Center for the Study of Development and Learning, which is a university-affiliated program that conducts research, training, technical assistance, and clinical evaluation and monitoring for individuals with developmental disabilities.

Dr. Levine graduated summa cum laude from Brown University and was a Rhodes Scholar at Magdalen College, Oxford. He graduated from Harvard Medical School and completed residency training in pediatrics at the Children's Hospital in Boston. He served with the United States Air Force as a pediatrician at which time he received The Meritorious Service Award for his work with children. Following his military service, Dr. Levine was Chief of Ambulatory Pediatrics at the Children's Hospital for fourteen years until he assumed his present position in North Carolina.

Dr. Mel Levine has always had a strong interest in the health and function of school-age children. He has had a compelling orientation toward various forms of dysfunction as they emerge and manifest themselves during this period of life. Dr. Levine has conducted considerable research and written many books and articles about learning disorders and other kinds of functional difficulty confronting children. In addition, he has been actively involved in educating pediatricians, educators, and others to understand childhood neurodevelopmental variation and its effects.

Dr. Levine is an unwavering child advocate. He is particularly concerned about the lives of young people whose innate characteristics are not well understood by adults or by the children themselves. Over the years he has worked to help such children succeed and feel good about their kinds of minds.

Dr. Levine lives on Sanctuary Farm in North Carolina. For many years he has raised and advocated for nearly every variety of domestic and wild goose. He encounters many kinds of minds among his approximately two hundred birds and ardently enjoys and respects the ever-changing display of observable phenomena within the gaggles.